Gender and Politics Series

Series editors: **Johanna Kantola**, Senior Lecturer in Gender Studies, University of Helsinki, Finland, and **Sarah Childs**, Professor of Politics and Gender, University of Bristol, UK

This timely new series publishes leading monographs and edited collections from scholars working in the disciplinary areas of politics, international relations and public policy with specific reference to questions of gender. The series showcases cutting-edge research in Gender and Politics, publishing topical and innovative approaches to gender and politics. It will include exciting work from new authors and well-known academics and will also publish high-impact writings by practitioners working in issues relating to gender and politics.

The series covers politics, international relations and public policy, including gendered engagement with mainstream political science issues, such as political systems and policymaking, representation and participation, citizenship and identity, equality, and women's movements; gender and international relations, including feminist approaches to international institutions, political economy and global politics; and interdisciplinary and emergent areas of study, such as masculinities studies, gender and multiculturalism, and intersectionality.

Series Advisory Board:
Louise Chappell, University of New South Wales, Australia
Joni Lovenduksi, Birkbeck College, University of London,UK
Amy Mazur, Washington State University, USA
Judith Squires, University of Bristol, UK
Jacqui True, Monash University, Australia
Mieke Verloo, Radboud University Nijmegen, the Netherlands
Laurel Weldon, Purdue University, USA

Titles include:

Gabriele Abels and Joyce Marie Mushaben (*editors*)
GENDERING THE EUROPEAN UNION
New Approaches to Old Democratic Deficits

Phillip Ayoub and David Paternotte
LGBT ACTIVISM AND THE MAKING OF EUROPE
A Rainbow Europe?

Elin Bjarnegård
GENDER, INFORMAL INSTITUTIONS AND POLITICAL RECRUITMENT
Explaining Male Dominance in Parliamentary Representation

Elgin Brunner
FOREIGN SECURITY POLICY, GENDER, AND US MILITARY IDENTITY

Andrea Chandler
DEMOCRACY, GENDER, AND SOCIAL POLICY IN RUSSIA
A Wayward Society

Sarah Childs and Paul Webb
SEX, GENDER AND THE CONSERVATIVE PARTY
From Iron Lady to Kitten Heels

Jonathan Dean
RETHINKING CONTEMPORARY FEMINIST POLITICS

Meryl Kenny
GENDER AND POLITICAL RECRUITMENT
Theorising Institutional Change

Andrea Krizsan, Hege Skjeie and Judith Squires (*editors*)
INSTITUTIONALIZING INTERSECTIONALITY
The Changing Nature of European Equality Regimes

Mona Lena Krook and Fiona Mackay (*editors*)
GENDER, POLITICS AND INSTITUTIONS
Towards a Feminist Institutionalism

Emanuela Lombardo and Maxime Forest (*editors*)
THE EUROPEANIZATION OF GENDER EQUALITY POLICIES
A Discursive–Sociological Approach

Emma-Louise Anderson
GENDER, HIV AND RISK
Navigating Structural Violence

Birte Siim and Monika Mokre (*editors*)
NEGOTIATING GENDER AND DIVERSITY IN AN EMERGENT EUROPEAN
PUBLIC SPHERE

Anna van der Vleuten, Anouka van Eerdewijk and Conny Roggeband (*editors*)
GENDER EQUALITY NORMS IN REGIONAL GOVERNANCE
Transnational Dynamics in Europe, South America and Southern Africa

Polly Wilding
NEGOTIATING BOUNDARIES
Gender, Violence and Transformation in Brazil

Gender and Politics Series
**Series Standing Order ISBNs 978–0–230–23917–3 (hardback) and
978–0–230–23918–0 (paperback)**
(*outside North America only*)

You can receive future titles in this series as they are published by placing a
standing order. Please contact your bookseller or, in case of difficulty, write to
us at the address below with your name and address, the title of the series and
the ISBN quoted above.

Customer Services Department, Macmillan Distribution Ltd, Houndmills,
Basingstoke, Hampshire RG21 6XS, England

Gender, HIV and Risk

Navigating Structural Violence

Emma-Louise Anderson
The University of Leeds, UK

First published 2015 by
PALGRAVE MACMILLAN

Palgrave Macmillan in the UK is an imprint of Macmillan Publishers Limited,
registered in England, company number 785998, of Houndmills, Basingstoke,
Hampshire RG21 6XS.

Palgrave Macmillan in the US is a division of St Martin's Press LLC,
175 Fifth Avenue, New York, NY 10010.

Palgrave Macmillan is the global academic imprint of the above companies
and has companies and representatives throughout the world.

Palgrave® and Macmillan® are registered trademarks in the United States,
the United Kingdom, Europe and other countries.

ISBN 978–0–230–29288–8

This book is printed on paper suitable for recycling and made from fully
managed and sustained forest sources. Logging, pulping and manufacturing
processes are expected to conform to the environmental regulations of the
country of origin.

A catalogue record for this book is available from the British Library.

A catalog record for this book is available from the Library of Congress.

For Jon

Contents

Acknowledgements

This work would not have been possible without the support, guidance and participation of many people over the years.

I would first like to extend my gratitude to everyone in Malawi who made this research possible. I am particularly grateful to Justice Jane Ansah, the former Attorney General, Hon. Kate Kainja, the former Minister for Women and Child Development, Anthony Kamanga, the then Law Commissioner, and Francis Cooke, the Headmaster at Kamuzu Academy, who helped me to gain access to the key informants in 2007. I am grateful to Professor Emmanuel Fabiano, the former Vice Chancellor at the University of Malawi, and Professor Paul Kishindo, Director of the Centre for Social Research (CSR), for welcoming me as a Visiting Research Fellow in 2011. I appreciate the advice and guidance I received from Professor Alister Munthali. I thank Professor Al Mtenje for his language instruction, Dr Stella Kachiwanda for arranging my language course and the Centre for Language Studies for warmly welcoming me during my studies in 2006.

The fieldwork in 2011 benefited from the advice and guidance of the National Coordinator of the Women, Girls and HIV/AIDS – Programme and National Plan of Action, the Head of Monitoring and Evaluation at the National AIDS Commission (NAC), a representative of the Department for Nutrition, HIV and AIDS, the Programme Officer for Monitoring and Evaluation (and Coordinator for Stigma Survey 2010) at the Malawi Network of People Living with HIV (MANET+), the Assistant Programme Manager at the National Association for People Living with HIV and AIDS in Malawi (NAPHAM), the National Coordinator at the Coalition of Women and Girls Living with HIV/AIDS, the National Coordinator of the Malawi Network of Religious Leaders Living with HIV and AIDS (MANERELA), the Programme Coordinator, Malawi Network of AIDS Service Organisations (MANASO) and the representative of the National Statistics Office (NSO) in Zomba. I also thank MANET+ in Lilongwe and NAPHAM in Zomba and Karonga for permitting me to observe their training sessions. I am grateful for the assistance of the staff at the National Archives Office, the National Statistics Office and the Chancellor College Library. I am indebted to Russell Msiska who acted as the facilitator and translator for the focus group discussions in Zomba and Karonga in 2011. I am also grateful to Kondwani

Klinga for his patience in assisting us to access the more remote parts of Zomba district by motorbike during the fuel shortages. I also thank the members of the Support Groups for PLHIV who welcomed us into their meetings, shared their experiences and showed us great hospitality. In particular, I would like to thank the Chairperson of Nsondole Support Group, who invited us to their group meeting where I had the opportunity to conduct a pilot study. I thank all the participants in the 44 key-informant interviews in 2011 and the 44 focus group discussions, 110 interviews and informal discussions in 2011. I extend my appreciation to all my Malawian friends and everyone who welcomed me into their homes and, in fundamental ways, contributed to my broader understanding of these issues. I am especially grateful to Diana Shaba for her hospitality.

I would like to thank the scholars from the newly established Global Health Section of the International Studies Association (ISA). I am particularly grateful to Simon Rushton (Sheffield) for his feedback on earlier drafts of the first two chapters and Stefan Elbe (Sussex), Sophie Harman (Queen Mary), Valerie Percival (Carleton) and Anne Buffardi (ODI) for the encouraging feedback they have given as discussants on the papers I have presented. I also thank Jeremy Youde (Minnesota), Peter Hill (Queensland), Owain Williams (Aberystwth), Amy Patterson (Sewanee), Steven Hoffman (Harvard) and Sara Davies (Queensland University of Technology) for their comments and support.

I appreciate being part of an inspiring and supportive research culture in the School of Politics and International Studies (POLIS) at the University of Leeds. I am indebted to Alexander Beresford for his considerable support, feedback and encouragement in the final drafting of the manuscript. I am particularly grateful to the POLIS reading group for their feedback on two of the chapters: Graeme Davies, Adrian Gallagher, Jelke Boesten, Polly Wilding, Jonathan Dean, Charlotte Burns, Jason Ralph and Nick Robinson. I am grateful to Ray Bush, Gordon Crawford and Michael Thomson for their feedback on associated work. I also appreciate the support I received from the School of Politics, International Relations and Philosophy (SPIRE) at Keele University. I particularly thank Barry Ryan, Helen Parr, Monica Mokherjee, Chris Zebrowski, Zoe Groves, Reuben Loffman and Juliette Hallaire for their feedback on my work. I am grateful to Tim Doyal and Hannes Stephan for their encouragement in developing this work into a book. From the University of Southampton, I would like to thank my PhD supervisor Tony Evans for his support and my external examiner Jill Steans (Birmingham). I am also grateful to David Owen, Frank Gregory, Chris

Armstrong, Darryl Howlett and Alex Kirkup for their feedback on my work. This work was inspired by the teaching of Nana Poku when I was an undergraduate. I also thank the anonymous reviewers for their invaluable comments on this and related work.

I appreciate the support I have received in developing my career from the Heads of School I have worked under: Kevin Theakston, Graham Smith, Bulent Gokay and Chris Bailey. I have also benefited from the excellent mentoring and support I have received from Brian Doherty, Andy Dobson and Lorna Lloyd. For their friendship and support I thank Katherine Brown (Kings), Egle Cesnulyte (Leeds), Susan Gaines (Leeds), Adam Newmark (Appalachian), Oliver Fritsch (Leeds), Laura Sandy (Keele), Rob Gray (Keele), Rachael Bright (Keele), Kelcey Swain (Bristol), Cathryn Spence (Guelph), Anthony Carrigan (Leeds), Nick Seager (Keele), Kingsley Edney (Leeds), Daniel Hausknost (Keele), Claire Saunders (Southampton) and Claire Duncanson (Edinburgh).

I thank the undergraduate and postgraduate students I have had the pleasure of teaching and working with over the years at Southampton, Winchester, Keele and Leeds. I particularly appreciate the engaging discussions I have had on issues closely relating to this work with my former PhD student Betty Chinyamunyamu and the dissertation students I have supervised – including Laura Holt, Malin Hagman, Edd Colbert, Vineeta Sehmbi, Naomi Dunn and Ella Foggitt.

I could not have completed this work without the love and support of my father, mother, brother, James and my friends Miranda, Justine, Laura and Rachel. I also thank Mark, Bailey, Darren, Han, James, Phil, Jezz and my father for reading drafts of my earlier work. I would particularly like to thank Ross Wilson for his help with editing my photograph that is used for the front cover. I dedicate this work to the memory of my friend, Jon.

This research was partially funded by the Economic Social Research Council (ESRC), UK and Keele University.

Abbreviations

ABCs	abstain, be faithful, use condoms
AGREDS	Assemblies of God Relief and Development Services
ARVs	antiretroviral drugs
AWFFI	African Women Food Farmers Initiative
BLM	Banja La Mtsogola
CAPRISA	Centre for the AIDS Programme of Research in South Africa
CBOs	community-based organisations
CHRR	Centre for Human Rights and Rehabilitation
CIDA	Canadian International Development Agency
COWLHA	Coalition of Women Living with HIV
DfID	Department for International Development
FHI	Family Health International
IR	International Relations
MACRO	Malawi AIDS Counselling and Resource Organisation
Malawi CARER	Malawi Centre for Advice, Research and Education on Rights
MANASO	Malawi Network of AIDS Service Organisations
MANERELA	Malawi Network of Religious Leaders Living with HIV and AIDS
MANET+	Malawi Network of People Living with HIV
MDGs	Millennium Development Goals
MDHS	Malawi Demographic and Health Survey
MHRC	Malawi Human Rights Commission
MK	Malawi Kwacha
NAC	National AIDS Commission
NAPHAM	National Association for People Living with HIV and AIDS
NGOs	non-governmental organisations
NICE	National Initiative for Civic Education
NSO	National Statistics Office
OPC	Office of the President and Cabinet
PEPFAR	President's Emergency Plan for AIDS Relief
PLHIV	people living with HIV
PSI	Population Services International

SAPs	Structural Adjustment Programmes
SAW	Society for the Advancement of Women
STDs	sexually transmitted diseases
STIs	sexually transmitted infections
UNAIDS	Joint UN Programme on HIV/AIDS
UNFPA	UN Population Fund
WFP	World Food Programme
WGHPPA	Women, Girls and HIV/AIDS – Programme and Plan of Action
WHO	World Health Organization
WLA	Women Lawyers Association
WLHIV	women living with HIV
WLSA	Women and the Law in Southern Africa

Introduction

Gendered Risk as Structural Violence

With the end of the UN Millennium Development Goals (MDGs) in 2015 there is the opportunity to critically reflect upon where we are now in terms of progress towards global development, what challenges remain and the very nature of development itself. Health had a prominent place in the MDGs and HIV was one of the 'big winners' – its inclusion in goal six recognised that addressing the virus is fundamental to sustainable development.[1] The virus was seen to stand apart from other global health issues because of the exceptional nature and sheer scale of the challenges it posed. The MDG agenda, coupled with the role of powerful advocates and the recognition of the UN Security Council that HIV posed an international security threat, contributed to the rise of 'AIDS exceptionalism', whereby the virus has attracted global commitments and resources on an unprecedented level as compared to other health concerns (see Smith and Whiteside, 2010; Nguyen, 2010, p. 13). Today, after three decades of HIV, crucial progress has been made. In recent years there have been encouraging reports that the pandemic, following what can be considered the natural cycle of viruses, is stabilising and the spread has begun to reverse. In 2012, the Executive Director of UNAIDS (the Joint UN Programme on HIV/AIDS), Michel Sidibé, expressed in his Statement for World AIDS Day how 'We have moved from despair to hope. Far fewer people are dying from AIDS. 25 countries have reduced new infections by more than 50 percent' (UNAIDS, 2012). Vital progress has been made in terms of treatment in the development of antiretroviral drugs (ARVs). And yet, despite the promise that these achievements bring, crucial challenges remain. In 2012, 35.3 million people were living with HIV worldwide. As is the case for development more broadly, the greatest challenges continue to be in Sub-Saharan

1

Africa: the region accounted for 71 per cent of the global population living with HIV (equating to 25 million people) and 70 per cent of all new HIV infections (UNAIDS, 2013, p. 12, A13). The concern of this book is that challenges remain in addressing the gender dynamics of the pandemic. Back in 2004, UNIFEM reported that 'A decade ago women seemed to be on the periphery of the epidemic. Today they are at the centre of concern' (Nath, 2004; see also UN, 2004b). The leading cause of death among women of reproductive age globally is HIV and in Sub-Saharan Africa women represent 57 per cent of infected adults (UNAIDS, 2010, 2013, p. 78).

It is well established that the spread of HIV is embedded in the socio-economic context (Gillespie, 2006; Kalipeni et al., 2004). This links to a broader recognition that, in order to address the challenges for global health more generally, it is vital to engage with the social and structural determinants of health (see WHO, 2008, 2010, 2011; Solar and Irwin, 2007; Williams, 2003; Graham, 2000, 2002; Navarro and Shi, 2001; Marmot and Wilkinson, 1999). This understanding is evident in the policy response to HIV. UNAIDS propounds that to meet its vision of 'zero new infections' will require taking a 'hard look at the societal structures, beliefs and value systems that present obstacles to effective prevention efforts. Poverty, gender inequality, inequity in health and the education system, discrimination against marginalised people, and unequal resource pathways all affect – and often slow – the HIV response' (2010a, p. 12). Policy makers have long highlighted gender as one of the key 'drivers' of the spread of the virus (Piot, 2006, cited in Boesten and Poku, 2009, p. 9; USAID Malawi, 2008, p. 70) and there have been widespread calls for women to be empowered to mitigate their particular risk (UNAIDS, 2010a, 2011; Global Coalition on Women and AIDS, 2008; UNAIDS et al., 2004). In 1992, the International Community of Women Living with HIV/AIDS was established by HIV-positive women at the 8th International Conference on HIV/AIDS in Amsterdam to allow the voices of women to be heard and to advocate for change. In 2004, the 'Global Coalition on Women and HIV/AIDS' was launched by UNAIDS. And yet, although recognition of the gender-HIV nexus infiltrates policies, it is still not fully understood and it does not effectively feed into practice.

The main objective of this work is to examine the nuances of the gender context of HIV risk in Malawi – how it is produced, experienced and responded to at the local level – and this is linked to a broader critique of the policy response.

Gendered risk as structural violence in Malawi

Malawi is a landlocked country in Southern Africa that borders Tanzania in the north, Mozambique in the east and south and Zambia in the west. The population is 13 million, of whom 49 per cent are men (6.4 million) and 51 per cent are women (6.7 million) (NSO, 2008).

On the surface, Malawi appears to be relatively 'peaceful' as compared to other contemporary African countries which have experienced civil war, genocide and apartheid. However, as Scheper-Hughes and Bourgois (2004) and Cockburn (2004, p. 43) highlight, it is necessary to recognise that violence extends beyond conflict, into peace-building processes and permeates even seemingly 'peaceful' contexts. Although post-colonial Malawi has not experienced these forms of mass violence, it is not a country at peace in the broadest sense of 'at peace'. As Galtung (1969) argues in his seminal work in the field of Peace Studies, 'positive peace', and thus meaningful social justice, encompasses more than the absence of personal violence; it requires the absence of structural violence. Structural violence is where social structures (including economic, political, legal, religious and cultural structures) engender inequality; they prevent individuals or groups from achieving their full potential – their 'potential realizations' (see also Farmer et al., 2006; Scheper-Hughes and Bourgois, 2004, p. 1). It impacts on longevity (see Høivik, 1977; Galtung and Høivik, 1971) and the quality of life in terms of broader psychological and physical well-being (Farmer, 2004, p. 308; Anglin, 1998, p. 145; Kim, 1984). This understanding of positive peace and structural violence is useful for shifting our gaze to what Scheper-Hughes (1993) conceptualises as the 'everyday violence' of the enduring, lived reality of 'small wars and invisible genocides' that are a normalised feature of contemporary Malawian society.

Malawi has some of the worst development statistics in the world for a non-conflict-affected state. Between 2000 and 2008, Malawi ranked among the seven poorest countries, with gross national income per capita fluctuating between US$150 and $280 (World Bank, 2010); 40 per cent of the population are living below the poverty-line, equating to approximately 5 million people surviving on less than one US$1 per day (World Bank, 2010). Parts of the country experience periodic food insecurity, with an annual 'hunger season' from November to March (MVAC, 2012; WFP, 2007). HIV prevalence escalated from 1.7 per cent in 1987 to 14.3 per cent ten years later. By 2006, Malawi was one of ten countries with highest prevalence (UNAIDS, 2006). Between 1990 and

2007, the number of people living with HIV (PLHIV) had increased over tenfold, to almost a million. In more recent years the trend in prevalence indicates a slight decline to 11 per cent as the epidemic matures, but overall the downward trend is relatively shallow and the epidemic continues to be severe (GoM, 2010, p. 29; NAC, 2009, p. 4).[2] This situation of poverty, under-development and poor health can be understood as a form of structural violence (see Mowforth, 2014; A. Gupta, 2012; Allen, 2001). It reduces longevity: Malawi has one of the lowest life expectancies in the world at 53 years (NSO, 2008). It also negatively impacts upon an individual's capabilities to live a life that can be considered fit for a human being (Sen, 1985; Sen and Nussbaum, 1993; Nussbaum, 1992, 2000). Nussbaum points to ten 'functionings' that are identified as central to human life, which include life, bodily health, practical reasoning and control over one's environment (1999, pp. 41–2, 2000, pp. 72–80).

As elsewhere, poverty, under-development and poor health are gendered. The Malawi *Population and Housing Census 2008, Analytical Report 4: Gender* (NSO, 2010a) considers how gender can impede growth and development in general, and for women in particular. It highlights how women are seriously disadvantaged with respect to their access to higher education, literacy, ownership of housing and household assets, and household basics including safe drinking water, cooking and lighting fuel (NSO, 2010a, p. iii; see also UN, 2004a). Women disproportionately experience poverty, hunger and poor nutrition, even in situations where there is no food scarcity (GoM, 2006, pp. xx, 33; NSO Malawi and ORC Macro, 2005, pp. 177, 182; Hindin, 2005, p. 93).[3] And, as women comprise 70 per cent of full-time farmers, they tend to take the pressure during times of shortage, especially in female-headed households (WFP, 2007; GoM, 2000, 1.4; UN, 2004a). Women smallholder farmers are typically limited to subsistence agriculture that focuses on household survival rather than market-orientated production, and are often marginalised from technical developments in farming. They often have the narrowest margins to deal with crop shortfalls and they tend to have smaller, less fertile plots of land. The particular concern in this book is that HIV disproportionately impacts on women. In 2004, prevalence among people aged 15–49 was higher among women (13 per cent) than men (10 per cent); 40 per cent of newly reported infection occurred in people under the age of 30 and, of these, almost 60 per cent were women and girls (NSO Malawi and ORC Macro, 2005; NAC, 2004).[4] By 2010, the gender gap in prevalence had widened: prevalence for men had reduced to 8 per cent but remained constant for women at 13 per cent. HIV prevalence was highest among women aged 35–9 (24 per cent) (NSO and ICF Macro, 2011, pp. 196–7).

It has long been established that gender-based violence is a key aspect of HIV risk and the World Health Organization (WHO) recognises the implications of coercive or forced sex, and how the fear of violence hinders access to Voluntary Counselling and Testing (VCT) (Türmen, 2003, p. 412). Gender-based violence is pervasive in Malawi. The Intimate Partner Violence survey (Pelser et al., 2005) reveals that a third of women experienced physical abuse, a tenth experienced sexual abuse and half have experienced some form of abuse.[5] As elsewhere, the family is one of the most violent of social institutions and women are at greatest risk of violence from their husbands (see Scheper-Hughes, 1993). The Malawi Demographic and Health Survey (MDHS) revealed that in 2004, 77 per cent of currently married women who have experienced physical violence reported that either a current or previous husband was the perpetrator (NSO Malawi and ORC Macro, 2005, pp. 267–8; see also CILIC, 2007, p. 7; Pelser et al., 2005, p. 8). These figures, however, only scratch the surface of gender as violence in Malawi and the implications for HIV risk. It is likely that the extent of the abuse is underestimated because cultural norms discourage the discussion of sexual or conjugal issues (NSO Malawi and ORC Macro, 2005, pp. 267–8, 273). Moreover, as Kelly (1988, p. 95) considers, gender-based violence extends along a continuum that goes beyond direct, personal violence (including physical and sexual abuse) to structural violence.

As Anglin considers, gender as structural violence manifests itself in terms of inequitable distribution of resources and social categorisation in accordance with gender norms (1998, p. 145). Gender is socially constructed and refers to the complex characteristics that denote what counts as 'female' and 'male'. Although gender is not fixed, stable or universal, gendered structures are pervasive and justify men's domination over women across class, race and cultural differences. Male contributions are typically more highly valued and privileged in society than female ones, and this underscores a hierarchy whereby women are considered inferior to men (see Squires and Weldes, 2007, p. 186; Baum, 2004, p. 1074; Spike Peterson and Runyan, 1998; Charlesworth, 1994; Steans, 1998, pp. 10–12; Tickner, 1992, p. 7, 1997, p. 615; Hawkesworth, 1997; R. Grant, 1991, p. 8; Squires, 1990, p. 54; Fraser and Nicholson, 1989, p. 92; Harding, 1986, p. 18; de Beauvoir, 1953, p. 192). Oppressive patriarchal structures tend towards inequalities and differences of gender that support asymmetric power relations and mean that women disproportionately experience HIV risk (see Nkenza, 2000, pp. 221–2).

It is, however, crucial to recognise that gender issues cannot be conflated to women; gendered inequalities and sexuality impact upon both men and women (see also Boesten and Poku, 2009). Gender norms place both men and women at risk of HIV: this includes, for example, both women's subordination and associations of risk-taking with masculinity and sexual conquest (Türmen, 2003; on South Africa see Jewkes et al., 2003; on Malawi see Kaler, 2003). Moreover, gender is politically, culturally and historically situated. The categories of 'men' and 'women' are not cross-culturally singular, homogeneous groups; they are unstable and contested, not always coherently or consistently constituted in different contexts. Gender intersects with a multiplicity of other aspects of identity – including race, ethnicity, class and religion (see Squires and Weldes, 2007, p. 191; Yuval-Davis, 2006; Phoenix and Pattynama, 2006; Steans, 1998, p. 15; Mohanty, 1998, p. 258; Hawkesworth, 1997, p. 680; Crenshaw, 1993). Where multiple inequalities of poverty, gender and ethnic marginalisation intersect, HIV risk is heightened. These structural inequalities are violent because they directly impact on HIV risk, which also diminishes health and well-being more broadly.

In order to fully understand these contemporary patterns of violence, Scheper-Hughes and Bourgois (2004, p. 5) argue that it is vital to recognise how they have been shaped by historical experiences of conquest and colonialism. The analysis here identifies what is historically general and what is specific to the Malawi case. Colonial rule was established in 1891, when present-day Malawi was incorporated within the British Central Africa Protectorate, which was later to become the Protectorate of Nyasaland in 1907 until independence in 1964. There were three decades of single-party rule under President Hastings Kamuzu Banda (1966–93) and the first multi-party elections were held in 1994 under a provisional constitution, which took full effect the following year. As elsewhere across the continent, Malawi has experienced successive neoliberal policies since independence that have been differentially experienced, have been contradictory and have changed over time (Bezner Kerr and Mkandawire, 2012).[6] The historical specificity is essential because it avoids the totalising fiction of permanent relations of domination and subordination. Gender is historically situated and patriarchal relations are transformed over time (Baum, 2004, p. 1097; Hawkesworth, 1997, p. 681; Mohanty, 1998, p. 259). As Williams (2003, p. 131) argues with respect to what is missing in work on the social and structural determinants of health in medical sociology, a more historically informed analysis, situated in the specificities of place, is necessary to understand relationships between social structures and health based upon the narratives of people. This is important for appreciating the magnitude of the task of responding to gender as a driver of HIV.

One of the challenges in advancing gender social justice is that, where structural violence permeates societal structures, it is obscured from view and the policy response is itself embedded within it. As Galtung explains: 'Structural violence is silent, it does not show – it is essentially static, it *is* the tranquil waters... even though the tranquil waters of structural violence may contain much more violence' (1969, pp. 173–4). The system legitimises and reinforces structural inequalities and power relations because violence also runs through the social, economic and political structures (Galtung, 1969, p. 179; see also Cockburn, 2004, p. 43; Anglin, 1998a; Susser, 1998; Gailey, 1998). There is widespread recognition that HIV is gendered and that the policy response needs to engage with the gender context of HIV risk. And yet the tendency is to focus on treatment and technological fixes within prevention strategies, especially where those are easier to implement and evaluate. With respect to behaviour change, the preoccupation is with changing so-called 'risky behaviours' of 'high-risk' or 'at-risk' groups or 'key populations' because, within the constraints of insufficient resources, this is deemed 'cost-effective'. However, in doing so it implies that risk is something that is contained within these groups and, for a long time, this has resulted in little action or progress (Craddock, 2006, pp. 153–68). Bezner Kerr and Mkandawire (2012) highlight how the dominant neoliberal responses contribute to and reinforce certain gender roles in Malawi: popular narratives about HIV in policy, public health promotion efforts and political speeches create 'gendered spaces of violence'.

This book contributes to the broader feminist task of de-invisibilising these gendered structures. Although structural power is deeply embedded in the societal structures, its operation, as Lukes (2005, p. 64) propounds in his work on power, can be understood through observing whose interests are furthered by the dominant ideas of the current system and whose interests are harmed. Of interest here is that where HIV spreads along the fault lines of society, it highlights the existing social, economic and cultural patterns of exclusion – including the gender patterns (Baylies, 2004, p. 71; see also Seckinelgin, 2008, p. 147). People are harmed, in that gender structures underscore the spread of HIV and there are particular ramifications for women. UNAIDS (2013, p. 79), for example, highlights the complications among women of tuberculosis and cervical cancer, and how the impact of the care-taking burden shouldered by women and girls diminishes their educational and economic opportunities.

Moreover, it is essential to recognise that gender as structural violence is not fixed or static. This work provides an actor-orientated and social constructionist analysis, as propounded by Norman Long (2001, p. 1), which responds to the shortcomings of the 'people-less' development orthodoxy and contributes to deconstructing 'received wisdoms' of expert knowledge. The findings reveal some of the complexities of the agency of the seemingly 'powerless' to navigate these structural inequalities in spite of the limited options available to them – what Lonsdale (2000, p. 6) terms as agency in 'tight corners'. This book examines the plethora of ways in which, in the absence of a more effective policy response, people at the local level (particularly women) navigate the gendered structural constraints to bring about their immediate security and well-being. It contributes to the feminist literature that examines and how gender as structural violence is produced, experienced and responded to (see Anglin, 1998; Susser, 1998; Gailey, 1998). More specifically, it complements the body of literature on HIV in Malawi that exposes the plethora of ways in which people are navigating their situations of dependency. For example, the work of Watkins (2004) that exposes local strategies of prevention behaviours, including reducing the number of sexual partners, partner selection and divorce, and the work of Bryceson and Fonseca (2006) that examines how people engage in risk to meet their food needs. This understanding is linked to a critique of the implications of the dominant ways of conceptualising and responding to HIV, which has implications for achieving gender social justice.

The analysis draws upon the wealth of interdisciplinary research in Global Health, geography, medical sociology, medical anthropology, history, feminism and African Studies (notably from Malawian scholars). It makes a particularly valuable contribution to the emerging area of Global Health, which is establishing its place within International Relations (IR) and, in turn, contributes to the broader task of challenging the traditional boundaries of the discipline. The global challenges of health bring the significance of analyses at multiple levels to the fore; contesting the traditional, disembodied, state-centricism of IR. HIV is a global pandemic that is experienced at the local, familial and individual levels. And yet, much of the Global Health literature focuses on the global level of governance and obscures other scales, particularly the local level where health is actually experienced (see for example McInnes and Lee, 2012; Harman, 2007, 2009a, 2009b, 2010, 2012; Rushton and Williams, 2011; Davies, 2010; Elbe, 2010; Hill, 2011; Rushton, 2010b; Goeman et al., 2010; Feldbaum et al., 2010; Lee, 2003, 2004a,

2004b, 2010). Despite a long history of feminist scholarship highlighting the significance of the personal level (Tickner, 2005, pp. 7–8) and the interconnectedness of the global, national and local (Mohanty, 1991, 2003, p. 501; Elshtain, 1981), these remain marginalised and under-researched within IR (Parpart, 2011; Young, 2005, p. 1). This work complements the wealth of interdisciplinary literature that highlights the importance of bringing in different scales and re-orientates the analysis along the global–local axis by offering a contextualised, empirical analysis of people's lived experiences of HIV (in geography see Kalipeni and Zulu, 2012; Koch, 2011; in sociology see Flynn, 2006, p. 84; Adam and Van Loon, 2000, p. 4; in feminism see Tickner, 2005; Mohanty, 1991, 2003; Webb, 1997). The analysis benefits from fieldwork in Malawi since 2005, which included work in two indigenous languages (Chichewa and Chitumbuka). It asks what we can learn about the gender context of risk from marginalised African perspectives, including PLHIV in more remote parts of the country. This refocusing of Global Health is important because viruses spread between bodies and impacts on the health of individuals. An understanding of the position and relations of women and men at the local level allows for a more complete approach to understanding the linkages between gender, peace, security and risk. In doing so, it exposes some of the different forms agency takes within the structural constraints of gender, and contributes to work that seeks to locate African agency within IR (see Brown, 2012).

Chapter outlines

Chapter 1 examines the implications of the dominant ways of conceptualising and responding to HIV for engaging with the gender context of risk. Where HIV has become an 'exceptional' global health concern it has been prioritised over other public health issues. The analysis questions the ways in which it is framed in development and security terms. It then moves on to critique the dominant neoliberal response, which emphasises the primacy of medical expertise, and the tendency to impose policies aimed at behaviour change from the top down. It is argued that the dominant policies aimed at treatment and behaviour change (most notably the ABCs – abstain, be faithful and use condoms) are embedded within the very structures of violence that underscore the gender dimensions of risk in the first place. The policy response is blind to the local gender context and obscures the complexities of people's lived experiences of risk. This work therefore asks what we can learn from marginalised African perspectives to fill gaps in policy and understanding.

Chapter 2 introduces the methodology. Following on from the critique of the policy response, the main objective of this work is to examine the nuances of the gender context of HIV risk in Malawi and how it is produced, experienced and responded to at the local level. The analysis in this work takes a social constructivist and actor-orientated approach. The research design has been informed and developed through engaging Malawians at all levels of society in a dialogue. The qualitative methodology included national-level key-informant interviews in 2007 to understand the broader issues across the country and the country-level policy response. This was then complemented by local level work in 2011 in two indigenous languages (Chichewa and Chitumbuka), which included consultations, observations, and focus group discussions with PLHIV, individual interviews and informal discussions. The local-level work explores the politics of health 'from below', focusing on the micro level of everyday experiences of HIV risk as serious objects of study. The thorough discussion critically reflects upon a number of critical incidents that particularly informed the research design.

The empirical chapters then move on to analyse the historically situated and culturally unique ways in which gender as a form of structural violence manifests itself in terms of inequitable distribution of resources and social categorisation in accordance with gender norms. In doing so they expose some of the various ways in which, in the context of limited other options, people respond to these structures. Chapter 3 examines the gender dimensions of poverty and argues that this is a form of structural violence that means women are the traditional dependants, which underscores their particular risk of HIV infection. The analysis exposes how these structures are maintained, resisted and navigated to secure immediate survival and also as a strategy for upward social mobility. Chapter 4 builds upon this to explore the gendered ways in which the identities of men and women are constructed and their lives are valued, which is linked to the gendered division of labour. The chapter argues that this social categorisation is a form of structural violence that underscores HIV risk. The analysis exposes some of the ways in which it is navigated to bring value and meaning to life. The understanding in these chapters helps to further highlight why the dominant neoliberal interventions are not working. In the absence of an effective response, risk-taking provides a fundamental means for navigating situations of gendered inequality and dependency. Where HIV has become normalised and accepted as part of life, people engage in risk-taking in sex for security (in terms of survival and upward social mobility) and well-being (in terms of identity and fulfilment). Although aspects of these practices exacerbate the spread of the virus, strategies to eliminate these practices are problematic because these are key safety nets.

It has long been recognised that gender issues are among the main drivers of the spread of HIV risk, with widespread calls for women to be empowered. Empowerment encompasses more than political or economic empowerment. It is vital for wider cognitive and psychological empowerment whereby people can critically understand their own reality, challenge their disempowerment, have a sense of self-worth, and have the self-esteem and courage to challenge their oppression, including through taking risks. Chapter 5 critiques the ways empowerment is being addressed and argues that these are limited in terms of engaging with gender as structural violence. Technological fixes, including female condoms and microbicides, offer the potential to circumvent some of the gendered power structures but do not address gender as structural violence. Empowerment through social protection has been hailed as the 'innovative' solution to gendered poverty, but it faces challenges in scaling up and entrenches some of the gendered structures. Education is important, but it is not sufficient. Initiatives such as support groups for PLHIV aim at psychological empowerment in terms of valuing people's lives and their contributions to society. And yet, despite the appeal of empowering people to solve their own problems, as Swidler and Watkins (2009) have argued, people are often empowered only far enough to be able to compete for aid resources, thus entrenching existing inequalities of power and the structural violence they reproduce.

The conclusion begins by exploring what this all means for de-invisibilising gender as structural violence before considering the challenges for the academy and the policy response. This book contributes to the Global Health scholarship, which typically obscures the micro level where health is experienced. It contributes to dispelling the gender silences in the security discourses. Gender as structural violence permeates even seemingly 'peaceful' and 'secure' contexts and underscores HIV risk. Global Health raises questions of what IR can understand from African experiences and perspectives. The challenge for the post-2015 development agenda is to augment gender social justice – promoting freedom from structural violence. Although this is difficult, it is fundamental because these structures undermine the current policy response to HIV. An effective response must understand context, be participatory and reflect on the impact it has.

1
Framing the Virus
The Policy Response to HIV

HIV has had a prominent place on the global health agenda as an 'exceptional' issue for global governance, attracting unprecedented levels of political commitment and resources as compared to other health concerns (see Smith and Whiteside, 2010; Nguyen, 2010, p. 13). The Global Fund to Fight AIDS, Tuberculosis and Malaria was established in 2001 and up to April 2010, US$19.3 billion had been committed in 144 countries. Seven grants were awarded to Malawi from October 2003 to 30 June 2010, totalling US$460 million ($343 million of which had been disbursed) (OIG, 2012, p. 1). In addition, the US President's Emergency Plan for AIDS Relief (PEPFAR) was launched by former President, George W. Bush in 2003 and subsequently extended by President Obama. On 30 July 2008, the United States Global Leadership Against HIV, Tuberculosis, and Malaria Reauthorization Act was signed, authorising the commitment of up to US$48 billion over the ensuing five years. For the fiscal year 2008, President Bush requested US$5.4 billion to support treatment for 2 million HIV-infected people, prevention of 7 million new infections, and care for 10 million people infected or affected by HIV.

Crucial to understanding the rise of 'AIDS exceptionalism' is the ways in which the complex challenges the virus poses have been framed. As Elbe (2006, p. 125) argues, it is a political decision how to frame HIV and this serves to circumscribe the parameters for the response (see also Shiffman and Smith, 2007; Labonté and Gagnon, 2010, p. 14). This chapter is concerned with examining the implications of the ways in which HIV has been conceptualised and responded to for engaging with the gender dimensions of the pandemic. First, the analysis questions the ramifications of these frames for engaging with gender as a structural determinant of risk. As Butler (2009, pp. 9–10) considers in her work on the 'frames of war', these can be challenged by showing that the 'frame' never contained the reality it was supposed to depict. It is argued that the ways in which the pandemic is conceptualised invisibilises the gender dimensions of people's lived experiences of insecurity and risk. Second, the dominant neoliberal responses that emphasise the medicalisation of risk and changing so-called 'risky' behaviour from the top down are critiqued. It is argued that, as is the case for neoliberalism more broadly, these serve to legitimise, manage, reinforce and even perpetuate the very structural inequalities and power relations that heighten risk rather than challenge them. In doing so, this chapter highlights the importance of context and provides the rationale for the subsequent analysis of the nuances of gender as a structural violence in Malawi.

Framing the global response

The analysis here focuses on examining the implications of the development and security frames for engaging with the gender dimensions of the pandemic. Since the mid-1990s HIV has been included within a global development framework (see Linking, 1996). In 1994 the International Conference on Population and Development highlighted in its Programme of Action the challenges HIV posed for population and development (UNFPA, 1995). Moreover, in 2000 combating HIV was included in goal six of the Millennium Development Goals, recognising that addressing the pandemic was critical to achieving 'sustainable development' (see Hulme, 2007). Ahead of the Millennium Summit, Kofi Annan (the then Secretary-General of the UN [United Nations]) highlighted in his report *We the Peoples* that, despite the multiple health challenges that are fundamental to development:

> It is beyond the scope of this report to explore all of these challenges. I wish here to focus on a specific health crisis that threatens to reverse a generation of accomplishments in human development, and which is rapidly becoming a social crisis on a global scale: the spread of HIV/AIDS. (Annan, 2000, cited in Rushton, 2010a, p. 8)

Framing HIV in development terms is important for recognising the complex challenges that the virus poses for development at all levels, including global development, states, the private and public sector, communities, households and individuals (see UNAIDS, 2009, p. 21; Commission for Africa, 2005, p. 204; Hope, 2001, pp. 22–9). For the case of Malawi, the National HIV/AIDS Policy (GoM, 2003) highlighted how the virus is threatening development by undermining previous gains and changing the very nature of development. Labour productivity and economic growth were diminishing, families were losing their bread-winners and the burden on elderly family members and older siblings was heightened. In the health sector, HIV patients were occupying more than 50 per cent of hospital beds and the maternal mortality rate more than doubled, a large part of which was attributed to AIDS-related ill-nesses. Agricultural extension workers were dying at a faster rate than replacements could be trained and it was estimated that by 2020 the agricultural workforce would be 14 per cent smaller than it would have been without HIV. Chronic illness was reducing productivity with the result that land was being left fallow. Where adults were absent for long periods to nurse sick relatives they were unable guard their land and livestock against theft. Women were identified as being particularly at risk of property grabbing on the death of their spouse. The persistence of a short-term outlook meant that people invest in petty trading rather than agricultural enterprises and children left orphaned do not have the skills to perform agricultural activities. Furthermore, HIV impacts on the capacity of the political system to effectively and efficiently perform its mandates, and thereby respond to the multiplicity of challenges posed by the epidemic. It exacerbates the demand on the public services to respond to the plethora of challenges and yet it decreases the capacity of these services (see UNAIDS, 2006, ch. 4; GoM, 2003, 1.1–1.4; Ngwira et al., 2001, pp. 15–16). The *Malawi Human Development Report* in 2005 therefore propounds that 'unless HIV and AIDS is placed at the centre of national planning processes Malawi's chances of stimulating eco-nomic growth, reducing poverty and promoting human development are dramatically reduced' (UNDP, 2005, p. 1).

And yet the dominant neoliberal 'Development' discourse (capitalised here to distinguish it from development more broadly defined) serves to manage and reinforce the structural inequalities that underscore HIV risk in the first place. There is a long history of 'top-down' neolib-eral development in Malawi. Structural Adjustment Programmes (SAPs) were introduced from 1981 and, as was the case in other so-called 'developing' countries, these conditional loans were dictated by the 'good governance' prescriptions of the Bretton Woods Institutions (the World Bank and the International Monetary Fund). The underlying free-market ideology required the rolling back of the state, efficiency cuts (with particular ramifications for health and education with the intro-duction of user fees) and export-orientated agriculture (see Chilowa and Chirwa, 1997; Lele, 1990; for the situation in general see Hay,

2004; Harvey, 2005). The SAPs did not include a systematic evaluation of the impact of adjustment on the poor, who are predominantly women (Kydd and Hewitt, 1986, p. 362). In the aftermath, facing growing criticisms, including the calls for adjustment with a 'human face' (UNICEF, 1987), the World Bank recognised that in countries with extreme poverty, such as Malawi, the SAPs compounded the adverse effects on the poor, highlighting the need for investment in broader agricultural development (Lele, 1990, pp. 1207–8). This led to the promotion of broader economic restructuring through the Enhanced Structural Adjustment Facility. Structural adjustment was replaced in 2001 by the Poverty Reduction Strategy Papers, following criticism of the limitations of the previous Poverty Action Plans and the Interim Poverty Reduction Strategy Plans of the 1990s. It stressed the importance of empowerment and creating an enabling environment 'whereby the poor can reduce their own poverty' (GoM, 2001, p. 90), but it remained vague in how this is to be achieved (Ellis et al., 2003, p. 1496).

Despite Malawi being hailed as one of the strictest adherers to neoliberal policies, at the end of the 1990s it was highlighted that increases in foreign direct investment and economic growth failed to materialise (Chilowa, 1998). The shift to export-orientated agriculture – most notably burley tobacco – has left the economy vulnerable to exogenous shocks in global trade prices. Agriculture accounted for 35 per cent of gross domestic product in 2008. For the period 2000 to 2010 there was an increase in the trade deficit to166 billion Malawi Kwacha (MK). Tobacco is the main export but there is an increase in non-traditional export commodities, including garments and cotton (NSO, 2011, p. 4). The government is still dependent on foreign aid for 40 per cent of national budget and the UK's Department for International Development (DfID) provides the largest bilateral aid programme. Given the situation of dependency on the external environment there is a pressure to enact donor-driven policies, as is the case for gender mainstreaming, democratisation and the Farm Input Subsidy Programme (see Moser, 2005; Chinyamunyamu, 2014), a point I return to in chapter 5.

Neoliberalism focuses the attention of agencies, particularly the World Bank, on technocratic and universalising policy initiatives in poor countries such as Malawi. As J. Ferguson (1990) famously argues in *The Anti-Politics Machine*, the deeper issues of development that underscore poverty (including inequalities, dependency and gender) are left suspended in mid-air, rendered non-political and are not talked about on the ground. As Mowforth's (2014) recent work considers, development is predicated on force and systemic violence, which permeates the policy response. The concern here is that the inherently political nature of many development problems, including inequality, discrimination and the local and national political processes, is obscured (see Hickey, 2009; Green, 2006). Hickey (2009) argues that, despite some lip-service paid to new forms of political analysis and efforts to support 'pro-poor' initiatives, these are limited and the agenda of liberalism – based on ideology rather than evidence – is entrenched. A stronger political perspective is therefore essential and this includes a gender perspective. These reforms have had a particularly negative impact on women, as chapters 3 and 4 explore. As Moser (1989) famously argues, women are a resource for development within neoliberal policies: their unpaid labour mitigates the negative impact of, for example, the SAPs and shocks to food production, including droughts and floods. Neoliberalism continues to be the dominant paradigm of international development today, which Bezner Kerr and Mkandawire (2012) argue includes the policies on HIV and gender. Despite the attention paid to the 'female face' of issues of development (including HIV), this is only at a superficial level, which invisibilises the deeper aspects of gender as structural violence, a point returned to in chapter 5, when I look at empowerment.

Since the turn of the twenty-first century there has been an emphasis on conceptualising HIV in international security terms and this has been extensively debated within the Global Health IR literature (see Rushton and McInnes, 2012; McInnes and Rushton, 2010; Rushton, 2010a, 2010b; Elbe, 2003, 2005, 2006, 2009; Ostergard, 2002, 2008; Barnett and Prins, 2006; McInnes, 2006; Whiteside, 2006; Garrett, 2005). In January 2000, the UN Security Council took the extraordinary step of highlighting the pandemic as 'a threat to international peace and security'. The speed with which it has spread across Sub-Saharan Africa and the absence of an effective response has entrenched the perception that HIV is a crisis situation. The rapid increase in AIDS-related mortality brought about uncertainty about the magnitude of the risk, which is compounded by the time lag between infection and AIDS-related deaths a decade later; HIV is a 'lentivirus' – taking a long time to manifest itself (see Boesten and Poku, 2009, p. 3). The long-term impact of HIV is hard to measure, which impairs the response to HIV as a systemic condition (Poku and Whiteside, 2004, p. xvii). The combination of the uncertainty of the situation and the fact that healthy looking people can be infected exacerbates the sense of emergency (Anglewicz and Kohler, 2009, pp. 65–7). In April 2001, the Abuja Declaration and Framework for Action for the Fight Against HIV, Tuberculosis, and Other Related

Infectious Diseases in Africa was created at a special summit of the Organization of African Unity, describing the AIDS situation as 'a state of emergency facing the continent' (OAU, 2001). The aim was to foster African leadership in the response to AIDS and African governments were required to commit at least 15 per cent of national budgets to the health sector to assist in the fight against HIV, tuberculosis and other infectious diseases. The UN General Assembly held a special session on AIDS at the end of June 2001, which represented 'the most concerted, high level and comprehensive gathering of nations ever held to discuss AIDS' (Piot and Seck, 2001, p. 1107) and a declaration of commitment was created.

This shift in how HIV is conceptualised was important because, as Labonté and Gagnon consider, the 'high' politics of security trumps the 'low' politics of human rights and development – allowing them to be taken more seriously in IR (2010, p. 14). Peter Piot (2005), founding Executive Director of UNAIDS and Under Secretary-General of the United Nations from 1995 until 2008, propounds how framing HIV as an 'extraordinary security threat' is advantageous: it engages with some of the complexities of the military, political and economic impact, appealing to material and strategic interests of states. The UN Political Declaration on HIV/AIDS (2 June 2006) recognised that 'HIV/AIDS constitutes a global emergency and poses one of the most formidable challenges to the development, progress and stability of our respective societies and the world at large, and requires an exceptional and comprehensive global response'. Emphasis is laid on the alarming statistics to highlight the sheer scale of the pandemic and quantify risk. The UN Political Declaration on HIV/AIDS (UN, 2006) for example states that:

[We] [n]ote with alarm that we are facing an unprecedented human catastrophe; that a quarter of a century into the pandemic, AIDS has inflicted immense suffering on countries and communities throughout the world; and that more than 65 million people have been infected with HIV, more than 25 million people have died of AIDS, 15 million children have been orphaned by AIDS and millions more made vulnerable, and 40 million people are currently living with HIV, more than 95 percent of whom live in developing countries.

UNAIDS (2009, pp. 7, 21) reports that over the past three decades a total of almost 60 million people have been infected and there have been 25 million AIDS-related deaths. Sub-Saharan Africa is the area hardest hit by the pandemic, accounting for 67 per cent of the global population living with HIV and 72 per cent of all new HIV infections in 2008. Against this backdrop there has been a proliferation of global and regional treaties, conventions and organisations, particularly over the first decade of the twenty-first century, committing governments to respond (see for example UNAIDS, 2008a, 2009; UN, 2000, 2006; OAU, 2001).

However, the securitisation of HIV lays emphasis on the more traditional, state-centric concerns about the impact on military security, particularly through diminishing the capacity and effectiveness of armed forces (see discussion in Elbe, 2006, pp. 125–6; for the debate on pandemic influenza see Enemark, 2007, 2009; Lee, 2006). HIV emerges onto the agenda as a security concern because of the connections with national stability and conflict (see McInnes, 2011; de Waal, 2010; Singer, 2002, p. 145). Narrow national security interests lie in protecting a state's territory, its population and its economic, social and political interests from the external threat of AIDS 'the invader' (Feldbaum et al., 2006a, p. 774; Elbe, 2006, pp. 120, 129). This rhetoric permeates even the United Nations discourse: when the former Secretary-General, Kofi Annan addressed the African Summit on HIV/AIDS, Tuberculosis and Other Infectious Diseases on 21 April 2001, he declared that 'The war on AIDS will not be won without a war chest, of a size far beyond what is available so far' (UN, 2001). Scarce resources target strategically important populations for national and international stability and security, in particular prioritising the elites and army. The virus is considered a threat to the operational capability of the military because it depletes highly trained human resources that are difficult to replace, interrupts training of new recruits, reduces the pool of new recruits and then there are the costs associated with treating infected soldiers. UN Resolution 1308 was formulated six months later, which mandated UNAIDS to take action with regard to the effect on peacekeeping missions. There was a dual concern to prevent diseases being spread to the civil population by peacekeepers and the peacekeepers becoming infected and introducing infections when they return home (Elbe, 2006, pp. 119–44; Barnett and Prins, 2006, pp. 367–8; Feldbaum et al., 2006a, p. 775). The US National Intelligence Council report *Global Infectious Disease Threat and Its Implications for the United States* drew attention to the impact of infectious diseases on national security: they 'endanger US citizens at home and abroad, threaten US armed forces deployed overseas, and exacerbate social and political instability in key countries and regions in which the United States has significant interests'

(US National Intelligence Council, 2000, pp. 33–65). As recognised by the human security discourse introduced by the 1994 *Human Development Report* (UNDP, 1994), problematising HIV in narrow security terms ignores individual women, men and children who are infected or coping with the impact, and, more specifically, the ability of women to identify with and contribute to the creation of security (see also Hoogensen and Stuvøy, 2006, pp. 208, 210). Furthermore, feminist scholars highlight that security is a gendered term, dominated by masculine characteristics of war and violence (see Tickner, 1992; Enloe, 1989).

Seckinelgin et al. (2010), in their work on Burundi, argue that the narrow security frame does not effectively engage with the ways in which conflicts place people (and women in particular) at HIV risk. They expose how the security–HIV nexus fails account for the gendered vulnerabilities, how these are instrumentalised in conflict and post-conflict, and how they are also maintained and changed as a result of people's experiences during conflict. The concern here is that it invisiblises gender as structural violence, which permeates even seemingly 'peaceful' contexts. Although Malawi is heavily affected by HIV, it does not have a history of conflict, and yet it is not a country at peace in the broadest sense of what Galtung (1969) defines as 'positive peace'. HIV risk is part of a 'continuum of violence' (see Kelly, 1988; Cockburn, 2004) that is interlinked with broader experiences of under-development and insecurity that is entrenched in a long history of colonialism and neoliberal development. As de Bruijn and van Dijk (1999, pp. 115–16) consider in their research on insecurity and pastoral development in the Sahel, 'crisis situations are not just calamities for an unhappy minority, but rather a dominant feature of life for millions of people in numerous societies throughout the world.... For them insecurity is a total experience not confined to one life sphere or another, but integrated in their lives and society.' The linkages between HIV and (in)security have resonance, particularly in terms of poverty, under-development and poor health as a structural violence – and these are experienced in gendered ways. This brings to the fore questions of what we can learn about the complexities of structural inequalities of gender in 'peaceful' contexts such as Malawi.

The sense of a 'crisis' within the security discourse is at odds with people's lived experiences of the normalisation of risk. Although it is over 30 years since the first clinical evidence of AIDS was reported in 1981, the pandemic is still treated as an emergency situation. Framing HIV as a 'crisis' is attractive because it fits the short-term view of the governments, non-governmental organisations (NGOs) and media, which respond to current events and emergency situations (Melesse, 2008). The virus has long been normalised and accepted as an inescapable fact of life, as is the situation across Sub-Saharan Africa (see also Caldwell, 1997, p. 180). The fieldwork in Malawi revealed that, despite the continuing fear surrounding the virus, the popular perception is that 'HIV comes for people, it does not come for animals. It comes for people.' There is also a pervasive Christian discourse that reflects: 'Don't be afraid of HIV, because God knows that there is HIV. So if God knows, what is the problem of getting it?' The normalisation of HIV has ramifications for how risk is perceived at the local level and this fuels the spread of the virus. This is compounded by the belief that the virus is pervasive in the community and transmission is certain if you have sex with an infected person. As Anglewicz and Kohler (2009, p. 67) reveal, the tendency is to overestimate the prevalence in their community and the likelihood of transmission: 95 per cent of women in rural areas believe transmission is certain during sexual intercourse with an infected person. If you believe that you have already placed yourself at risk it may be considered not worth changing your behaviour, because of the perception that you are already infected.

HIV is not a crisis situation, instead, as Barnett and Prins propound, it is a 'long-wave event' that requires a long-term political commitment to engaging with the structures of inequalities that underscore risk. They critique how 'the resultant rising political priority has worked to fore-close prematurely the research phase in a rush to define responses'. This is problematic because it is likely that actions that are believed to be best in the short term will exacerbate the problem in the long-term (Barnett and Prins, 2006, p. 360; see also Barnett, 2006). Rather than imposing emergency measures, the response instead should be part of the nor-mal, routine political process (Elbe, 2006, p. 13; see also Seckinelgin, 2012b). An HIV specialist working with CIDA (Canadian International Development Agency) in Malawi explains:

> Emergency situations always allow you to make quick decisions *ad hoc*. I would like to move away from an emergency situation. This is not an emergency; this is the situation. So we need to work on it. We cannot always be just running around with the fire extinguisher, just to spray out a little bit here and a little bit there.

Moreover, the emergency response situation leaves little room to engage more effectively with the complexities of the gender context of risk as a structural violence that places women at particular risk, which is rooted in a long history (see also O'Manique, 2005, p. 35). The complexities of which are explored in chapters 3 and 4.

Neoliberalism and governing HIV risk

Neoliberalism dominates the governance of HIV risk and the concern here is to examine the implications for engaging effectively with gender, focusing on the medicalisation of risk and the ABCs as the dominant approach to behaviour change. It is argued that the neoliberal orthodoxy legitimises, manages, reinforces and exacerbates the very gender structures of violence that underscore the spread of the virus, rather than challenging them (for the situation of neoliberalism in Haiti see Farmer, 2004, p. 313). This connects with work on Malawi by Bezner Kerr and Mkandawire (2012) in critical feminist geography, which considers how popular narratives about HIV in policy, public health promotion efforts and political speeches create 'gendered spaces of violence'.

The invisibility and uncertainty of the risk posed by HIV has been confronted by medical science and clinical risk assessment, with an emphasis on the responsibilities of individuals for managing risks to their own bodies and selves, as the literature from sociology reveals for risk more generally (see Flynn, 2006, p. 83). To understand the governance of HIV risk it is useful to draw upon Foucault's understandings of the rise of the 'clinical gaze', 'governmentality' and 'surveillance' as a new part of disciplinary power from the eighteenth century:

> Bio-power spread under the banner of making people healthy and protecting them. Where there was resistance, or failure to achieve its stated aims, this was construed as further proof of the need to reinforce and extend the power of experts. A technical matrix was established. By definition there ought to be a way of solving any technical problem. Once this matrix was established, the spread of bio-power was assured, for there was nothing else to appeal to: any other standards could be shown to be abnormal or to present merely technical problems. We are promised that normalisation and happiness through science and law. When they fail, this only justifies more of the same. (in Dreyfus and Rainbow, 1982, p. 196; see also Flynn, 2006, p. 82; Lemke, 2001; Dean, 1999; Peterson, 1997)

As Elbe (2012a, 2012b) considers in his work on swine flu and the antiviral drug Tamiflu, security is linked to the medicalisation of society and insecurity, amplifying what he terms 'pharmaceuticalisation'. Within modern western societies, a scientific way of knowing the world – albeit contested – prevails: there is the dominance of rational thought, scientific knowledge and the desire to control and predict (Capra, 1983, p. 39). Despite shifts in the ways health, illness and disease are defined, medical science dominates most people's routine understanding of health, based on the assumption that 'medical science can produce rational, objective and value-free knowledge about disease and its treatment' (Flynn, 2006, p. 80). As Seckinelgin propounds, 'the experience of the disease as a social phenomenon is transformed into solely medical experience as constructed by medical expert knowledge' (2008, p. 1). The response to HIV lays emphasis on the conviction that science will find a solution, which has eclipsed an understanding of the social and cultural circumstances of risk (see Fauci, 2003; McFadden, 1992). Complex technologies (so-called 'silver bullets') are developed to solve problems and resolve human needs, and primacy is accorded to the power of 'experts' (Oakley, 1986, p. 144).

Until a scientific solution to the virus is found, the global response has sought to develop coping technologies and technological fixes that can mitigate the impact, including through the Global Fund and PEPFAR. It is clear that over the past three decades important scientific achievements have been realised in responding to the virus and that crucial challenges remain (Lewin, 2010). Antiretroviral drugs (ARVs) have been developed that slow down the onset of AIDS and prolong the time until the full impact is felt. UNAIDS estimates that a total of 2.5 million deaths have been averted in low- and middle-income countries since 1995 due to the introduction of antiretroviral therapy and the scaling up of access to medicines could reduce the number of people newly infected by up to 1 million annually (UNAIDS, 2010, p. 8, 2011, p. 10). With the availability of free ARVs in Malawi from 2005 at the major hospitals (and from 2008 in the village health centres), there is a reason for people to get tested: to access the ARVs and prolong their life. Previously, the impact of HIV was more apparent on businesses and services. People living with HIV (PLHIV) who were infected prior to the availability of ARVs widely report how they were bed-bound and 'like skeletons'. In recent years however, PLHIV can return to work and the Chief Executive of Zomba City (Malawi's fourth largest city) reflects, for example, that few people are off sick at the City Council, despite a number of its staff being HIV-positive. Furthermore, potential strategies are emerging for a cure, including the successful trials in Thailand in September 2010 that indicate advances in the development of a vaccine for particular HIV strains. Microbicides (gels, creams, films, diaphragms or suppositories that can be applied or inserted inside the vagina or rectum to protect against HIV) are under development to offer women more opportunities to control their bodies, and in July 2010 the success of the CAPRISA (Centre for the AIDS Programme of Research in South Africa) trials was hailed as a major breakthrough.

Of course, these 'silver bullets' are a vital part of the response. With respect to the gender dynamics of HIV risk, women need better tools to protect their own bodies from infection – including female condoms and microbicides (Serour, 2008). And yet, they obscure the deeper structures that act as pervasive barriers to women actually using them that the empirical analysis here explores – a point that chapter 5 returns to. Policy makers recognise the necessity to go beyond these technological solutions and medical interventions (Boesten and Poku, 2009, p. 10). To effectively respond to the pandemic, the contributions of social scientists are essential to further understand and engage with the structures that place populations at heightened risk, and to recognise why the current interventions are not working.

In the absence of a scientific solution to the spread of HIV the dominant neoliberal policy response to HIV focuses on behaviour change. The concern here is that this response is embedded within and reinforces the very structures of violence that underscore the gender dimensions of risk in the first place (see also Bezner Kerr and Mkandawire, 2012).

The dominant discourses of risk are applied to certain sexual behaviour and identities, acting as a control mechanism to regulate the 'other'. As Lupton (1994) highlights, people's bodies are seen as dangerous sources of disease, posing risks to self and wider society. The focus of the policy response has been on changing the behaviour of individuals who fall within so-called 'high-risk' groups from the top down. The neoliberal 'one size fits all' model is based on a philosophy of 'best practice' in other countries. As is the situation elsewhere, behaviour change programmes in Malawi – such as the Population Services International's (PSI) *Chisango* Condom Programme and Family Health International's (FHI) Behaviour Change Monitoring Programme – target truck drivers, traders, police officers, teachers, fishermen, estate workers, sex workers, young people and, more recently, men who have sex with men. In 2011 the Head of Monitoring and Evaluation at the National AIDS Commission (NAC), when asked about HIV risk in the country, highlighted how 'NAC nationwide has identified risk groups that include sex workers, truck drivers, men who have sex with men, non-common drug users, 70 per cent prevalence in sex workers'. With scarce resources, this targeted approach – based on assumptions of the high rates of partner change among these groups – is deemed to be cost effective by the World Bank (Tinker et al., 2000, p. 18). And yet, although the language of 'risk' is useful, it cannot be narrowly conceived. The continuing labelling of certain populations as 'high-risk' or 'at-risk' in the policy response implies that risk is something that is contained within these groups and has resulted in little action or progress. In particular, the focus on sex workers eclipses the importance of understanding the experiences of women in marriage who live in 'situations of risk' (see UNAIDS, 2008; Craddock, 2006). The Director of Planning, Research and Evaluation at the Department for Nutrition, HIV and AIDS reflects in 2007, 'most of the transmission now is through the husbands in the family' (see also Craddock, 2006, pp. 153–68).

A more sophisticated understanding requires a shift in focus beyond the appeals to expert opinion to understand how risk is differentially experienced, understood and contested at the local level (see Flynn, 2006, p. 84; Adam and Van Loon, 2000, p. 4). Risk is differentially experienced and resisted, along what Sanders (2006) conceptualises as a 'continuum of risk'. Of particular interest here is how gender (as a social construct) is a fundamental way in which power operates and risk is experienced (on gender and power see Squires and Weldes, 2007, p. 187).[1] As chapters 3 and 4 explore, differences and inequalities of gender support asymmetric power relations between men and women that underscore a structural violence whereby women disproportionately bear the brunt of the virus (see also Anderson, 2012).

Most HIV prevention aims at reducing immediate risk through Information and Education Campaigns and the main strategy had long been the ABCs (see Poku and Whiteside, 2004, p. xvii; Piot and Seck, 2001, p. 1107). Information and Education Campaigns were attractive because they have an impact that can be measured. They were deemed to be the most successful phase of the response in Malawi, resulting in high levels of HIV awareness (Lwanda, 2005, p. 128). By 2004, there was almost universal knowledge of AIDS: over 90 per cent of people realised HIV can be transmitted from someone who appears healthy and more than 80 per cent knew that the presence of sexually transmitted infections (STIs) can increase the likelihood of transmission (NSO Malawi and ORC Macro, 2005, p. 186; Watkins et al., 2004). By 2010, knowledge of HIV transmission and prevention had become more comprehensive: two-thirds of people aged 15–49 knew that you can reduce risk of HIV infection by using a condom every time you have sexual intercourse, and having one uninfected sex partner who has no other partners (NSO and ICF Macro, 2011, p. 167).

As is the case for health interventions more generally, the measures that are promoted to encourage risk avoidance are informed by neoliberal conceptualisations that individuals are responsible for their own health (see Flynn, 2006, p. 83; Beck-Gernsheim, 2000, p. 123). The neoliberal individual is rational, competitive, economically motivated and self-interested. Life is not a 'gift from God', as is widely believed across Sub-Saharan Africa, rather life is individual property and it is expected that the individual will behave in ways that ensure they will continue living (Kohli, 1986, p. 185, cited in Beck-Gernsheim, 2000, p. 123; Lwanda, 2005, p. 53). Beck explains that, 'In the industrialized society, the individual must... learn on pain of permanent disadvantage to conceive himself or herself as the centre of action, as the planning office with respect to his/her own biography, abilities, orientations, relationships and so on' (1992, p. 135). However, individuals are not rational neoliberal subjects and, as is the situation for health behaviour more generally, knowledge does not tend to result in behaviour change (Nguyen and Stovel, 2004; Ngwira et al., 2001, p. 7; Caldwell, 2000, p. 120). As the Principal Officer at the Department for HIV, AIDS and Nutrition considers in the case of Malawi, people are aware of HIV and transmission and yet, despite the high level of knowledge, there is limited behaviour change.

Furthermore the neoliberal subject is based on a male individual, which Bezner Kerr and Mkandawire (2012) argue ignores other motivations for behaviour, including altruism, collective strategies, empathy, love, reciprocity and care. And yet, typically it is women who bear the responsibility for behaviour change. They tend to be the first in the family to know their serostatus because they are tested when they attend antenatal clinics. As the Gender Network National Coordinator at Action Aid reflects, this is mostly in the absence of their spouse (see also Muula and Mfutso-Bengo, 2004, p. 482; Maluwa-Banda, 2005, p. 16). As Anne Ntombela highlighted at the Third Africa Conference on Sexual Health and Rights in 2008 for the situation more generally, when women are found to be HIV-positive at the health clinics they assume the burden of being the moral guardians: they are the ones responsible for informing their husbands and ensuring the couple uses condoms (see also Campbell et al., 2005). When those women return with STIs or pregnant they are told that 'you must learn to be more responsible', even though it is overwhelmingly their male partner who will not use a condom. This responsibilisation of women obscures the reality at the local level in Malawi that typically women are 'on the receiving end' of their sexual relationships, as the representatives of NAC, the Family Planning Association and the *Packachere* Programme consider. Women may fear informing their spouses because they are often blamed for infecting her husband, as the Director of Planning, Research and Evaluation, Department of HIV, AIDS and Nutrition considers. As is the case more generally, the topic of sex is particularly taboo for women and they face greater stigma and discrimination from society if they disclose that they are HIV-positive than men do (see CILIC, 2007, pp. 6–7; in general see CHGA, 2004, p. 8). The Gender Network National Coordinator at Action Aid for example outlines that 'your friends they desert you, your family they desert you and you are stigmatised. You are denied your rights – your right to association is denied.' This is supported by a number of media reports that reveal that if a woman disclosed to her husband that she was HIV-positive, she may be subjected to violence, accused of infidelity, lose the marriage and be excluded from her family (Nkulembe, 2004; Paliani-Kamanga, 2004; Mwafulirwa, 2006, p. 4; Maluwa-Banda, 2005, p. 16; for the situation across Sub-Saharan Africa see Muula and Mfutso-Bengo, 2004, p. 482). In one article, a woman from Masanjala in Chiradzulu is quoted as reporting that when she disclosed she was HIV-positive:

> My husband together with my in-laws were blaming me, saying that I brought them HIV and decide to chase me out of the house the moment I revealed my serostatus, I became a pariah and was dispossessed of everything except personal clothes in spite of my huge contribution to the construction of the house and several other efforts towards our well-being as a family. (Nkulembe, 2004)

In response to these issues the Programme Officer at the World Food Programme (WFP) explains how couple-testing initiatives have been developed and considers, for example, how a Prevention of Mother-to-Child Transmission programme in Namete did this through providing food support to couples who attended. However, the focus group discussions and interviews revealed this is based upon a western model of the nuclear family, which is at odds with African families, which include polygamous marriages and extended families.

The ABCs in particular were not effective strategies for women because they are fundamentally at odds with the pervasive gender norms. Regular sex and bearing children is central to marriage (for the situation in general see Holland et al., 1991, p. 128; on Malawi see Zulu and Chepngeno, 2003, p. 250). The 2004 MDHS reports that 'women are taught to never refuse having sex with their husbands, regardless of the number of partners he may have or his unwillingness to use condoms, even if he is suspected of having HIV or another STI' (NSO Malawi and

ORC Macro, 2005, p. 17). This is supported by the Head of the Society for the Advancement of Women, a women's rights NGO, who explains that 'If a man wants to have sex without a condom as long as a man is the "breadwinner" in that house [the wife] cannot say no, because then she is afraid that if she says no he is going to marry another woman and then she is out.' In stark contrast, women traditionally cannot negotiate sex for example, as the men consider in the focus group discussion with Kapora Support Group, and Gregory emphasises that 'if a woman asks for sex a man will think she is a "prostitute" and has *wanjala chomene* (lots of [sexual] appetite)'. Typically, women are not in a position to ensure that their husbands are faithful. As the Senior Programme Manager for the *Packachere* Programme reflects, the popular belief is that the wife must ensure her husband is satisfied sexually to keep him from seeking other sexual partners (Fielder, 2000, p. 38). Typically wives cannot confront their husbands if their demands for safer sex are ignored and they are not in a position to leave a relationship that places them at risk. Whereas women who refuse their husbands sex are vulnerable to being divorced, as the National Coordinator of the Malawi Network of Religious Leaders Living with HIV and AIDS (MANERELA) reflects.

It is widely reported that women typically lack the power to negotiate for condom use, particularly women in marriage, and this includes situations where the husband is HIV-positive or has other STIs (NSO Malawi and ORC Macro, 2005). The FHI Behaviour Surveillance Survey (2004), for example, reports that condom use was almost non-existent (3 per cent) in the marriage situation. The lack of power women have to negotiate for the use of condoms is illustrated by one case of 'husband abuse' reported to the Victim Support Unit in Mulanje in 2006. It was recorded by the Investigating Officer that: 'the husband complains that despite of practising "Loop Contraceptive" (a type of child spacing) the wife insists on using condoms whenever they want to do sexual intercourse'. The resolution of the case was reported to be that: 'The wife admitted her weakness and agreed to give herself fully to her husband on condition that her husband supports the family both physically and financially.'[2] The interviews and focus group discussions indicate that a couple can only use condoms if the man wants to and therefore, as is the case more generally, use is more consistent where the wife is infected than where the husband is infected (Blanc, 2001, p. 198; for a study of Rakai, Uganda see Porter et al., 2004, p. 477).

The use of condoms within stable relationships is problematic because of the stigma associating them with sexual immorality and protection against infected women, as the Product Manager for HIV Prevention at PSI's *Chisango* Condom Programme considers. Condoms are criticised by some church leaders for promoting promiscuity and many of the churches, including the Catholic Church, refuse to distribute them and condone their use (see also IPPF et al., 2006, p. 5; Rankin et al., 1995, p. 6; for the situation on general see Schoepf, 2003, p. 555; Baylies and Bujra, 1995, p. 202). Condoms have also met cultural resistance, with traditional leaders opposing their use because they believe they promote promiscuity. Lwanda reports that 'those initial few who accepted condoms were seen, because of their breaking with local customs, as promiscuous' (2005, p. 117). The mixed messages and falsehoods spread by some churches have contributed to widespread fear among the general population based on a lack of understanding; this includes doubts that condoms really control HIV, and people believe that they have holes that permit HIV to leak through (Muula and Mfutso-Bengo, 2004, p. 486; Banda, 2005, p. 183; for the situation in general see Schoepf, 2003, p. 559; Grown et al., 2005, p. 183). The social marketing of condoms exacerbates the stigma of immorality. As elsewhere, in Malawi condoms are marketed for use in casual and commercial sex (Mabala, 2006, p. 421). Driven largely by American funding, the social marketing of condoms is targeted at high-risk groups with a high rate of partner exchange, including: policemen, men in the army, truck drivers, fishermen, field workers, sex workers and sexually active young people (for the situation in Nigeria see Orubuloye and Oguntiniehin, 1999, pp. 121–9). They are marketed to be pleasure-orientated; they come scented, flavoured and studded, and they are packaged with provocative images of women on the front. The packaging of studded and flavoured *Manyuchi* condoms sparked controversy in September 2004, and MP Patricia Kaliati called for the removal of the women from the packaging because it was disrespectful to them. A representative of Banja La Mtsologolo (BLM), a reproductive health NGO, explained that the condoms were marketed in this way to appeal to adults and youths (see also Namangal, 2004). Similarly, the Product Manager at *Chisango*, who is responsible for the social marketing of that condom brand, explained in 2007 that:

> This condom is basically for the 15 to 24 age group and what it was meant to be is, it was meant to be a lifestyle product [that] said 'look if you are cool this is what you need to have'. We sort of wanted to break [with the taboos] to say nobody ever has sex whilst fully dressed, you know and this sort of thing where people are putting on

miniskirts and stuff like that, that is what you see when you go to all these nightclubs and bars. We are targeting people who are already sexually active, we are not saying that if you are not having sex you better had because this is what you are missing. What we are saying is you are having sex, ok then you need to protect yourself.

He recognises that the marketing of most condoms may be part of the reason for the stigma of sexual misconduct, and as a result 'people then think you only use condoms when you want to sleep with somebody who is like a stranger to you, somebody who is outside of the marriage context'. Women were only targeted by the social marketing as sex workers, rather than as women in marriage who are in situations of risk. This adheres to the ideology that condoms are a means of protection against infected women; women with multiple sexual partners are blamed for the spread of HIV (see also Van Den Borne, 2005, p. 1). However, it is beginning to be recognised that women are becoming infected in increasing numbers and they are actually at greatest risk from their husbands. *Chisango* was launching the female condom that year to specifically target women, and male condoms were to be targeted at couples as a means of family planning alongside the marketing of the female condom.

Where condoms are primarily considered as a means of protection against HIV and STDs (sexually transmitted diseases) in extra-marital relationships, use within marriage is negligible and the condom is considered to be an intruder in the domestic space (Chimbiri, 2007, pp. 1102–15). As the Technical Advisor to the Women, Girls and HIV/AIDS – Programme and National Plan for Action considers, the stigma acts as a barrier for even the more educated women to buy condoms and negotiate for the use of a condom in the marriage situation (PSI/Malawi, 2006, p. 20). It was widely reported by the interviewees and focus group discussions that women often fear that if they suggest the use of condoms then they will be perceived as sexually experienced and labelled as promiscuous; if a woman suggests the use of condoms in the marriage context, the husband will become suspicious that the wife has been engaging in extra-marital affairs. As the Technical Advisor to the Women, Girls and HIV/AIDS – Programme and National Plan for Action explains:

The man will not look at himself to say 'yes, I think let's do it because I think I have not been faithful'. No he will say 'why do you want to use a condom? It is because you are sleeping around with other men and therefore I do not want it in my house.' So it is put back to the woman.

The MDHS reports that 17.4 per cent of men aged 15–54 who know of a contraceptive method believe that women who use contraception may become promiscuous. This view is strongly expressed by men who are not living together with their partners (29.8 per cent) (NSO Malawi and ORC Macro, 2005, p. 92). As the Strategic Manager of the Youth Alert! Programme considers 'a young woman who carries a condom is looked at as a prostitute, a young lady who talks about condom use is looked at as some who has been there, experiencing sexual matters and they look at you as "ah, a prostitute"'. It may also suggest that she is accusing her husband of infidelity, which will instigate a negative reaction from the husband, even though it may be true. The Strategic Manager of the Youth Alert! Programme at PSI/Malawi explains that trust is central to steady relationships, even where the husband has another partner:

A lot of people do not use condoms because they trust their partners. So it is very likely that in a casual one or in a one-night stand people will use condoms. But where people are in a more established relationship that has been there for some time they have probably slept with each other for a number of times...most people tend to stop using condoms.

The Strategic Manager considers how many women believe 'trusting to love' is a role for a wife or a regular partner, and therefore prevention methods are unnecessary and undesirable in a committed and loving relationship. This 'trusted partner myth' exists among young people, that when you have been with a partner for a long time you can stop using condoms (see also Muula and Mfutso-Bengo, 2004, pp. 485–6).

There has been a lot of sensitisation of faith-based organisations and traditional leaders, particularly by the NAC. As a result, as the Product Manager for *Chisango* reports, some faith-based organisations 'are warming up to that idea of encouraging people to use condoms in the marriage setting when the man is positive and the woman is negative'. During one meeting of traditional leaders, church elders and birth attendants organised by BLM in Thekerani, Thyolo, the participants were given the chance to brainstorm on uncertainties surrounding family planning methods. The discussions revealed that modern contraceptives mitigate the effects of HIV, allowed couples to follow child spacing, and to provide for the health and well-being of their children (Nkawire,

2006). The NAC and faith-based organisations have broadly reached an agreement that, although they may not necessarily support the use of condoms, they will not speak against them either. As the HIV Advisor at DfID explains, 'the National AIDS Commission and the churches have reached a consensus that they will focus on their strengths without discrediting the areas that they do not believe in, which has worked very well now that NAC has stepped in with behaviour change messages'. The Assemblies of God Church supports the use of condoms within marriage, however the Catholic Church and the Seventh Day Adventist Church continue to raise concerns that condoms do not work.

Currently, male condoms are the most available barrier against HIV infection and, as the key informants widely consider, this increases the man's control over the sexual reproductive health of the couple. As the Director of Planning, Research and Evaluation at the Department for Nutrition, HIV and AIDS reflects 'It's the man who uses [them], if the man wants to have protected sex then it is all up to the man, so then the woman is just on the receiving end.' This is supported by research from PSI/Malawi that reveals that men are overwhelmingly likely to be the ones to buy, carry and suggest the use of a condom, because it is a male product socially marketed at sexually active men who have a disposable income to spend on them. PSI/Malawi reports that 'males are willing to pay an average maximum price of MK16.56 for a three-pack of *Chisango* condoms, and females, MK11.79' (2006, pp. 3, 12). As a result, where condoms are controlled by men, women tend to only have very limited powers for negotiating safer sex: they can either try to persuade their husbands to use condoms or refuse sex. Female condoms and microbicides have been hailed as having the potential to empower women with control over their bodies – as explored in further depth in chapter 5. Piloting of the female condom began in 2007 and the development of microbicides – gels, creams, or suppositories that can be applied inside the vagina to protect against STIs including HIV – is also under way. Research trials have been conducted by the Johns Hopkins Project since 2005 (Chikoko, 2006, p. 3). However, microbicides are still in the research phase and an effective microbicide is not available.

Conclusions

With the rise of 'AIDS exceptionalism' the virus has a prominent place on the global health agenda. The concern here is that the ways in which the pandemic is framed has repercussions for the response, and this has particular ramifications for effectively engaging with gender as a structural determinant of risk. The 'Development' and 'Security' frames situate the pandemic within the more conventional understandings of the national interests of states and global interests. However, the dominant neoliberal discourse of 'Development' focuses upon technocratic and universal initiatives, which obscure the political nature of HIV, including its gender dimensions. The 'Security' discourse is undeniably powerful, but is a gendered term that ignores how the virus is experienced by individuals and obscures women's agency. The narrow security frame invisibilises gender as a form of structural violence, which permeates even seemingly 'peaceful' contexts such as Malawi. Crucially, the perception that HIV is a 'crisis' is fundamentally at odds with the normalisation of HIV as a 'part of life', which will be examined in the ensuing chapters. This is not a crisis – it is a 'long-wave event' (Barnett and Prins, 2006). The emergency response situation leaves little room to engage effectively with the complexities of the structural constraints that place women at particular risk.

HIV has flourished due to the convergence of the global and the local, and yet top-down policy initiatives are largely blind to the complexities of gender power relations and so have failed to instigate meaningful social change on the ground. In accordance with neoliberalism, policy has mostly tried to find a technological fix (through a vaccine and ARVs) and impose behaviour change from the top down. In the absence of a scientific solution, the emphasis over the past two decades has been on individual behaviour change. Current HIV interventions focus on changing the behaviours of certain populations that have been identified as engaging in so-called 'risky' sexual behaviour, as the preceding chapter considered. The labelling of these groups as 'high-risk' or 'at-risk' implies that risk is something that is contained within these groups, obscuring some of the complexities of people's lived experiences of risk. Although the language of risk is useful, it is important to recognise that it cannot be narrowly conceived. Health interventions are predicated on western neoliberal conceptualisations of responsible, rational individuals. And yet knowledge does not tend to result in behaviour change because this ignores the structures around people. Despite the widespread currency of the ABCs, the assumption that behaviour is under the individual's control ignores the social, structural and environmental constraints that are inextricably linked to gender. This has particular ramifications for women, who are typically the ones responsible for behaviour change (as they are the ones who are targeted through antenatal clinics) and yet, in the context of entrenched patriarchy, are unable to do so.

This chapter identifies how structural violence permeates the ways in which the pandemic is framed and responded to – this reinforces and perpetuates the invisibilisation of gender and the very structures that heighten risk. Rather than responding to the HIV pandemic from the top down, a more effective response must be informed by greater understanding of specific economic, political and social contexts. As Webb considers, 'generalizations negate the reality of the great diversity and variety in which people react to this unprecedented situation' (1997, p. xii–xiii). 'The feminist gaze' that informs the analysis here seeks to locate what Sylvester (2006) talks of as being missing from the picture: 'the excesses that a certain visualisation, characterisation, or measurement tries to control or keep out'. The focus in chapters 3 and 4 is to provide a more nuanced understanding of the culturally specific and historically situated complexities of the gendered dimensions of HIV risk in Malawi. The focus is first on gendered poverty and, second, on the gendered ways in which life is valued, which is particularly obscured by the top-down policy response based on appeals to 'best practice' in other contexts. This requires us to draw upon local-level expertise. The next chapter moves on to outline the methodology.

2
Methodology

The ways in which HIV is conceptualised and responded to serves to invisiblise gender as structural violence, as the preceding chapter has considered. Despite the rhetoric, top-down policy initiatives are largely blind to the complexities of the gender context of risk and so have failed to instigate meaningful social change on the ground. Instead, the dominant neoliberal response justifies, manages, reinforces and even perpetuates the structures that underscore risk in the first place. This book therefore contributes to the feminist task of de-invisibilising gender as a form of structural violence to locate what is missing.

This chapter begins by introducing the Malawi case study and the research design. This work provides a social constructivist and actor-orientated analysis to fill gaps in the understanding. The research design has been informed by engaging Malawians at all levels of society in a dialogue. It employs qualitative methodology to understand the gender context of people's experiences of risk. The chapter then moves on to provide thorough discussion of the methodology, which is necessary because a key contribution of this book is the richness of the fieldwork. At the national level this included initial fieldwork in 2005 and 2006, and 44 key-informant interviews in 2007 to understand the broader issues across the country and the country-level policy response. This was complemented by local-level work in 2011 in two indigenous languages (Chichewa and Chitumbuka) to explore the politics of health 'from below'. This included consultations, a series of participant observations, 44 focus group discussions, 110 individual interviews and informal discussions at the local level. There was continuous reflexivity as the research developed and a number of critical incidents that particularly revealed the limitations of some of my initial assumptions are included here.

The Malawi case study

This book examines the nuances of what is historically general and what is unique to the specific gender context of risk for the Malawi case. On the one hand, Malawi is an exemplifying case (Bryman, 2008, p. 56) that represents a broader category of countries in Sub-Saharan Africa that experienced similarities in terms of colonisation and disproportionately experience under-development, severe HIV epidemics and some similarities in the gender context of HIV risk. And yet, on the other hand, Malawi stands in stark contrast to other African countries that have experienced mass violence such as apartheid, genocide and conflict since independence. The concern here is to examine gender as a form of structural violence in this seemingly 'peaceful' context.

The case study approach allows a contextualised, detailed examination of the complexity and particular nature of the gender context of HIV in Malawi, rather than aiming at generalisability (see Mahoney and Goertz, 2006, p. 230; Stake, 1995; Fontana and Frey, 1994, p. 652). The analysis exposes some aspects of the culturally unique way in which gender as structural violence manifests itself in Malawi and for this reason it is worth briefly introducing the ethnic groups. The Chewa is the largest ethnic group (33 per cent), followed by the Lomwe (17 per cent), Yao (13 per cent), Ngoni (13 per cent), Tumbuka (9 per cent), Sena (4.5 per cent), Mang'anja (3 per cent), Tonga (2 per cent), Nkhonde (1 per cent), Nyanja (1.5 per cent), Ndali (0.4 per cent), Lambya (0.4 per cent) and other groups (2 per cent) (NSO and ICF Macro, 2011, p. 26). The Chewa are the dominant ethnic group both politically and culturally. This is rooted in historical experience whereby the first President of Malawi, Hastings Kamuzu Banda, manipulated culture and capitalised on Chewa cultural values to entrench his political power (Forster, 1994, pp. 477, 481). Of particular interest is how gender norms differ between ethnic groups. A key distinction is that the Ngoni, Tumbuka, Tonga and Nkonde (the main ethnic groups in the north) and the Sena (in Nsanje District in the south) are patrilineal: the wife moves to the husband's village on marriage, land is inherited through the man's lineage and women access land through their husbands. Men dominate in the family and the woman's father or husband is the highest authority. In contrast, the Chewa, Yao, Mang'anja and Lomwe (the main ethnic groups in the central and southern regions) are matrilineal: the husband moves to the wife's village on marriage and the lineage is traced through the women. Although women in the matrilineal areas have some powers, they are still under male control, a point I will return to in chapter

3 (see Peters, 1992). The analysis explores some of the specific cultural practices of these groups.

This understanding of the complexities of the gender context of risk in Malawi is important for filling gaps in understanding because there is insufficient evidence and data to inform policy and planning despite the National HIV Prevention Strategy 2009–2013's emphasis on the need for evidence-based and data-driven prevention (NAC, 2009, p. 1). The UNGASS Country Progress Report for 2008–9 (GoM, 2010) highlights the limitations of its findings, which relied upon the 2004 MDHS, the Multiple Indicator Cluster Survey (MICS; UNICEF and NSO Malawi, 2006) and the Behaviour Surveillance Survey (FHI, 2006). Another Demographic and Health Survey was planned for 2008, but it was postponed until 2010 because of the plan for a national census that same year, and the results were released in July 2011. The policy discussions in 2014 on the preparation of the new National Strategic Plan for HIV highlighted the sheer inadequacies of the data. Although a plethora of research is undertaken by the various organisations involved in the response, the findings are not always effectively shared. Moreover, the analysis here also generates issues and questions that can be applied to other contexts. Although the situation of HIV is different between contexts, the issues are not always unique and, where appropriate, I draw upon the broader interdisciplinary literature on other contexts throughout the analysis in order to contribute to that literature.

Research design

This research aims to understand the complexities of the gender context of HIV risk: how it is produced, experienced and responded to. It provides an actor-orientated and social constructionist analysis which, as Norman Long (2001, p. 1) propounds, responds to the shortcomings of the development orthodoxy, which he argues is ' "people-less" and obsessed with the conditions, contexts and "driving forces" of social life rather than the self-organising practices of those inhabiting, experiencing and transforming the contours and details of social landscape'. Such an approach contributes to 'deconstructing "received wisdoms" of this specialised niche of knowledge production and prescription' (Long, 2001, p. 1). Social constructivism recognises knowledge, views, understandings, experiences and interactions as meaningful in terms of understanding the social reality. An interpretivist methodology is used to facilitate detailed understanding of the meaning derived from gender-based cultural norms and practices, the intricacies of behaviours, motivations and experiences, and how they contribute to the spread of HIV (see Mason, 2002, p. 3; Denzin and Lincoln, 2000, p. 3; Blaikie, 2000, p. 115). This work analyses a wide range of people's knowledge and lived experiences to fill gaps in understanding (Flyvbjerg, 2001; Rhodes, 2002). The purposive sampling (Vromen, 2010, p. 259) included policy makers and other actors engaged in the response, and people whose perspectives are marginalised, including people living with HIV (PLHIV) in more remote areas who speak indigenous languages. This work benefits from my cultural understanding and working knowledge of the Chichewa and Chitumbuka languages. This is important because, as Pass highlights, command of English is restricted:

> Development requires comprehension and comprehension requires understanding the most important things in life in one's own mother tongue, or at least in a tongue that is familiar to the culture and psychology of the average African. (Pass, 2005, p. 3)

English was imposed as the official language during colonial rule and it is the language of the official documents, including the language of legislation, reports and the press. Chichewa (the language of the Chewa) is the second national language and it is the language that policy and legislation is typically translated into for popular consumption. Chichewa/Chinyanja is probably the most widely spoken language in Southern and South-Central Africa and it is spoken in parts of Zambia, Mozambique, Zimbabwe and South Africa (see Pass, 2005). Chitumbuka (the language of the Tumbuka) is the dominant language of the north.

Since this work is critical of the top-down policy response based upon appeals to western 'expertise', the research design has been informed and developed through engaging Malawians at all levels of society in dialogue. This allows these voices to shape the research questions and rectify initial stances (see Schratz and Walker, 1995) because, as Chabal and Daloz (1999, p. 141) consider, perceptions of Africa as the 'other' have had a profound impact on the approaches employed to analyse Africa. A series of consultations were undertaken with key actors engaged in the response, and local-level understandings were incorporated through observations, piloting and the guidance of the local research assistant. Where power permeates the research process it is necessary to be continuously reflexive of the lens through which the researcher is interpreting these dynamics, and how structures of gender, discourses of HIV and relationships with the 'researched' change over time. The inductive data collection and analysis sought to adapt to changing circumstances, follow new paths of discovery as they emerged and allow the previously marginalised perspectives of the participants to be heard (Rhodes, 2002).

Qualitative methodology was considered the appropriate methodology given the criticisms raised of the neoliberal orthodoxy and the concern to understand the gender context of people's experiences of risk. As Semu and Binauli argue in their research on gender inequalities in Malawi, statistical measures 'do not present complete pictures of specific country situations, being more concerned with just the figures and not the dynamics that lead to such inequalities' (1997, p. 86). Charmes and Wierenga conclude in their evaluation of measuring women's empowerment that 'there are many issues related to women's empowerment that escape quantification in the traditional sense' and identify the need for more sensitive approaches (2003, p. 434). Therefore a combination of qualitative methods was used, which included documentary analysis, semi-structured key-informant interviews, participant observations, focus group discussions, individual interviews and informal discussions. The particular emphasis on dialogical approaches is in accordance with the epistemological position that a legitimate and meaningful way to generate data is to talk interactively with people (Mason, 2002, pp. 3, 63–5; Marková et al., 2007; Wells, 1999). The analysis is undertaken from the 'bottom up' to allow the theorising to emerge out of the data and meaningful categories arise from the ground (Glaser and Strauss, 1967; Mason, 2002; Wengraf, 2001, p. 2; Bryman, 1988, p. 46). The local, contextual data facilitates a culturally respectful critique of those gendered structures that are oppressive, presenting important, and yet neglected, areas for further research.

Quantitative methods are utilised only to a limited extent in order to further understand the issues generated from the qualitative research. In doing so, it is important to be mindful of the issues surrounding the reliability of this data. As the HIV/AIDS specialist working with CIDA in Malawi highlights in 2007, there are concerns surrounding the quality and relevance of the available data, as well as the methods used to gather data. CIDA workers reflect upon the contradictions in the information that the Health Sector-Wide Approach (SWAp) receives. Personal sexual relations are hard to quantify and, with the stigma surrounding issues of sex and HIV, the data cannot always be precise or predictable. The data on HIV prevalence prior to 2010 is problematic because the methodology involves monitoring data obtained primarily through antenatal clinic sentinel surveillance. The 2004 MDHS recognises that the biases include the following factors:

health facilities are not randomly selected and tend to be urban; pregnant women may have unprotected sex at a greater rate than the general population, which could overestimate the prevalence; the prevalence in ANC [antenatal clinic] attendees may underestimate what is happening with the general population because women with HIV associated infertility are not captured; and men and non-pregnant women are not included in the sentinel surveillance sample. (NSO Malawi and ORC Macro, 2005, p. 225)

In addition, there are variations in the quality of population surveys, and some uncertainty concerning the magnitude and direction of biases being introduced due to refusal and absence (see NSO Malawi and ORC Macro, 2005, p. 226; Dzekedzeke and Fylkesnes, 2004). A scenario assuming that non-responders have twice the HIV prevalence of those who fully participated in the survey suggests that individual non-response could result in an adjusted HIV prevalence 1.03 to 1.34 times higher than the observed prevalence (García-Calleja et al., 2006). HIV testing in the 2011 MDHS enabled the inclusion of men age 15–54 (NSO and ICF Macro, 2011). However, 87 per cent of eligible participants were interviewed and consented to testing – and coverage was higher for women than men (91 and 84 per cent respectively). Among men, coverage was lowest among those in urban areas (80 per cent), those aged 30–34 (81 per cent) and in the lowest wealth quintile (82 per cent) (NSO and ICF Macro, 2011, p. 193). Furthermore, although national gender statistics have become available and key data for HIV/AIDS are disaggregated by gender (IPPF et al., 2006, p. 3), it is important to note that the statistics beyond these national surveys are still partial. For example, many organisations did not compile basic statistics, including the Victim Support Units and Magistrates Offices, which were approached during the fieldwork in 2005–7.

Nvivo was used to facilitate extensive qualitative analysis of large volumes of rich data. The qualitative methods are not neutral tools but active social interactions between people that produce negotiated and contextually based results. As a result, knowledge was reconstructed and meanings created, rather than facts reported (Mason, 2002, p. 62). Therefore this research does not aim to uncover established truths but instead to understand the worldview of the participants; how they make sense of multiple and often conflicting 'truths' about gender and

HIV risk (King and Horrocks, 2010, pp. 61–2; Wilkinson, 1999, p. 65). Although risk is underscored by the realities of structures of the global political economy, the sociology literature argues that it is simultaneously real and constructed (Flynn, 2006; Beck, 2000, p. 212; Lupton, 1994; Douglas, 1992). Drawing upon Habermas, people's health can be considered as part of their interpretative and symbolic 'life worlds' (see Flynn, 2006, p. 90). As Lupton (1999) argues, risks are not realities that are 'out there' but instead encompass beliefs, meanings and understandings about a phenomenon (see also Adam and Loon, 2000, p. 4; Beck, 1992, p. 23). Although there is not necessarily a clear way of determining the validity or legitimacy of the data, it is important for exposing indeterminacy of risk. It is the generation and regeneration of these perceptions that motivates action, directly and indirectly influencing so-called 'risky' behaviour (see Castaneda, 2000). It is this 'psychological reality' that informs personal beliefs and actions (see Yow, 1994, pp. 10–14). This understanding sheds light on the reasons why people behave in the ways they do, and why behaviour change policy has limited impact. A degree of judgement was necessary in the analysis and the results are subjective (Mason, 2002). Qualitative validity is achieved through trustworthiness based on credibility, dependability, plausibility, transferability and conformability (Guba and Lincoln, 1994, pp. 105–17; Hammersley, 1992). A process of 'triangulation' was used to verify, contextualise and clarify the data, which involved returning to the literature and data on Malawi, Sub-Saharan Africa and HIV to provide greater analytical rigour (Mason, 2002, p. 108).

National-level fieldwork 2005–7

The first stage of this research aimed to understand the gender context of risk across the country and the policy response. Two initial periods of fieldwork were undertaken in 2005 and 2006 in order to plan the subsequent fieldwork and commence language training. A series of informal consultations were undertaken in Zomba, Blantyre and Mulanje in the south; Lilongwe, Kasungu and Dedza in the centre; and, Karonga, Mzuzu, Nkhata Bay and Rumphi in the north. These included District Commissioners, the offices of the National Initiative for Civic Education (NICE), Traditional Authorities and NGOs working on HIV and gender. Primary and secondary data was collected, including legislation, policy proposals, reports and media articles. These resources were added to during the key-informant interviews in 2007 and consultations and interviews in 2011. I undertook a one-to-one, intensive Chichewa language course in 2006 at the Centre for Language Studies at the University of Malawi (funded by the Economic and Social Research Council). I built upon these skills throughout the course of the fieldwork and I also learnt Chitumbuka. Where there are not words in their own vocabulary the Chichewa and Chitumbuka languages both adopt words of other languages (including from English and from each other) and this expedited my learning (see Pass, 2005, p. 9). These skills were particularly strengthened in 2011 when I was immersed in Chichewa and Chitumbuka throughout the focus group discussions, the informal discussions, working with the research assistant (who is a native Chitumbuka and Chichewa speaker) and staying with Malawians.

In June and July 2011, 44 individual key-informant interviews were conducted in Lilongwe and Blantyre with representatives of organisations involved in responding to the gendered dimensions of HIV. Theoretical sampling was conducted whereby a specific sample of key informants with relevant experience and knowledge was identified (Mason, 2002). The participants included representatives from government ministries, the NAC, the Women, Girls and HIV/AIDS – Programme and Plan of Action (WGHPPA), Malawi Law Commission, CIDA, World Bank, Joint United Nations Programme on HIV/AIDS (UNAIDS), FHI, PSI, Society for the Advancement of Women, Family Planning Association of Malawi, Malawi Centre for Advice, Research and Education on Rights (Malawi CARER), Malawi Network of People Living with HIV (MANET+), Coalition of Women Living with HIV (COWLHA), Catholic Church and Assemblies of God. (The full details for the participants are included in Appendix 1.) The interviewees were officials and special informants with relevant knowledge and expertise, often in positions where they can shape, reflect on and critique popular opinions. They were identified, approached and recruited through the organisations they represent. The willingness with which interviewees were prepared to recommend me to further interview subjects enabled the research to achieve a much broader and deeper level of data collection than was originally planned. The representatives tended to be HIV or gender focal points rather than the heads of organisations because they had specialist understanding. Many of the organisations have had a long-term presence and work across the country. The interviewees were often in a position to draw upon their organisation's research findings and feedback from the regional and district offices to reflect upon the situation countrywide. It is important to note that the interviewees were also intimately connected to, and a part of, the social

world they reported on. Many interviewees drew upon their own experience and that of their friends, colleagues and family to substantiate
the issues they were presenting. The HIV Advisor to DfID, for example,
came from a patrilineal ethnic group and reflected on how her mother
had been inherited by another relative after her husband died.

Although key issues were generated from the literature and preliminary research trips, the interviews were exploratory (Mason, 2002, p. 3).
The semi-structured interview framework allowed the respondents to
intellectualise about the gender dimensions of HIV risk and critically
reflect upon the response in their own terms (Patton, 1980). It also
ensured that similar themes were explored in the interviews and this
allowed for comparison in the data analysis. The interview method
was sensitive to the social context in which the data was generated.
The participants received an information sheet prior to their interview and gave their informed consent on a signed form. It was made
clear that the participants could withdraw at any time. The interviewees were assured of the anonymity of their responses and identified
as representatives of their respective organisations.[1] The interviews
were conducted in English but a working understanding of Chichewa
enabled greater access to the interviewees that could not have been
achieved otherwise, facilitating travel to the offices and access through
the gatekeepers.

Local-level fieldwork 2011

Building upon the findings from 2007, a three-month research project
was undertaken in 2011 to provide an in-depth analysis of the complexities of the gender context of risk at the local level. Initially, a series
of consultations were undertaken in Lilongwe to determine how best
to design the research to complement current understandings. These
included the National Coordinator of the WGHPPA; the Head of Monitoring and Evaluation at the NAC; a representative of the Department
for Nutrition, HIV and AIDS; Programme Officer for Monitoring and
Evaluation (and Coordinator for Stigma Survey 2010) at MANET+; Assistant Programme Manager at the National Association for People Living
with HIV and AIDS (NAPHAM); National Coordinator at the Coalition
of Women and Girls Living with HIV/AIDS; and the National Coordinator of the Malawi Network of Religious Leaders Living with HIV and
AIDS (MANERELA).

A key concern when designing the fieldwork at the local level was
how to discuss issues such as HIV, sex and violence in the family when

there is reportedly such pervasive silence and stigma surrounding these issues (especially for women). The key-informant interviews in 2007 highlighted that the human body, especially the sexual parts, is traditionally shrouded in secrecy and cannot be talked about. There has been a long history of stigma surrounding these issues: under the rule of Banda, it was officially taboo to discuss sexual behaviour publicly and within the Chichewa language there are only limited references to sexual behaviour and euphemisms are often used (CILIC, 2007, p. 7; Rankin et al., 2005, p. 11; Mhone, 1996, p. 16). The Head of the Assemblies of God Relief and Development Services (AGREDS) explained how this is problematic because 'you cannot talk about HIV without talking about that, we cannot talk about STIs'. He reflected upon a training workshop on STIs he attended when a video was shown: 'you could see people shying off, not looking at the screen, things like that, because it was really showing how the STIs have destroyed the sexual parts. But looking at what they were showing that – no! It was as if they stripped you naked or something like that.' Moreover, it was widely reported that sex is particularly taboo for women. As the Programme Officer at UNAIDS (a Malawian woman) reflects:

[Malawian people] are reserved in certain matters, like sex is a non-starter for discussion with other people. So can you imagine every other time going to this kind of set up and saying 'Oh my husband keeps on forcing me, he doesn't want to use a condom.' You become shy, you do not want people to get to know that private life and say 'I will deal with it in my own house; even though he might end up killing me – but I will deal with it in my house.' So women suffer in silence.

It is reported that sex is rarely discussed openly between the husband and wife, and that often women can only use non-verbal communication to coax men into sex (see Rankin et al., 2005, p. 11; Rivers et al., 1998, p. 280). Cultural norms suggest that women should not be knowledgeable about sexual matters nor talk about issues of sex outside of marriage, including issues surrounding their HIV risk. The Director of Planning, Research and Evaluation at the Department for Nutrition, HIV and AIDS outlines, that:

if the woman is fore frontal about sex then they [people] say 'you are a prostitute' ... so there is also cultural factors that prevent them from talking about sex openly.

Women cannot negotiate for safer sex or defend and protect their sexual rights if they do not have the appropriate language to do so.

However, the observations and participant observations in 2011 revealed how limited this understanding was, and exposed the multifaceted nature of the agency of the seeming 'powerless' and 'marginalised'. Following the consultation with MANET+, I was invited to observe a week-long training workshop on Community Mobilisation in June 2011 in Mponela for representatives of support groups for PLHIV from across Malawi. On the first day of the observation photos were shown of genital ulcers to an audience of women and men. Ironically, my own reaction was just as the Head of AGREDS had described four years before: I found myself shying away from looking at the images and, as I did, I recalled his depiction of that very situation. But as I shifted my gaze around the room I realised that the women and men participating in the workshop were studying the images. The facilitator asked them why he was showing them – to which one man replied that 'we need to know, we need to see, so we can go to the hospital to find treatment. We are not afraid.'

On the final day of these training sessions the facilitator asked the participants 'What makes sex enjoyable for you?' I was a little taken aback by his question because of the pervasive reports that sex is taboo for Malawian people. The facilitator gestured to one of the women and asked her, moving on to the other women. The first couple of women appeared to be embarrassed, but they responded. One woman hid behind her hands and, after talking, fanned herself with her top to cool down. The other participants laughed; dissipating the tension in the room. As the facilitator moved around the room, asking each of the women in turn, they appeared to gain some confidence from each other's responses. I was sitting behind the group, watching closely and listening to the answers, mostly in Chichewa, writing this all down. Another woman talked more confidently, but laughed and looked down as she talked. And then, much to my surprise, the facilitator directed his question to me. I felt myself flush; everyone in the room had their eyes on me, the 'researcher', shattering any illusion I might have had about a division between research and reality. I could not find the Chichewa to express myself; so, in English, I shared a few vague thoughts about love, avoiding saying anything about sex. I had no idea what would be the appropriate thing to say in front of this group. Interestingly, when the other female facilitator was asked she also avoided answering the question. The third representative of MANET+ left the room, perhaps fearing he would also be asked. This raised interesting questions of whether he was more disempowered than the participants because he would not talk about this in front of them, or if he was more empowered to leave and not to have to answer the question. The facilitator then asked the men. The first man talked of 'kissing here and there' and how 'both have a contribution: the wife must take her part, but also the wife is free to touch every part because it is for her, so when we go into the actual sex it is sweeter'. The others laughed. The facilitator asked the next man, who replied. There was more laughter, some shook their heads, others cried 'ayii'. Another man replied 'not the traditional one: "the woman comes on top" '. Some people looked away, others engaged as the men talked.

Although, the sense of the sensitivity of the topic varies in different contexts, for PLHIV participating in the support groups some of the taboos surrounding sex and HIV may have been broken down. Where the participants have already discussed issues of sex and HIV risk within these groups, they may be considered more neutral in front of peers within these groups. Sexuality and sex are important sites of power and resistance (Farquhar and Das, 1999, pp. 49, 51). Although professionals are vocal about these issues when discussing the situations of others, they often lack a voice when it comes to expressing their own lived experiences. As the Programme Officer for Monitoring and Evaluation at MANET+ reflects – and my own research suggest – men and professionals tend to conceal their HIV status and do not join support groups.

The consultations and observations in Lilongwe were followed by consultations in Zomba with the Programme Coordinator for the Malawi Network of AIDS Service Organisations (MANASO); a representative of the National Statistics Office (NSO); and Professor Alister Munthali, the leading authority on the politics of HIV at the University of Malawi.[2] The consultations allowed important but neglected areas for research to be identified and to determine the research sites. The research sites were identified through consultation with the NSO and the Centre for Social Research at the University of Malawi to explore how my research could best complement research already being undertaken in country.

Through these consultations, Zomba District in the south and Karonga District in the north were identified as important case studies. Malawi is divided into three regions: the Northern, Central and Southern regions. There are 28 districts in all: 6 districts in the Northern Region, 9 in the Central Region and 13 in the Southern Region (NSO and ICF Macro, 2011, p. 1). HIV prevalence is highest in the south at 14.5 per cent, as compared to 6.6 per cent in the north and 7.6 per cent in the central region (NSO and ICF Macro, 2011, p. 198). Both Zomba and Karonga districts are important urban trading centres and have high levels of migration, which facilitates the spread of HIV (NSO, 2010b). Forty-five per cent of Malawi's population resides in the Southern Region, as compared to 13 per cent in the Northern and 42 per cent in the Central Region (NSO, 2008). The two districts also allow the research to explore the differing cultural practices of the matrilineal and patrilineal communities (where land inheritance is traced through female and male line respectively). They also enable comparison between the major urban centres of Zomba City and Karonga Municipality with the rural areas of these districts. This is important because the majority of HIV-positive people are in rural areas. Moreover, there are differences between people's lived experiences of gendered inequalities in urban and rural areas.

Zomba District is one of 12 districts of the Southern Region, bordering the districts of Chiradzulu, Blantyre, Mulanje, Phalombe, Machinga, Balaka and Mozambique to the east. The population in 2008 was 587,167 and population density was 230 per km^2 (NSO, 2008). The main ethnic groups are the Yao, Mang'anja, Lomwe and Ngoni and they are matrilineal: customary land inheritance is traced through the female line (ZDA, 2009, p. 12). The focus group discussions included participants who self-identified as Yao, Chewa, Lomwe, Ngoni and Nyanja. In 2004 Zomba District had the fifth highest HIV prevalence, at 18 per cent (NSO Malawi and ORC Macro, 2005). Zomba City is situated 290 km south-south-east of Lilongwe. It is an important urban centre and is one of the four major cities of Malawi (along with Lilongwe, Blantyre and Mzuzu). In terms of size, it is a sub-regional centre (ZDA, 2009, p. xiv). Zomba City is an important trading centre, conference centre and tourist destination. There is extensive migration at local, district, regional and international levels. Zomba City has the highest gross lifetime migration rate (the total number of in-migrants and out-migrants divided by the total population) at 101.5. The in-migration rate (the number of in-migrants divided by the total population) is 59.0; only Mzuzu has a higher rate at 60.9. The out-migration rate (the number of out-migrants divided by the total population) is the highest in Malawi at 42.5 (NSO, 2010b, p. 13). Moreover there is extensive temporary migration, including to Chancellor College, police stations, colleges, the army barracks, trading centre, training sessions, conferences and the tourist destinations of Zomba plateau and Lake Chilwa. Zomba District had the fifth highest HIV prevalence at 18 per cent in 2004 (NSO Malawi and ORC Macro, 2005). The Zomba Municipality Urban Development

Plan 2007–2012 identifies HIV as the second of the 15 most pressing development issues in the city, after health issues more broadly defined (ZDA, 2009, p. 7). The number of PLHIV in the district is estimated to be 19,000, of which 13,000 are women (NSO, 2010a). The district had the highest HIV prevalence for women at 25 per cent, as compared to 10.5 per cent for men (NSO Malawi and ORC Macro, 2005). The Urban Development Plan suggests that the rate of HIV transmission is a result of unprotected sex, sexual intercourse at a young age, high-risk groups, mother-to-child transmission, rape and sexual exploitation, and commercial sex workers (ZDA, 2009, p. 12).

Karonga District is one of six districts of the Northern Region, bordering the districts of Chitipa to west, Rumphi in the south and Tanzania to the north (KDA, 2008, p. ii). It has a population of 270,960 and the population density was 80.76 per km² but is experiencing population growth of 2.86 per cent and the crude birth rate is the third highest in the country at 43.5 (NSO, 2010a, p. 15). The Tumbuka and Nkonde are the dominant ethnic groups and they are patrilineal: customary land inheritance is traced through the male line (KDA, 2008, pp. ii, 22–3). The focus group discussions included participants who self-identified as Tumbuka, Nkonde, Lambya, Nyakusa, Nthuka, Ndali, Yao, Chewa, Sena, Msukwa and Mundale. HIV is identified by the Karonga District Assembly as the 'single most important social challenge – contributing to a high mortality rate, high morbidity rate, orphans, shortage of skilled staff, chronically in need of support, overcrowding of hospital wards and overstretching of HIV/AIDS services' (KDA, 2008, pp. 94–5). There was particular interest in Karonga District among the stakeholders in Lilongwe during the key-informant interviews in 2007 and the consultations in 2011. It is a neglected area for research and it is marginalised politically because of its location in the far north of the country. The Tumbuka and Nkonde speak Chitumbuka and KyaNgonde/ChiNkonde: the latter is a particularly under-researched ethnic group. The Malawi Human Rights Commission report (MHRC, 2006) drew attention to a practice among the Nkonde ethnic group known as *Kupimbira* in Chitipa and Karonga districts, whereby daughters are married off by their parents as a form of debt repayment, heightening their risk of HIV infection. HIV risk is entrenched in the political economy because of high levels of trade and migration. Karonga Municipality is situated 50 km south of the Tanzania border and 585 km north of Lilongwe (KDA, 2008, p. ii). It is an important transit hub situated on the main M1 road that runs the entire length of the district, along the lakeshore, and connects the rest of Malawi with Tanzania through the Songwe border and Zambia through neighbouring Chitipa. The gross migration rate is below average for country at 26.2 (NSO, 2010b, pp. 10–12) but this figure does not capture the temporary migration through the district, for example to the trading areas and from the mines for leisure in Karonga *Boma* (municipality). With the exception of the four major cities Karonga District has the highest urban male and female populations (both 17 per cent) (NSO, 2010a, p. 12). Most of the major trading centres are situated along the M1 at Songwe border, Pusi/Kaporo, Mwenitete, Miyombo, Karonga *Boma*, Mwenilondo, Mlare, Ngara, Nyugwe, Chilumba Jetty and Uliwa. The major mining activities include uranium at Kayerekera (40 km west of Karonga Municipality along the Karonga–Chitipa Road), coal at Kayerekera and Mwaulambo (20 km north), lime at Hara in Chilumba area and Mpata (16 km along Chitipa Road) and golden beach sands at Chifyo and Chilumba (KDA, 2008, p. 6).

The research was first conducted in Zomba District. I contacted the District Commissioner's Office to request permission to undertake research and to identify the Traditional Authorities, NGOs, District HIV/AIDS Officer, religious leaders and other stakeholders for key-informant interviews. Further consultations were undertaken with the Chief Executive at Zomba City Council, Zomba City AIDS Coordinator and the District Coordinator of NAPHAM. Through these contacts a series of participant observations of HIV-related activities were conducted through a process of 'snowballing'. This included shadowing the work of the Zomba AIDS Coordinator and conducting participant observations of trainings by MANET+ on Community Mobilisation, NAPHAM on Group Therapy and Child Therapy, the MANASO on the Community Scorecard, cultural ceremonies, the meetings of community-based organisations (CBOs) and support groups for PLHIV. These are all important social contexts in which meanings and understandings about HIV and gender are generated. The consultations and observations were vital for designing the subsequent research at the local level, including in terms of learning how to conduct myself in culturally appropriate ways.

The fieldwork was originally conceived to 'give a voice' to those people who are particularly powerless – women living with HIV (WLHIV). However, the naivety of this was highlighted during the four participant observations with CBOs and support groups from across Zomba District in June and July 2011 (*Yankho* Support Group at the Zomba Police College; NAPHAM training sessions; Nsondole Support Group meeting; Makunganya Village Support Group). Instead these observations exposed multiple aspects of the agency of seemingly 'powerless'

WLHIV. While shadowing the work of the Zomba AIDS Coordinator there was the opportunity to observe a meeting with *Yankho* Support Group. When the seven women arrived at the meeting there was a strong sense of community among them and they chatted, hugged and greeted one another and began their meeting with dancing and singing. The three men in the group arrived late and sat separately in the farthest corners of the room. At the end of the meeting there was the opportunity for me to ask questions related to my work. The women dominated the discussion, so I enquired why the men were quiet. One man replied: 'Usually the men are seen as the ones that are involved in promiscuous behaviours, like risky behaviours, so mostly people don't support them that much. But that is not true because for the man to get infected it means there was also a woman.' To which the women all laughed and the woman chairperson called out 'There was a woman somewhere, not your wife!' At which the women all laughed.

I also had the opportunity to observe the NAPHAM training sessions for support groups and CBOs, which were the first of their kind in Zomba District following the establishment of the new District Office in February 2011. The local research assistant, Russell Msiska was recruited to the research following observation of his work as a trainer on 'positive living' as part of the Group Therapy training sessions. Mr Msiska is a social worker with a decade of experience working in HIV and health, including HIV testing and counselling at the NGO BLM, which is important because of the potential sensitivity of conducting the research. He is fluent in Chichewa and Chitumbuka, the dominant languages of the south and north of Malawi respectively. He was integral to the local research acting as my advisor, assistant and translator. With the assistance of Mr Msiska and my Chichewa skills, a series of initial interviews were conducted with one representative of each of the support groups for PLHIV attending the training sessions. We also collected their mobile numbers and the details of where they held their meetings.

We were invited to attend three support group meetings and this provided the opportunity to conduct a pilot study with the Nsondole Support Group. Throughout my observations of the support group meetings and the subsequent focus group discussions there was a tendency for WLHIV to be able to talk about sex and their own personal experiences. Perhaps most surprising was that some women could talk about sex in ways that went against traditional norms, including for example the pervasive notion that women are faithful while their husbands are unfaithful. Following the observation of the Nsondole Support Group meeting, I asked the group of women and men 'Why is HIV high in your area?' In response one woman stood up and revealed that 'I'm HIV-positive because of revenge: I discovered my husband was having affairs, so I decided to do the same, now I am the one who is HIV-positive.' It was at this moment that I realised the focus group discussions I had originally planned to undertake with groups of PLHIV had the potential to explore areas that went against traditional norms and understandings. Although, the sense of the sensitivity of the topic varies in different contexts, for PLHIV participating in the support groups some of the taboos surrounding sex and HIV may have been broken down. Sexuality and sex are important sites of power (see Farquhar and Das, 1999, pp. 49–51). The subsequent focus group discussions further revealed that where the participants have already discussed issues of sex and HIV risk within these groups, they may be considered more neutral in this context.

Moreover, it was apparent throughout the fieldwork that it tended to be the men who lacked a voice in relation to talking about their HIV status. As Seckinelgin (2013) reveals in his work on Burundi, men find it hard to talk about issues of gender and sex. His work raises questions about masculinities that challenge the preoccupation with gender as to do with women, focusing on men's victimhood and experiences of sexual violence. It was widely reported and frequently observed that men tend not to join support groups in the same numbers as their female counterparts. This is of particular resonance at a juncture when the government was embarking on a new Gender and HIV Programme, following the end of the WGHPPA in 2010. Men must be included for a more effective response, including better empowerment outcomes for women vis-à-vis their risk of HIV infection. Gender is constructed by both men and women, and ultimately HIV risk is determined by the behaviour of both sexual partners.

Eleven of the support groups involved in the NAPHAM trainings from across Zomba District were included in focus group discussions and one group in Makunganya Village that was not part of the trainings was accessed through local contacts. We were keen to include a broad coverage of groups from across a range of rural and urban areas throughout Zomba. We coordinated the meetings with our transport options, which was particularly problematic in the context of the fuel crisis and we had to negotiate transport options by motorbike, minibus, *matola* (open-back trucks) and *cargo* (bicycle taxis). North of Zomba City this included four support groups: Chisomo Support Group, Tikondone Support Group, Nsondole Support Group and Tukamanerane Support Group. One group was included in Zomba

City: St Charles Lwanga Home-Based Care. South of Zomba City six groups were included: Makunganya Village Support Group (outside of NAPHAM), Omodzi Support Group in Nambande, Nanchenga Support Group, One Voice Support Group Nkolokosa, Tigwirisani Support Group and Talandira Support Group located on the border of Zomba and close to the Namadzi Trading Centre in Chiradzulu. All of the focus group discussions were conducted in July and August.

Based on the success of the fieldwork in Zomba, the research was extended to Karonga District. Although neither of us had worked in the district before, we had contacts through officials we had met in other parts of Malawi and used a process of snowballing. Consultations were undertaken with a number of representatives of the District AIDS Coordination Committee, which meets quarterly and is responsible for coordination, networking and monitoring in accordance with the District Implementation Plan. This included the Karonga District AIDS Coordinator, the NAPHAM District Coordinator, the Reverend of the Anglican Church (and part of the District Interfaith Alliance) and the District Coordinator for the Centre for Human Rights and Rehabilitation (CHRR). These consultations enabled the opportunity for participant observation of the NAPHAM Executive Meeting and the District Interfaith AIDS Committee training on Behaviour Change and Life Skills for the youth.

Eleven support groups for PLHIV were recruited to the study in Karonga through the NAPHAM Executive Meeting, and one group in Mwiketere that was outside NAPHAM affiliation who were associated with a CBO. We wanted to include groups that covered a wide geographical area within the limitations of the transport options and the timing of their weekly or fortnightly support group meetings. In the context of the fuel crisis there were particularly limited transport options to reach the communities across Karonga District: the minibuses, buses and *matola* were infrequent and the majority of those that did have fuel were carrying passengers to and from Mzuzu City in Rumphi District and Tanzania. The minibuses and buses could wait for several hours to fill up in Karonga *Boma*, so we hired bicycles to access the communities in the north of the district. In northern Karonga we included six support groups: Lughano Support Group in Karonga *Boma*; three groups towards the Songwe border with Tanzania (Pokani Omoyo Support in Kasowa, Kapora Support Group in Kapora and a support group associated with Lufiya CBO in Mwiketere); Lupembe Support Group to the south of Karonga *Boma* and Nbande Support Group to the west of Karonga *Boma* along the main road to Chitipa. Ideally we would have included further groups in the Nbande area because of the close proximity to the Kayerekera mine, however given the transport difficulties few groups were in contact with NAPHAM or other stakeholders in Karonga *Boma*. We cycled for almost three hours to reach the group. The journey was problematic because of the difficult terrain where the road was unpaved and broken up. In central Karonga we included two groups: Chigomezgo Support Group in Ngara and Temwanani Support Group in Nyungwe. Both support group meetings were close to major fishing and trading centres so we could travel by minibus. In the south of the district we included four groups: Majaliro Support Group at Chilumba Galizon, Chilumba Support Group at Chilumba Jetty, Hangalawe Support Group in Uliwa and Fuliwira Support Group in Fuliwira. We relocated to Chitimba and accessed the meetings by minibus and then on foot. Hailing the minibuses at the roadside in Chilumba was problematic because of the limited traffic on the road and the vehicles that were passing were often full. Given the greater time spent travelling to all of the groups in Karonga it was not within the scope of the research to include the interviews with Village Headmen and health centres in the villages.

In total, 44 focus group discussions were conducted with men and women from the 24 support groups in August and September 2011 (see Appendix for full details of the support groups involved). The original intention in designing the fieldwork was to conduct two focus group discussions with eight men and eight women for each support group. However, it was not always appropriate to exclude people who were part of the support group meeting so, depending on numbers who attended, the discussions included up to 14 people. The focus group discussions with the women were particularly fluid because they arrived late or had to leave during the discussion to attend to their children or to prepare food. Where men typically do not join the support groups and attend the meetings in the same numbers as women, on two occasions there was only one man present so we conducted an individual interview, and on two occasions no men were present. Women and men are included because gender is constructed by men and women and HIV risk is determined by the behaviour of both sexual partners. It is pertinent to note that, despite the tendency to focus on the importance of empowering women, men often control the couple's sexual reproductive health and it tends to be their risky sexual behaviour that puts women at risk: men are the perpetrators of gender-based violence; cultural practices favour men; where men migrate to work they are at heightened risk of contracting HIV and other STIs; and men do not seek treatment when they have early signs of STIs. While we conducted the focus group discussion the rest of the group were asked to complete a form detailing their age, sex, ethnic group, village and home village, marital status, number of children and date they were diagnosed HIV-positive. This gave the rest of support group a task to focus on and they were encouraged to sit in a location away from the focus group discussions so as not to disrupt the discussion. The data collected provided useful background information and allows the analysis to draw out some of the nuances of who said what because these details could be matched by the system of coding to who said what in the focus group discussion. Depending on time, we would usually break between the two groups for lunch.

Where the focus group discussions were undertaken during the regular monthly or fortnightly support group meetings it gave the research participants greater control over the norms and conduct of the session. The means through which we arrived stood in stark contrast to the arrivals of NGOs and other development actors in their 4×4s. We joined the group members in dancing and singing when we arrived. The meeting would commence with introductions from the group and from myself and the research assistant, Mr Msiska. We explained the details of the research and all the support group members were given the opportunity to ask questions about the research, researcher and research assistant. The chairperson explained the background to their activities and we observed the meeting. Once we had permission to begin the focus group discussions we would divide the members into groups of men and women to conduct the discussions and to complete participant background forms. The groups that participated in the focus group discussions were initially recruited through the chairperson but the decision on whether to participate and the terms of participation was negotiated with the individual members on the day – including those participants who arrived late and joined the focus group discussion after it had commenced. The participants were made aware that they could choose if and when to participate, were allowed to leave at any time and could request that their answers be omitted from the transcripts. This was important for developing a relationship of trust. The participants have greater power over whether and how to participate with greater opportunity to set the research agenda and develop themes that are perceived to be important to them (see Farquhar and Das, 1999, p. 52; Wilkinson, 1999, pp. 72–3). The participants were granted anonymity. The findings are presented using pseudonyms for participants in the focus group discussions and interviews to allow them to be more accessible to the reader.[3] The discussions were conducted in

Chichewa in Zomba and in Chitumbuka in Karonga. Mr Msiska was the facilitator and he took notes of the main issues that were raised. I made more nuanced notes of what was said and by whom to capture the deliberative elements of the discussions, which increases the richness of the data. It is presented in the analysis to capture the dialogue.

The questions were developed by reflecting on the issues raised in the secondary literature, primary data, interviews, consultations, the observations and pilot study. The way the questions were phrased in Chichewa and Chitumbuka was developed in collaboration with Mr Msiska and the questions were initially piloted and revised. The semi-structured format allowed the knowledge and perceptions of the participants to guide the discussion. The introduction of less sensitive topics earlier on was useful for building up trust among the group, so that the participants feel at ease, and we moved on to more sensitive topics later on. A general question about HIV in the local area provided a relatively 'neutral' area to open the discussion, the topics of food distribution in the household and negotiating for sex typically proved to be uplifting and worked well before asking about violence that is experienced in the home. The participants were encouraged to build on, improve and modify the points being raised (Stewart et al., 2007; King and Horrocks, 2010, p. 64).

There were particular language issues in Karonga because there were occasions where participants were unfamiliar with a term in Chitumbuka, which was the language in which the focus group discussions were conducted. Mr Msiska spoke some KyaNgonde and he was aided by the participants who negotiated the understanding of the term. Furthermore, I was not familiar with the Chitumbuka and KyaNgonde for cultural practices that, for the most part, I had only heard referred to in Chichewa by the stakeholders in Lilongwe and in the reports. For example bride price is known as *lobola* in Chichewa but among the Tumbuka and Nkonde who engage in the practice it is known as *malobola* and *chuma* respectively. Wife inheritance is known as *Chokolo* in Chichewa and as *Chihalo* among the Tumbuka and *Chilingo* among the Nkonde. The focus group discussion respondents would use all three languages in labelling these practices so the discussions were interrupted to clarify what practices they were referring to, especially given that some of the participants were of other ethnic groups. Areas of potential misunderstanding were either clarified during the discussion or highlighted and discussed in the debriefing session in the evening following the focus group discussions.

Focus group discussions can be relatively less threatening than individual interviews because power relations shift and the researcher's relative power and influence are reduced (see Wilkinson, 1999, pp. 70–3; Farquhar and Das, 1999, pp. 55–6; Schratz and Walker, 1995, p. 12). The participants can feel supported in the presence of people they perceive to be like them (Farquhar and Das, 1999, pp. 47, 58), enabling connections to be made between individual and group experiences, to challenge pervasive beliefs and allow space to discuss and reflect upon gender issues that are relevant to their lives (Pini, 2002). Where the groups of PLHIV already know each other this increases their sense of safety and helps them feel comfortable with participating in the research. Despite some concerns about using focus group discussions to explore sensitive topics, people are more likely to share personal experiences in a group setting and the group interaction produces data and insights that are less accessible otherwise (Frith, 2000; Farquhar and Das, 1999). PLHIV have already disclosed their status to their support group and some of the traditional taboos surrounding the discussion of sex and sexual behaviour have already been broken down. Where I am an outsider (speaking a different language, from a different culture) the participants may feel more comfortable disclosing personal experiences. Single-sex discussion groups were used to open up taboo topics. The literature suggests that focus group discussions can be relatively successful if carried out by women with women (Farquhar and Das, 1999, p. 50) but that men prefer female interviewers (see Spencer et al., 1988). In this research, working with a male facilitator created an interesting dynamic because the groups of women would talk through the facilitator to me, whereas the men could speak to the facilitator who acted as a buffer between them and the female researcher. That I could introduce myself, my work and my intentions in the local languages, could follow the focus group discussions and raise questions when I needed further clarification, enabled me to develop a relationship with the groups we met. It also allowed for clarification of language and understanding where words in vernacular languages may not have the same nuance of meaning that I might have otherwise read into them. And yet, since my linguistic skills are still limited, this meant I communicated in this environment with less authority than everyone else. This I see as important in mitigating the power structures of the researcher and the researched. Though of course this must not obscure the reality that I was still very much an outsider and the structures of power are pervasive.

The focus group discussions provide the space for the research participants to reflect upon the situation of HIV in their area, why people are at risk and the effectiveness of the policy response (Flyvbjerg, 2001; Rhodes, 2002). The dialogical approach is useful because it corresponds to the way opinions are produced, exchanged and addressed in everyday life (Pollock, 1955, p. 34, cited in Roberts, 2002, p. 245). The participants share experiences, explore the similarities and differences in their perspectives, learn from one another and re-evaluate existing positions (see King and Horrocks, 2010, p. 62). As Wilkinson (1999, p. 679) considers, the focus group discussions allowed insight into how the group engages in meaning generation about HIV through making collective sense of lived experiences, including through myths, stories and misinformation. For example, my previous fieldwork revealed how certain gender norms limit the power of women to negotiate for safer sex. Typically, women are in a subordinate position in general and in their sexual relationships specifically. As considered extensively by the key informants, women are socially conditioned throughout their lives to be submissive to men, especially to their husbands, and this is particularly entrenched in the rural areas. And yet, during the focus group discussions, women would reveal the limits of this understanding. For example, the discussion with the women in Makunganya Village Support Group about whether women can negotiate for sex echoes many of the focus group discussions in both districts:

> Bridget says yes, whilst Mercy contests that they cannot. The facilitator asks Mercy why not, to which she explains that it is 'because of our culture we are used to the man starting the "game" [sex]'. The facilitator then asks Bridget why she says they can, to which she explains 'a woman can say the "game" has to start because I am not satisfied, I have sexual feelings'.

Similarly when the women of Pokani Omoyo Support Group in Kasowa discuss whether women can negotiate for safer sex, the women overwhelmingly propound the view that they cannot, but this is then contested:

> Patricia explains 'women can but men here don't allow that. We have lots of condoms in our houses but we are not using them. Men say "Can you lick a bottle of Fanta when you are thirsty?" ' The facilitator asks whether women can negotiate sex, Lydia proposes that 'women are empowered to ask for sex' to which Sandra laughs. 'For example, elbowing husband' and Lydia demonstrates on Evelyn. Evelyn that adds that 'what I do is tell my husband "let's go inside the house

to discuss" there I tell him to have sex'. Patricia and Sandra laugh. Patricia says 'I know where to touch my husband', to which the others laugh, 'so when I want him it is very easy to have sex and I enjoy my husband.'

The dialogue can be empowering because 'allowing the person to have a voice and the opportunity for genuine self-expression are prerequisites for achieving a sense of control over life' (Coleman, 1994, pp. 8–9, cited in Roberts, 2002, p. 27). It can allow the participants to see their lives differently and inspire them to change (Wilkinson, 1999, pp. 74–5; Vaughn et al., 1996, p. 302; Atkinson, 1998, p. 28, cited in Roberts, 2002, p. 20)

It is crucial to recognise that the discussions bring potentially sensitive issues to the fore and can destabilise the security that people take from established understandings and constructed truths (Fay, 1977, p. 214; Farquhar and Das, 1999, p. 58). Following the group discussions Mr Msiska (as social worker and HIV counsellor and tester) would address the questions and concerns that the participants had (often about the problems they were having with their ARVs, issues of nutrition and personal experiences of stigma). This would allow some clarifications of areas where there was misinformation, a lack of understanding or concerns. In this respect the research process immediately gives something back to the participants. We were also mindful of information and support the participants might need following the focus group discussions and, where appropriate, we signposted groups to organisations working in their area.

Focus group discussions are a public arena of ongoing social relations and there may be constraints on what information is shared. Certain voices and perspectives may be marginalised or silenced during focus group discussions. For example, the majority of the focus group discussion participants in the north were Tumbuka and Nkonde, which meant that it was their cultural practices that dominated the discussions. The facilitator actively encouraged people to join in the group interview through directly asking their opinions, encouraging them when they made contributions and giving them time to answer. For example, during the focus group discussion with two men of Talandira Support Group, Eric initially dominated in answering the first few questions and the facilitator had to coax Lazarus to contribute through focusing the questions on him, clarifying what was being discussed when he misunderstood and nodding to encourage him when he did participate. It is crucial to recognise that the data produced may only represent ideas that are socially acceptable to the group. Therefore this was recognised when reading the data and the analysis draws upon a broader range of qualitative approaches.

Alongside the consultations, observations and focus group discussions, 110 individual informant interviews were conducted in Lilongwe, Zomba and Karonga between June and September 2011. These included (1) people from key bodies in the national response to HIV/AIDS such as the Department of HIV, AIDS and Nutrition with the Office of the President and Cabinet (OPC), the National Coordinator for the WGHPPA, the Head of Monitoring and Evaluation at the NAC, a Programme Coordinator at the MANASO, and the NSO Zomba. Also interviewed were (2) people involved in local governance of HIV/AIDS, including the Chief Executive at Zomba City Council, Zomba City AIDS Coordinator, Karonga District AIDS Coordinator; national and district coordinators of MANET+, NAPHAM, the Coalition of Women and Girls Living with HIV/AIDS and MANERELA. Further interviews took place with (3) people working for NGOs, including the Foundation for Community Support Services, Youth for Development and Productivity (YODEP), Malawi Carer, IMPACT, CHRR; (4) 20 leaders of religious communities and traditional leaders including Group Village Headmen and Village Headmen; (5) 15 local business people and traders including *matola* drivers, bar owners, hair salon owners, Fishing Chairman, accountants, hospitality staff; (6) the heads of 9 CBOs and 19 support groups in the communities and staff in hospitals and health centres.

A series of informal discussions and observations were also conducted in Lilongwe, Zomba and Karonga at bottle stores, rest houses, restaurants, markets, local businesses, travelling on local minibuses and *matolas*, including with shop workers, rest house staff, police officers, business people, students, NGO workers and migrant workers. Where gender and HIV affects all people in all settings it is not possible to clearly demarcate the population to be researched. The research extends beyond the traditional contours of the interviews and focus group discussions. People from a whole diversity of backgrounds would engage in a dialogue about the research outside the realm of 'the research process', including before and after the recorder was switched on, while waiting for interviewees to arrive, moving between interviews, shopping in the town and so forth. These presented opportunities to discuss issues that would not otherwise be raised.

Conclusions

Where the policy response tends to obscure the gender context of HIV risk, this research aims to understand the complexities of how this context is produced, experienced and responded to. This book examines what is historically general and what is specific to the Malawi context. On the one hand, Malawi is an exemplifying case for a broader category of countries in Sub-Saharan Africa that experience severe HIV pandemics and show similarities in the gender context of risk. On the other hand, the specific case study enables analysis of culturally unique ways in which gender as a form of structural violence permeates this seemingly 'peaceful' context. Although the situation of HIV is different between contexts, many of the issues are not necessarily unique and the broader interdisciplinary literature on other contexts is drawn upon throughout the analysis. The findings presented here generate issues and questions that can be applied to other contexts.

This work asks what we can learn from marginalised African perspectives. The research design has been informed and developed through engaging Malawians at all levels of society in dialogue. A series of consultations with stakeholders and experts were conducted throughout the research to ensure it contributes to existing knowledge. Crucially, local-level understandings were incorporated in the research design through observations, initial interviews and group discussions, piloting, the guidance of the local research assistant and the dialogical methods. The qualitative methods included national-level key-informant interviews in 2007 to understand the broader issues across the country and the policy response. This was complemented by local-level work in 2011 in two indigenous languages (Chichewa and Chitumbuka), which included consultations, observations, focus group discussions, individual interviews and informal discussions. The local-level work explores the politics of health 'from below', focusing on the micro-level of everyday lives as serious objects of study. In particular, it draws upon the perspectives of people living with HIV (PLHIV) in more remote areas of two districts – Zomba and Karonga. The district-level work in Zomba and Karonga enabled comparison between south and north and the cultural practices of the ethnic groups within matrilineage and patrilineage.

The research process involved continuous reflexivity of the lens through which the researcher is interpreting these dynamics, and how structures of gender, discourses of HIV and relationships with the 'researched' change over time. The inductive data collection and analysis sought to adapt to changing circumstances, follow new paths of discovery as they emerge and allow the previously marginalised or ignored perspectives of the participants to be heard. The critical reflection here exposes how limited my initial understanding was. For example, the popular perception is that there is a pervasive silence and stigma surrounding HIV, sex and violence in the family in Malawi, especially for women. And yet the observations and focus group discussions reveal that, for PLHIV participating in the support groups, some of the taboos surrounding sex and HIV may have been broken down. Malawian women living with HIV are empowered to talk about sex and their own sexual behaviour, and actually it is often men and professionals who 'lack a voice' when it comes to talking about their own HIV risk and sex. The analysis exposes the multifaceted nature of the agency of the seeming 'powerless' and 'marginalised' to navigate their situations of inequality and dependency.

Drawing upon the findings from the fieldwork, the next two chapters analyse how Malawians experience and respond to gendered poverty and the gendered ways in which life is valued.

3
Sex for Security
Gendered Poverty

The dominant ways of framing and responding to HIV obscure the gender context of risk and, in so doing, undermine the effectiveness of the response. This chapter is the first of two chapters that examine the culturally specific and historically situated complexities of the gendered dimensions of HIV risk in Malawi. The focus here is on examining the ways in which gendered poverty is produced, experienced and responded to. Since Malawi has long been one of the world's poorest countries, the linkages between poverty and HIV are pertinent. The concern here is the gendered dimensions. As Nattrass et al. (2012, p. 307) propound, 'poverty and sexual behaviour matter to individuals' HIV risk, but in gendered ways' (see also Boesten and Poku, 2009, p. 6).

Gendered poverty is a form of structural violence that exacerbates the spread of HIV. Inequalities of gender mean that women disproportionately experience poverty and are placed at particular risk of infection (see Ghosh and Kalipeni, 2005; Bryceson et al., 2004).[1] As is the situation more generally, women in Malawi are susceptible to hunger and poor nutrition, even in situations where there is no food scarcity (NSO Malawi and ORC Macro, 2005, pp. 177, 182; Hindin, 2005, p. 93; for the situation in general see Sen, 1990). And yet, where women comprise 70 per cent of full-time farmers, they tend to take the pressure during times of shortage especially in the case of female-headed households and *de facto* female-headed households (where the husband is in polygamous marriage or migrates for waged labour) (WFP, 2007; GoM, 2000, 1.4; UN, 2004a). These structural inequalities are rooted in a long history and yet, despite the pervasive structures and limited alternatives, it is argued here that this injustice is not experienced passively. With limited alternative options, women in particular engage in risk-taking in sex to bring about immediate security. As James Ferguson (1999, p. 186) considers in his work on the Zambian Copperbelt, in such contexts the concept of 'prostitution' is redundant because transactional sex takes on a different guise. Despite knowledge of the risks, there is a hierarchy of interests and, as the key-informant interviews and focus group discussions widely reported, short-term interests are typically prioritised over the risk of HIV infection.

To make this argument the analysis focuses on the gendered inequalities in three key areas and identifies the diverse ways in which the structural violence is maintained, subverted and challenged. First, it explores the inequalities in both the traditional and modern systems of land distribution. It identifies how a number of cultural practices have developed to maintain the status quo and ensure the security of the extended family, including wife inheritance and marriage for debt repayment. Women also use sex to maintain marriage. Second, it examines the inequalities that permeate agriculture and food security. It explores how women respond to the norms of feeding their husband first and exchange sex for food as a fundamental survival strategy. Third, it analyses how women are disadvantaged in terms of their labour opportunities. It considers how some women engage in commercial sex and find 'sugar daddies' as a survival strategy and for upward social mobility.

Gendered land distribution

To understand the gender dimensions of poverty in Malawi it is fundamental to understand the historically situated gendered inequalities that permeate land distribution. Since this is a predominantly agrarian economy, with over 95 per cent of the population living in rural areas, land ownership plays a crucial role in determining levels of poverty and is central to social differentiation. Land is not only essential to food security but, as Peters (2002, p. 155) considers, it is also a primary means for generating a livelihood and transferring wealth between generations. Economic survival is dependent on agricultural smallholdings, with rural households having on average 1.2 hectares of land (see GoM, 2006, p. 47; Mbaya, 2002). As is the situation across Sub-Saharan Africa, women are typically disadvantaged by land distribution because they experience discrimination under both the customary and modern systems of land inheritance. This plays out in subtly different ways under patrilineage and matrilineage (see White et al., 2003).

The Ngoni, Tumbuka, Tonga and Nkonde (the main ethnic groups in the north) and Sena (in Nsanje District in the south) are patrilineal. Customary land inheritance is traced through the male line and access to land is dependent on the presence of a male adult. The wife moves to the husband's village on marriage, men dominate in the family and the woman's father or husband is the highest authority. Traditionally, women live with their husband in his home village and the children belong to his lineage. A bride-price is paid to the wife's family in the form of cattle or the monetary equivalent to legitimate the marriage, which is known as *lobola* (Chichewa), *malobola* (Chitumbuka) or *chuma* (KyaNgonde). Traditionally this payment ensures that women are valued (Lwanda, 2005, p. 121). However, the HIV Advisor to DfID, reflecting on her own mother's experience, propounds that it essentially makes the wife the property of her husband and his family, and the wife surrenders her rights to ownership of property. As Saur et al. reflect in their work in Rumphi District, the husband's family has control over her productive and reproductive capacity (Saur et al., 2005, pp. 35–8).

In contrast, the Chewa, Yao, Mang'anja and Lomwe (the main ethnic groups in the Central and Southern Regions) are matrilineal. Customary land inheritance is traced through the female line and the husband moves to the wife's village on marriage. In some respects women within matriliny traditionally have a higher position in society and have a greater range of powers. Aguillar and Aguillar (1999) reveal, for example that women elders decide upon the village head and exert influence over decision-making, land is inherited through the woman's lineage, and children, a vital asset, belong to the woman's lineage. And yet, although women have greater security of tenure relative to the patrilineal system, it is well established in the literature that it is a patriarchal structure in reality. Women tend to access land through marriage, it is jointly owned by the husband, men act as the *nkhowse* (matrilineage heads), the *mwini mbumba* (the wife's brother) has authority over the land and property, and the husband has the rights to the use of the land and its products and control the household resources, including the income and crops (see Tango International, 2004, pp. 1–2; Mwale, 2002, pp. 134–5; Semu, 2002, pp. 78–9; Peters, 1992; for the situation across Sub-Saharan Africa see Kevane, 2004, pp. 47–66).

Gender as structural violence permeates land distribution and this has been transformed by colonialism and by neoliberal development since independence. In particular, the customary rights of women to land in matrilineal areas have been eroded over time. During the colonial period, individual ownership of land was introduced, benefiting men because they were the heads of household, and this continued after independence. The major land registration project registered all the land in the name of the senior man, ignoring the customary land rights of women in matrilineal areas. Women must be married in order for land to be registered through their husband's name and upon the husband's death the wife is not considered the heir (see Gray and Kevane, 1999, pp. 24, 25; Spring, 1995, p. 22). The involvement of men in waged labour activities, beginning in the 1890s, led to migration, and men could take their wives to their own villages or areas where they could find secure waged employment instead of residing in the wife's village (Davidson, 1993; Kishindo, 1994, p. 60). However, Davidson (1993) argues that women in matrilineage maintain a comparative advantage as compared to women in patrilineage. They continue to engage in individual *banja* (family) production rather than participating in gender-specific collaborative forms of production in order to maximise their own production and profits, and to mitigate further erosion of their economic power. The tradition of the husband moving to the wife's home is diminishing, with some men only agreeing to stay for one year to prove himself to the family, and where husbands do move to the wife's home they may spend the majority of their time away on business (Banda, 2005, pp. 10, 174; Semu, 2002, p. 79; K. Phiri, 1983, p. 273; I. Phiri, 1997, p. 48; Schoffeleers, 1997, pp. 34–7).

In more recent years, land distribution has been under pressure from population growth and reduced land fertility. As a result there has been the decline of traditional support systems for extended families, including land allocation for widows, and there is insufficient land to ensure women economic independence (Tango International, 2004, p. 2; Peters, 2002, p. 177; Hirschmann and Vaughan, 1983, p. 99). Modern neoliberal, financialised channels of land distribution often supersede customary channels, and these disproportionately benefit men. Women are restricted in their economic and social ability to access land in a multitude of ways: they rarely access land through direct purchase because they typically do not have pre-existing land assets to provide the financial security and do not earn enough to purchase outright (Butegwa, 1994, p. 499). In addition, women typically lack the knowledge and understanding of the procedures, bureaucracy and laws to manage modern market transactions (Kishindo, 2004; Tango International, 2004, p. 2). Some women gain from land registration, especially where it provides the basis of human rights programmes to protect widows from dispossession, but there has been a tendency for the manipulation of the social interpretation and enforcement of rights to benefit men. For example, the use of the land has been changed to put it under male control and inheritance rights tend to be interpreted in such a way that the wife does not inherit land. There are reports that widows living under both the patrilineal and matrilineal inheritance systems are being dispossessed of their land and assets, as the key informants widely reflect (see also Mbaya, 2002, p. 2). The Senior Assistant to the Chief State Advocate and Human Rights Coordinator at the Ministry of Justice and Constitutional Affairs reflects that women are more likely to experience being denied property than men (see also GoM, 2006, p. 33). According to traditional customs all the property is shared among the husband's family on his death to 'ease the pain of mourning' – with the exception of the kitchen items, which are considered to be the wife's personal belongings (Tango International, 2004, p. 2).

Preserving the family's support structures

In the context of entrenched poverty, the extended family system is vital to the survival of all of its members. A number of cultural practices have developed that are linked to land inheritance to preserve the status quo and maintain the extended family as a fundamental support structure. As the Population and Health Specialist at the World Bank and Head of the Women Lawyers Association (WLA) highlight, families are often keen to transfer the financial liability for the daughter to her husband (see also Manda and Meyer, 2005, p. 453; Kachiwanda, n.d., p. 7). Parents encourage their daughters to marry early to ensure security before they die (Fielder, 2005, p. 18). There is pressure on the daughters to marry young so that the family can raise the *lobola* (Kachiwanda, n.d., p. 7). Marriage for the daughter is believed to be of greater benefit for the family and the daughter than her education. It was widely reported during the consultations, key-informant interviews, focus group discussions and informal discussions that for families in patrilineal systems of inheritance in Karonga, marriage of their daughters provides a fundamental survival strategy, for example to preserve their support networks and repay debts. These practices are of cultural and economic significance, but some contribute to the spread of HIV, with particular ramifications for women.

Where the husband's support is a vital source of patronage for the wife's family, the focus group discussions and interviews reveal how a number of practices have developed to maintain that support. During the focus group discussion with the men of Pokani Omoyo Support Group in Kasowa in Karonga District for example, Sydney reports that in situations where the couple are not bearing any children, the wife's parents offer the husband another daughter to ensure he does not marry another wife from a different family. The family may also offer the husband a second daughter as a gesture of gratitude, as the Director of Planning, Research and Evaluation at the Department of HIV, AIDS and Nutrition and the HIV Programme Officer at UNFPA (UN Population Fund) report. And yet, it is widely reported by the key informants and the focus group discussions across Karonga District that polygamous unions are a key contributing factor to the spread of HIV. The MHRC explain in their report *Cultural Practices and Human Rights* that many people enter into such unions without knowing the serostatus of their would-be spouses (2006, p. 15). As the Senior Assistant to the Chief State Advocate considers, if the husband neglects some of the wives then they may engage in transactional sex for financial support. The focus group discussions also reveal this can also be to fulfil woman's sexual needs. In polygamous marriages, if one wife becomes infected with HIV, it can spread to the other wives (see also MHRC, 2006, p. 13; Chimgwede, 2004b). I will return to issues of polygamy in the next chapter, when I consider the crisis of male personhood.

The Tumbuka and the Nkonde practise wife inheritance (known as *Chihalo* in Chitumbuka and *Chilingo* in KyaNkonde) where a brother of the deceased inherits the wife. Traditionally this militates against the destitution of the widow and children and also ensures the daughter's family continued access to the deceased husband's assets (including the children as a valuable asset). It was found to be widespread in three districts of the north covered by a MHRC report in 2006 and this was supported by the interviews and focus group discussions across Karonga District. The women in Lughano Support Group and the District Coordinator for CHRR also reveal an associated practice of sister inheritance (known as *Kuhalira* in Chitumbuka and *Siyazi* in KyaNkonde), whereby the family offer the husband the deceased wife's sister as a wife. The MHRC reports that these practices occur because the parents fear that they will have to pay the bride-price back, because they wish to continue to access the husband's wealth or to provide a mother for the children left behind (2006, pp. 15–17). The practices can place the wife at heightened risk of contracting HIV from the brother-in-law, as the Head of Policy Support and Development at the NAC considers (see also Rankin et al., 2005, p. 12). The focus group discussions reveal some of the complexities of how the practice varies between families. Sometimes it is forced and at other times women are part of the decision-making, as the discussion between the men in Nbande Support Group illustrates:

Michael reflects that in their area '*Chilingo* in the past was rampant but now it is slowly ending'. To which Wyson adds, 'sometimes at *Chilingo*, the wife and the brother of the sick person can agree whilst the patient is still alive'. Wyson and Michael explain after just 14 days of the death they can marry. James interjects that 'Some *Chilingo* is forced – the wife has no choice. The parents of the deceased arrange it without consulting anyone, including the wife.' The men laugh, and James continues explaining that 'they do this in fear that the possessions could be used by another man who can marry the woman'.

Despite the risks involved, it is important to recognise that women are not simply passive recipients of these practices, as the focus group discussions reveal. As Annie explains during the focus group discussion with the women of Lughano Support Group in Karonga: 'After the husband dies the brothers assemble with sticks and the woman is asked to choose one of their sticks. When she chooses one it means she has accepted him [as her husband], but when she is not interested she takes all the sticks and gives them back.' However, in the context of entrenched poverty and dependency, women and girls often have limited alternative options.

The Nkonde (who are predominantly in Karonga and neighbouring Chitipa District) practise *Kupimbigha* (more commonly known as *Kupimbira* in Chichewa), where families marry their daughters as a form of repayment (MHRC, 2006, pp. 1, 19; Nyirenda, 2006, p. 25). The MHRC drew particular attention to the practice in its *Investigations Report of a Case on Young Girls (Minors) in Karonga Being Forced to Marry Elderly People in Exchange for Cattle or Repayment for Loans* (MHRC, 2002). It reported on incidences when the girls can be as young as 9 years old when they are married and the man could be as old as 40 or more. In one specific incident in Karonga the MHRC reported that a 13-year-old girl was forced to marry a man as repayment for the 4000 MK the parents owed the man (MHRC, 2002, p. 1). The District AIDS Coordinator (who has been working in the district since 2005) and the support groups report that this is a common practice across Karonga District. The District Coordinator for CHRR explained that during the rainy season families may use it as a strategy to purchase fertiliser or seeds. The focus group discussion with Luhango Support Group reveals that parents sometimes arrange marriage for their unborn babies. Across Karonga District it is common for parents to receive four or five cows from a man to give him their daughter without the girl's consent. The members of Mwenitete and Pokani Omoyo Support Groups also high-light the associated practice of *Kusingililira*, where fathers can organise a husband for the daughter without her consent, perhaps with their best friend. For example, from the focus group discussion with the women of Pokani Omoyo:

> Sandra explains that 'When the man is ready to get the girl, the father deliberately sends the girl for a walk' and Lydia adds 'and the man catches the girl and runs away with her.' Lydia then suggests that 'many families do not send their girls to school because they are afraid she might find another man'.

The older men begin having sex with the younger girls because, as the Technical Advisor to the WGHPPA explains, 'as long as he feels he can start having sex with the girl he will start having sex with the girl, he is already married'. The girls involved in these practices typically do not have a say in whether they marry the man in question or not (see Nyirenda, 2006, p. 25). The Karonga District Coordinator for CHRR reflects that the chiefs in the rural areas report that *Kupimbigha* is dimin-ishing and refuse to give information because it is their culture, but the community members report it still happens – the interviews, focus group discussions and informal discussions across the district reveal that it is still widely practised. This is also revealed through reports in the press: for example, in one report, Traditional Authority Kilipula reflected that: 'As traditional leaders, we also recognised the dangers of the prac-tice and we are very strict now, and if it exists it is just here and there and secretly though' (Nyirenda, 2006, p. 25). Although *Kupimbigha* and *Kuhalira* are not practised in the Southern Region, Tikondane Support Group reports similar practices in Zomba whereby girls are forced to marry by their parents to have children and for money.

Maintaining marriage: The sexual contract and persevering

There is pressure on women across Malawi to maintain their mar-riages for their own and their extended family's survival. As is the situation across Sub-Saharan Africa, within the extended family sys-tem marriage involves both families. The National Coordinator of MANERELA outlines:

> A marriage in our society is not just about two people. [Marriage] is about two families and perhaps two villages. So it is considered that once you break that chain of connection you are considered to have

breached a contract that is there. So then the effects they are not just about the two of you, they will extend to the others.

In accordance with what Pateman (1988) identifies as a universal 'sexual contract', the wife has a marital duty to fulfil her husband's sexual desires and provide him with children because he is the breadwinner and supports the family, as the interviewees widely report. This is a masculine sex-right that 'ensures that there is an orderly access by each man to a woman' (1988, pp. 109–10). An essential part of being a 'good wife' and having a successful marriage in Malawi is ensuring that the husband is sexually satisfied. Once women are married then they receive counselling and, as the Head of AGREDS reports, they are told that 'whatever [your husband] demands please give it to him, if he is demanding for sex give sex to him'. As William of Kapora Support Group reflects, this can even be at the expense of the wife's own pleasure and well-being (NAC, 2003, p. 17). It was widely reported that sexual intercourse is conducted according to the man's terms and for his pleasure (Tango International, 2004, p. 3; Ngwira et al., 2001, p. 7). In a study of *Nkanza* (gender-based violence), one man expressed that an 'ideal' man 'should be hard-working... that way the woman surrenders her body to you' (Saur et al., 2005, p. 50). This gendered construct has religious foundations. Ephesians 5:22, 23, a verse from the Bible that is well known in the south of the country and popularly cited, commands the wives to 'submit to your husbands as to the lord. For the husband is the head of the wife as Christ is the head of the church, his body, of which he is the saviour' (Banda, 2005, p. 182; Rankin et al., 2005, p. 14). In the study of *Nkanza*, one woman explained that an 'ideal' woman 'should positively assist her husband when having sex; should be able to wiggle her waist to satisfy his sexual needs otherwise he will go with other women' (Saur et al., 2005, p. 42). The focus group discussions reveal how women who fail to sexually satisfy their husband may risk divorce or their husband may cheat on them. For example, during the focus group discussion with Lupembe Support Group Doris explains how typically 'Women are not "free" in the family, then the husband goes and finds someone who is "free" in bed.' This was widely echoed throughout the interviews and Chief Chalunga in Nkolokosa explains, for example, that 'Malawian women are not free [extraverts] in the bedroom, men encourage women to wear miniskirts in the bedroom.... But lots of women are lazy in bed and if a man could do a game [have sex] one day then she refuses four or five days saying "I'm tired". The man then goes elsewhere.' Research by Rachel Fielder in southern Malawi, reveals for example how one woman in a focus group discussion in Mpirisi was divorced because she would not dance during lovemaking. The focus group discussion revealed that 'it was only when other women helped the woman to dance the sex dance that her husband took her back' (Fielder, 2000, p. 38). Women who leave or lose their marriage are likely to become dependent on other men for their own and their children's survival, as the Head of AGREDS propounds.

Women engage in riskier sexual practices in order to enhance sexual satisfaction. There is an emphasis on the importance of body contact during sex: it was widely reported by the focus group discussions and interviewees that *nyama-ku-nyama* (skin-to-skin) ejaculation is socially constructed as a sign of masculinity and it is widely believed that condoms deprive men of sexual fulfilment. It is also believed to be psychologically impossible or damaging for men to either abstain from sex or to have sex with a condom (IPPF et al., 2006, p. 3; Kaler, 2003, pp. 355, 362; Lwanda, 2005, pp. 116–17). As the then Health Minister, Heatherwick Ntaba, expressed in 2004, 'there are people who are very inflexible with their behaviour, they believe that the use of a condom is nothing but degradation of the sexual practice' (Namangal, 2004). Popular sentiments reported throughout the focus group discussions, interviews and informal discussions include that you cannot 'eat sweets in a wrapper', 'take a shower in a raincoat' or 'lick a bottle of Fanta when you are thirsty' (see also Banda, 2005, p. 183; Muula and Mfutso-Bengo, 2004, p. 486).

There are situations where violence is considered acceptable if a wife denies her husband his marital right to sex (Saur et al., 2005, pp. 8, 12; Tango International, 2004, p. 3). The Head of AGREDS reports that some women know that their husband is engaging in extra-marital sex, but they cannot refuse his demands for sex, because if they do, they may be forced to have sex or accused of engaging in extra-marital affairs. This is particularly entrenched in the patrilineal areas, where a *lobola* is paid on marriage. As the Principal Documentation Officer at the Ombudsman and Programme Manager at the Story Workshop report, it is believed that the husband has bought the wife and can use her as he wishes. In July 2006, one man was reported to have cut his pregnant wife's sexual organs for refusing sex when she had sores and she had to have seven stitches (Mwafulirwa, 2006). All matrimonial problems, including domestic violence and divorce, are taken to the marriage counsellors (*ankhowse*) who are usually the husband and wife's uncles (WLSA, 2000, p. 28). As the Behaviour Surveillance Research Coordinator at FHI explains:

So if you want to leave your husband... in [some] areas you will have to go to your uncle and tell him 'I am leaving him' and the uncle will have to talk to [the husband's] uncle and [say] 'she is leaving him'. So it is not as easy as just walking out that door.

In accordance with customary law the *ankhowse* try to reconcile the parties because of the belief in the notion that *'banja ndikupilira'* – that one has to persevere for the marriage to work (WLSA, 2000, p. 21).

Although in both regions gender-based norms persist that place women under the control of men, the capacity of a woman to leave a marital union differs between the matrilineal areas of the south and the patrilineal areas of the north, as the Principal Documentation Officer for the Ombudsman and the Behaviour Surveillance Research Coordinator at FHI consider. The payment of the *lobola* in patrilineal areas underscores a form of structural violence whereby the majority of women are not in a position where they can negotiate the terms of sex or leave marriage if they experience violence or are at risk of HIV, as the interviews in Lilongwe and Karonga widely report. The Principal Documentation Officer at the Ombudsman, who deals with such disputes, explains that the woman is bound to the husband's family and the family believe that 'We have paid this then you are ours and you will go by what we are going to say. You don't have to do what you want. You will do what we want because we have bought you.' If the wife does leave then she would have to abandon her children because they belong to the husband's lineage, as the HIV Advisor at DfID considers, 'It is difficult position for a woman to be in, to leave and to know that the children are being looked after by another women or just not being looked after at all.' It is also unlikely the wife or her family will be in a position to repay the bride-price to the husband's family, as the Population and Health Specialist working with the World Bank explains. There can be familial pressure on the daughters to marry young so that the family can raise the bride-price and in turn pay for their own sons to marry (Kachiwanda, n.d., p. 7). The Population and Health Specialist at the World Bank reflects that in the matrilineal areas women have at least some agency to leave a marital union (see also Saur et al., 2005, p. 35; Kaler, 2001, p. 530). The husband lives in the wife's village and power resides with the male family members on the wife's side: the woman is under the control of her maternal uncle or brother (*bambo aang'ano* or *bambo aakulu* – meaning small father or big father, depending on the age difference between the biological father and paternal uncle) (Banda, 2005, p. 9; Tango International, 2004, p. 1; I. Phiri, 1997, p. 1). This is supported by the findings of Women and the Law in Southern Africa (WLSA) for Mpondasi Village, Mangochi District, where women who wanted to end their relationship told their husbands to pack up and go (2000, p. 31). Matrilineage therefore empowers women with some ability to be able to leave an unsafe marital union.

Moreover, there is social pressure to persevere in marriage to maintain the status quo, as the Population and Health Specialist at the World Bank explains:

> A wife is supposed to persevere in a marriage because a marriage starts on a rocky ground, but later on things stabilise. So when you have had big problems, even if a lady goes to parents to say 'by the way he is doing this, he is doing that' they say 'just persevere, these things happen at the beginning, later on things will be fine, so don't worry'. Until it really comes to a critical level that is when maybe they can come out.

It is also believed to be in the best interests of the children for the family to remain together. Women are encouraged to persevere no matter what. The Head of AGREDS highlights that:

> Women are told when they are getting married 'you must persevere'. Some women are dying in the name of persevering or they are being infected in the name of persevering. [They are told] 'Even if your husband is going out with other women, please persevere.' Sometimes they tell them that 'a man is like a young kid he does naughty things, he can go out with a lot of women but never mind all that'. So because of that mentality a woman cannot question a husband's behaviour, so that again makes them more vulnerable to HIV infection.

The National Coordinator of MANERELA suggests that this applies to the extent that 'in some societies the woman is bound to stay with the husband until death'. Young girls are socialised not to leave an abusive relationship as a result of their experience in the home. The Programme Officer UNAIDS for example questions: 'What does happen if they [the mothers] stay in these abusive relationships? The tendency is that the kids are looking at that, and what kind of society are we building?' The ideology of persevering in marriage is institutionalised throughout society in all the places women may go to if they want to leave their marriage, which makes it difficult for women to actually leave. When women go to their parents they are often sent back to their husbands. The Head of AGREDS considers how they 'have heard of stories where a woman decides to leave, she goes to her home and the parents say "what are you doing here? You are given out on marriage, please go", so she is forced back.' Similarly the Programme Manager at the Story Workshop NGO considers how:

> Their parents will tell them to go back to the husband because what they are told is 'marriage is about perseverance so you have to persevere, whatever goes on, persevere'. So when they get back to their relatives they will surely send them back.

The churches also advocate for reconciliation and aim to ensure peace in family (Banda, 2005, p. 186). As the National Coordinator of MANERELA reflects, the churches 'consider divorce as being unreligious, even where there are reasons for that, so they will try to make sure that you unite'. The Roman Catholic Church, for example, places emphasis on the sanctity of marriage and assists couples to adhere to their marital promise. Likewise, in the Seventh Day Adventist Church, it is the duty of the pastor to reconcile a couple (WLSA, 2000, p. 40). The Head of the Seventh Day Adventist Church explains that 'What we encourage as a church is that they can still live as a family but they can negotiate. We don't encourage her to leave but we encourage her to stay and discuss. We do counsel them together so that they can understand each other.' In accordance with the dominant religious discourse, women feel obliged to follow God's wishes and submit to their husbands, even when a woman is abused by her husband or denied her rights in the family (Banda, 2005, p. 182). As a result of these barriers to women leaving an unsafe relationship, women endure a lot in their marriages. The Population and Health Specialist at the World Bank reflects:

> Sometimes the idea of going back to church and saying 'you know, this is happening in our family' or going say to your parents and saying 'this is happening'... it is not that easy. So sometimes it easier to say 'maybe this is just today, maybe next time it will be something different'. So with that maybe you will find that they will stay in that relationship a little bit longer until they are saying enough is enough.

However, some churches offer support to women who do divorce their husbands. The interviews with representatives of the Seventh Day Adventist Church and the Assemblies of God Church reveal that although they do not encourage the couple to separate, they support the couple's decision should they decide to dissolve the marriage. The Head of the Seventh Day Adventist Church explains: 'We can give pieces of advice but it is up to an individual to make a decision. Sometimes they can accept the advice or reject so when it comes to that it is an individual's decision.' The Baptist Church accepts divorced women into their membership and during the seminars for Baptist women in the Southern Region some are advised that, although they should show their husbands forgiveness when their husband engages in risky behaviour, in accordance with the Bible, they should 'not accept him as a husband; he will bring you AIDS' (Banda, 2005, pp. 174, 182).

Despite the barriers and stigma, it was widely reported that some women do leave. Where some women are stable and self-dependent they may be in a better position to leave an unsafe marriage, as the Programme Officer at the NICE considers. For example, the wife of the Paramount Chief M'mbelwa IV of Mzimba was filing for divorce because of claims of adultery, cruelty and desertion (Langa, 2006b, pp. 1–2). Furthermore, there is also a growing sense among WLHIV included in the focus group discussions that they can leave a relationship if it places them at risk. The women of Mwenitete Support Group reveal that in their area there are some options:

> Mary explains that 'in situations where the wife is at risk of being beaten the father of the woman intervenes and the marriage can end'. Gloria explains that 'the chiefs are just informed', to which Rachel adds 'and when the case is at court, the father still has more power'.

When the women of Lupembe Support Group in Karonga District were discussing the problems associated with HIV in their area, Hannah explains that she left her marriage despite the stigma she faced:

> In my case when I was tested HIV-positive I hated my husband and stopped talking to him. I packed up and came back home. My father called me '*lipumba*' [a dead person]. I stayed my family's village despite the problems I faced.

It is, however, important to recognise that where these women are more easily accessible by outreach and educational campaigns through their support group, they have been more exposed to the messages from NGOs. Jane and Hannah of Lupembe Support Group report that in their area the woman's family, the Coalition of Women Living with HIV (COWLHA) and the Victim Support Unit support them.

The numbers of women who do leave are very few, as the Head of the Seventh Day Adventist Church and the National Coordinator of MANERELA reflect. More educated women may be able to challenge the pervasive traditions, as the Strategic Manager of the Youth Alert! Programme identifies, but there are still barriers to leaving. Even more educated and wealthier women fear losing their social status, as the Programme Officer UNAIDS explains, 'They are a "Mrs", they are respectable people in society, they die in silence... because what is society going to say if they are respectable people?' The Senior Programme Manager of PSI's *Packachere* Programme considers how, because of the stigma and gossip, 'Some women do stay in the family as much as they are knowledgeable, as much as they are financially empowered because of trying to save their image or the image of the husband.' Some women can only leave once they have consulted their *ankhowse* several times. As the Head of AGREDS explains, 'There are times when you quarrel you leave. The marriage counsellors come in they help you, you come back again. The incidents have to happen several times before you finally make the decision of leaving.' However, this tends to mean that women will experience repeated incidents of violence before they can leave. In one case that was highly publicised in November 2006 Herbert Mankhwala chopped off both his wife's hands when she tried to leave him. Despite the abuse his wife experienced, the efforts of the marriage counsellors focused on reconciliation when she had tried to leave, including through convincing her it was in her unborn child's best interests. There was a history of abuse and one article in *The Nation* newspaper reported that 'the family said Mankhwala took his wife as a punch bag' and that her relatives were 'shocked but not surprised when they saw her coming from the *dimba* garden [vegetable garden] with both hands chopped' (Langa, 2006a).

Gendered agriculture and food insecurity

Since this is a predominantly agrarian economy, understanding the gendered structures that permeate agriculture is also fundamental. During colonial rule, as was the situation across the continent more generally, cash crop production on tea and tobacco plantations was prioritised in terms of investment over smallholder farming for subsistence food production (Harrigan, 2001). As elsewhere in Africa, a 'hut tax' was imposed, necessitating households to generate a cash income, so men could be targeted by the colonial authorities to migrate to work on the cash crop plantations. This impacts negatively on women because it undermines their control of crop production and, where the best land is reserved for cash crops, women's land access decreased. Furthermore, women's workload increased because they were responsible for subsistence farming to ensure survival of the family (see Bryceson and Fonseca, 2006, p. 1655; Bryceson, 1995; Boserup, 1970; on the Baule of Côte d'Ivoire see Etienne, 1997). Cash crop production was promoted under SAPs and the liberalisation of tobacco in the 1990s provided opportunities for more affluent male farmers (Ellis et al., 2003). The legacy of cash crop agriculture is evident in Malawi today. The most important cash crop continues to be burley tobacco, which is grown predominantly in the north and is primarily controlled by men. Despite the heavy workload women undertake during production, they have little or no control over the proceeds and it is widely reported that when the crop is harvested the husband leaves and takes the earnings. One man in focus group discussions conducted by Saur et al. draws the analogy that 'women are like trailers while the man is the truck driver so we have to control the resources' (2005, p. 28). For example, Banda reflects on a seminar conducted for her research with Baptist women in the south-east region where one woman revealed that 'At least four times, our marriage has been interrupted by him [the husband] running off with other women. He usually does this after harvest time, when we have sold our produce' (2005, p. 185). It is also reported that in Karonga District women are chased away from their homes after the crops are harvested (see Nyirenda, 2006, p. 25).

Women continue to bear the burden of the subsistence farm work and comprise an estimated 70 per cent of full-time farmers (GoM, 2000, 1.4; UN, 2004). Women are the major food producers and yet they lack control over the land and its produce, even in the matrilineal societies of the south, where land is inherited through the female line. Women have only limited access to and control of small holdings on typically less fertile land, or of subsistence crops and the sales of any excess of these crops. As Boserup (1970) highlights for the case in general, there is a long history of skills development benefiting men. Although women play a fundamental role in agriculture, gendered norms mean that they are largely excluded from agricultural education (Semu et al., 2005; Tango International, 2004, p. 5). Girls are under-represented and underachieve in maths, science and technology subjects and agricultural education. Women are also typically marginalised from technological and scientific advancements in farming (for the situation in general see Koopman, 1995, p. 21; A.E. Ferguson, 1994, pp. 544, 547). As is the situation across Africa in general, women are part of the 'underside of development' because they are engaged in subsistence production for home consumption (Spring and Hansen, 1985; Seidman, 1981). The informal and private sectors in which women are actively engaged do not benefit from agricultural development and, if anything, they experience increased burdens. In terms of the main crop, maize, men are more likely than women to use higher yielding hybrid strains that require fertiliser, which they can then sell, while women tend to use the lower yielding, seed-bearing strains chosen for domestic production. The involvement of women in decisions about farm inputs and planning is largely limited to crops that do not require fertiliser application (GoM, 2006, p. 33). The lack of access of women to technology begins with their lack of awareness of alternative methods of farming. The *Malawi Poverty and Vulnerability Assessment* reveals that:

> only 7 percent of female-headed households obtained such advice [on farming methods], compared to 13 percent of male-headed households. Based on [women's limited role in decision-making identified]...it can be presumed that within a household, agricultural advice provided to men is not always passed on to their wives, furthering this gender gap. (GoM, 2006, p. 33)

Despite being the major food producers, women are disadvantaged in intra-household resource allocation (Hindin, 2005, p. 93). The husband tends to control the family's food security and the focus group discussions revealed a whole plethora of ways in which husbands regulate the amount of food that their wives use: for example by counting the number of pieces of meat in the pot, catching a fly in a packet of sugar to ensure it is not opened and marking the levels on the milk and maize to warn their wives against using the supplies (see also Saur et al., 2005). As is the situation across Sub-Saharan Africa, women have a vital role in investing in children, typically investing a greater proportion of their earnings in the household needs, particularly for the children (Commission for Africa, 2005, p. 208); and yet their food output and income is rarely adequate for their responsibilities for managing the family (Koopman, 1995, p. 21).

Women's nutrition suffers where they do not have the time to eat properly, as the key informants widely report (see also UN, 2004b;

Rankin et al., 2005, p. 9). The Senior Programme Manager of PSI's *Packachere* Programme explains:

> in the rural areas the woman does most of the household work, she loses a lot of energy: that also can make her vulnerable because if she has got problems with nutrition, she is doing too much work she is not having enough food to recover the energy she is losing.

Women work a greater number of hours than men and there is a deeply engrained gender division of labour (Rankin et al., 2005, p. 9; Ngulube-Chinoko, 1995, p. 90; for the situation in general see Boserup, 1970, p. 35). This situation is especially severe for female-headed households, as the HIV Advisor at DfID outlines: 'She is now lumbered with the responsibility of going to the garden, going to collect firewood, chopping the firewood and this is a daily process. Drawing water, feeding her kids, and making sure that they have gone to school.' In female-headed households women have the responsibility of supporting themselves and their children in the absence of their husband. As a result women typically are 'time-poor' because they have to balance a multitude of tasks, as the key informants reveal:

> [The women] are not resting because everything depends on them, like looking after the children, they do the work in the gardens, from there they come home, some work is waiting for them .... They don't have time to rest, because if a man comes back and says 'where is [the] food?' they will expect the same woman to cook, to do everything. (Principal Documentation Officer at the Ombudsman's Office)

> [The husband] will wake up very early and go to the field. He will be at the field until 1 o'clock in the afternoon, he comes home, he will rest and do other things around the house, chop firewood, etc. At the same time his wife will wake up, she will draw water in the morning, give her kids a bath, and make sure they are fed. Some of them will go to school. Likely one of them will be an infant she will have to breastfeed. She has got to go the market; she has got to go to the maize mill. (HIV Advisor at DfID)

Women work an average of 16 hours a day, 10 hours more than men and 11 hours more than men in rural areas (GoM, 2006, p. 48; Wodon and Beegle, 2006, p. 104). The interviews conducted for the study of *Nkanza* by Saur et al. revealed that, despite some men and women believing that the labour demand on women is too great, it is popularly accepted as the norm (2005, p. 29). The HIV epidemic has exacerbated the burden because women have to care for the sick and support the family if the husband is infected (Rankin et al., 2005, p. 9).

There are also specific aspects of women's domestic role that heighten their susceptibility to under-nutrition. Domestic tasks including washing and water collection leave them vulnerable to nutrition-related diseases associated with water contamination, including giardia and dysentery. Women are particularly vulnerable because 93 per cent of women live in rural areas where water contamination is worse. Furthermore, where women immerse themselves in water for prolonged periods while washing clothes or collecting water, they are susceptible to schistosomiasis (also known as bilharzia) because the water turbulence and chemicals particularly stimulate the parasite's activity. Young girls are susceptible because they tend to assist their mother collecting water or washing laundry, as the Programme Officer for Reproductive Health and HIV at UNICEF highlights (Stillwaggon, 2006b, p. 57). This waterborne disease is endemic and increases the risk to women of contracting HIV because it can cause genital lesions and tumours in the vulva, which facilitate the transmission of the virus (Mabala, 2006, p. 410; A. Ferguson, 2005, p. 55; Kjetland et al., 1996; Feldmeier et al., 1994, pp. 368–72). Despite their impact on women these issues were not included in the formulation of the 2004 water policy, which did not take into account the gendered dimensions, mention HIV or consider the importance of water to mitigate illness (A. Ferguson, 2005, pp. 49–57).

There is a tendency for men to be in a position to access more diverse foods when they migrate to work in town and they have a disposable income to purchase this food. Whereas the food that is typically consumed within the home in the villages does not provide a balanced diet because it tends to consist predominantly of carbohydrates, as the Principal Documentation Officer at the Ombudsman and the Programme Officer for Reproductive Health and HIV at UNICEF consider. Maize is the principal crop and the staple food is *nsima*, which is made from maize flour, and is often served only with a small relish of leaves. Despite the necessity for alternatives rural households typically lack the capacity to diversify (Ellis et al., 2003, p. 1496). The representatives of the HIV Section at the Ministry of Education also consider how women in rural areas are vulnerable to malnutrition caused by intestinal worms because they lack access to clean water. As Stillwaggon (2006a) outlines, this makes it difficult to keep hands and food preparation areas clean, and women tend to walk around without shoes.

Satisfying the husband and 'salt-testing'

Traditionally, as part of maintaining marriage and satisfying men as the breadwinners, women have to ensure their husband is well fed. This is a practice the focus group discussions in both districts widely report and is known as *mkomia*. Nancy of Fulirwa Support Group in Karonga District explains that 'We are told that men are children and *mwanalume phatumbo'* [meaning "the whole man is at the belly"] – you do not look a man in the face, look at the belly. So when the house has little food, give it to the man.' Majidu of One Voice Support Group in Zomba District explains that men get priority for food in the homes because 'women want to get favours from husbands' and Eleck adds 'love', at which the other men all laugh, and Blessings explains, you get 'enough food – love – so you do not leave the house and go elsewhere'. The interviews and focus group discussions reveal the tendency for the nutrition of men to take priority. Traditionally men eat first and are fed the most nutritious food as the gender specialist with CIDA highlights:

> Women are the ones that prepare the food, but they are taught from a young age that they should serve the best food to the men. Whether it is during a function like a wedding ceremony or is a funeral or even the home. If there is the best part of a chicken, if there is just a little of a nutritious food that is available, women are supposed to give preference to the men. So in most cases they end up eating something that is less nutritious, and is inadequate, so that would lead to their being vulnerable to being low in nutrition levels.

During the focus group discussion with the women of Kaporo Support Group, Mary explains that men take priority 'because they buy every-thing for the family', to which Flora adds that 'when a piece of chicken is left in the pot the man is the one to finish', to which the other women agree. The focus group discussions with men and women in Zomba and Karonga Districts reveal how men prefer certain portions of the chicken such as the breasts and gizzard, while women receive the neck, legs and head. Although this situation is most entrenched in rural areas, as the Executive Director of Malawi AIDS Counselling and Resource Organisation (MACRO) explains, it is still evident among the middle-class educated urban women that the food preference goes to the husband. A representative of the HIV Section of the Ministry of Edu-cation, for example, reflects upon how she is 'yet to know a woman who does not feed her husband first'.

And yet, the focus group discussions reveal how the situation differs between families and shed light on some of the strategies women employ to navigate these gendered structures. The focus group discussions in Zomba and Karonga widely reveal how women would engage in 'salt-testing' while they were cooking, and thus eat a lot during food preparation. For example, when the women of Tikondane Support Group consider who takes priority in terms of food in their homes, Agatha immediately replied 'the man'. To which the other women all laughed and Elube and Magret argued it was women, explaining that 'women are full time in the home while the men are away'. These subtle ways in which women resist gender inequalities in terms of food link to James Scott's (1990) work on the 'weapons of the weak'. Power structures are navigated through public 'performances of compliance' with the established order. Scott distinguishes between the public 'mask' that is required by those subordinated (the public transcript) and the performance that takes place 'off stage' (the hidden transcript).

Fish-for-sex

Within the context of economic crisis, with increasing cost and scarcity of food and fuel coupled with rising unemployment, men increasingly struggle to fulfil their gender-based role as breadwinner, a point I return to in chapter 4. Where women are traditionally the dependents, exchanging sex for food provides a fundamental strategy of survival for them and their families. Women have an avenue for mitigating food insecurity that is, for the most part, not available to men, and they can use it to circumvent men's control over the household resources. This is particularly crucial where they are typically the ones who are responsible for their own and their children's welfare.

HIV is popularly accepted as a 'part of life' and the powerlessness concerning HIV risk leads to a focus on meeting immediate basic needs, particularly for food, as Bryceson and Fonseca (2006, p. 1655) consider in their research on the high levels of HIV risk among smallholder farmers during the 2001 3 famine. Even beyond famine situations, risk-taking in sex continues to be a strategy to mitigate normal shortage. Where 93 per cent of women live in the rural areas hardest hit by food shortages and water contamination, they are more susceptible to poor nutrition and tend to take the pressure of ensuring the survival of their families during the periodic food shortages (WFP, 2007; GoM, 2000, 1.4; UN, 2004a). Women may exchange sex for food with traders – especially between December and March when hunger peaks – to ensure food security of the family, as the HIV Advisor, DfID and the Director of

Planning, Research and Evaluation at the Department of HIV, AIDS and Nutrition report (Pinter, 2004; Bryceson et al., 2004). This is particularly the case for female-headed households because they have tighter margins and experience lower levels of health, education and employment (Tango International, 2004, p. 5; NSO Malawi and ORC Macro, 2005, p. 11; Ngwira and Mkandawire, 2003). However, it is also the case in situations where the husband is not adequately supporting the family. For example, Kondwani of Fulirwa Support Group proposes that 'every day men are drinking, with no time to find food and soup for the family, so the wife has sex to find food for the children'.

In 2007 the HIV coordinator at UNFPA reflected that a phenomenon known as 'fish-for-sex' had been reported in Nkhotakhota on Lake Malawi, whereby girls would be sent by their families to buy fish and they would get better prices. A Project Coordinator with an international NGO in Zomba conducted focus group discussions with fishermen in Nkhotakhota at the time and, when he was interviewed in 2011, he reported that the men would recognise that the practice was placing them at risk of infection but they admitted that they could not resist the women when they undressed. As is the situation more generally, the fishing industry in Malawi is highly gendered, as MacPherson et al. (2012) consider in their study of two villages in Mangochi in Southern Malawi, and Odotei (1992) considers for the canoe fishermen in Ghana. There are gender-based roles whereby men are the fishermen and women carry out processing, drying and selling the fish. Odotei describes the ways in which the 'fishmothers' in Ghana support the migration of canoe fishermen along the coast, who may travel without their wives and 'need the services of women to cook and wash their clothes for them' (1992, p. 93). Where men control the means of production, MacPherson et al. (2012) consider how it is difficult for women to negotiate for safer sex. They report that transactional sex was prevalent, including in the forms of gift-giving within relationships, sex-for-fish exchanges and sex worker encounters.

In the context of depleting fish stocks, the interviews and focus group discussions in 2011 reveal that the practice is widespread on Lake Chilwa in Zomba District and along Lake Malawi in Karonga District. The Chairman at Nkuba Beach on Lake Chilwa explained how the fishermen stay for extended periods and women migrate to exchange sex for free fish, for better prices or to get preference in buying limited stocks. Penny of Lughano Support Group in Karonga and Henry of Tikondane Support Group in Zomba report that fishermen have other sexual partners in the villages along the lakeshores because they travel long distances without their wives, particularly where the fish stocks are depleting. Henry explains that 'when they are alone at the lake they have lots of sexual feelings and they meet lots of women everywhere'. In Karonga District the fishing industry is small scale and yet contributes over 60 per cent of animal protein. In 2005 there were an estimated 5400 fishermen – an 80 per cent increase as compared to 2002 (Department of Fisheries Frame Survey, 2005, cited in KDA, 2008, p. 52). The annual catches are estimated between 1780 and 2817 tonnes, which equates to a value of 114 million MK. There has been a decline in catches since 1997 but the number of fishermen, fishing craft and fishing gear has reportedly increased two fold (KDA, 2008, pp. 52–3). There is a large fishing population but, as the Reverend of the Anglican Church reports, the fish stocks are depleting so the men migrate around the lake and in doing so still make a lot of money as compared to other professions. Men in the focus group discussions in Karonga report how they had travelled from as far as the southern lakeshore. Clement of Hangalawe Support Group in Uliwa in Karonga District explains in a one-to-one interview how he contracted HIV while he was living in Monkey Bay in Mangochi District for 13 years and working as a fisherman. He talks of his own experiences, which he believes led to him becoming infected with HIV:

> When a fisherman has caught fish the women come and visit him and they say 'give me fish for credit'. You go to their home at night, but when you go there they say 'I will do anything. I have already eaten your fish and you can eat me [have sex].' Men don't resist. Lots of women want to buy at cheaper prices, and the fishermen agree and say 'the deducted money will be replaced by sex'.

He reflects that he knows that lots of men in Karonga get HIV because of this practice: 'Here [near to Uliwa] and Ngala [further north along the coast] it is very common for fishermen to have sex with women; I have seen this with my eyes.' Women are the majority of the buyers of the fish and to maximise the profits they travel to the lakeshore to dry the fish. The exchange of sex is a vital strategy for women to compete to get free fish, better prices or to get preference in buying. It was also reported in the areas around Karonga *Boma*. For example, during the focus group discussions with the women of Lupembe Support Group, just south of the *Boma*:

> Mercy, Fran and Jane explain how 'we have relationships with fishermen to get free fish and *usipa* [small fish]'. Fran adds that 'when we

go to order fish at the lake we sleep at the same beach at night and we can have sex'.

As the Reverend of the Anglican Church explains, women traders would want to minimise their expenditures when they travel north through the area towards the Songwe border, 'They do not want to pay for guest houses so they look to find someone who will pay on their behalf. They develop relationships where they go to sell the fish and they build up a ready market so they do not need to stay too long.' In the context of depleting fish stocks, the interviews and focus group discussions in 2011 reveal that the practice is widespread along the lake shore, which extends along the length of Karonga District.

The exchange of sex for food extends beyond the practice of 'fish-for-sex'. In Karonga District there are four main markets at Songwe, Nyungwe, Miyombo and Chilumba, with other satellite markets. These are particularly vibrant with the scale of trade across the Tanzanian border, especially in clothes and household goods from Tanzania, and sugar, beers and rice from Malawi (KDA, 2008, p. 70). Most of the major trading centres are along the M1 road, including Songwe border, Pusi/Kaporo, Mwiketere, Miyombo, Karonga *Boma*, Mwenilondo, Mlare, Ngara, Nyugwe, Chilumba Jetty, Uliwa and Fulirwa near Wovwe mini-hydroelectric power plant. The men of Kapora Support Group in the Pusi/Kapora area and the women in Mwiketere Support Group report how women in those markets in the north of the district offer sex to the traders to get better prices for commodities such as vegetables, tomatoes, rice and flour (see Bryceson and Fonseca, 2006; Shah, 2002). Similarly, Clement of Hangalawe Support Group reports that in the Uliwa area 'Lots of women think people with grocery businesses [small stalls] are rich. They go there without money and seduce the owner.'

Gendered labour opportunities

As elsewhere, women are typically are disadvantaged in terms of labour opportunities. Employment opportunities for men have long been associated with labour mobility, where men migrate for work opportunities, for example to the mines etc. More men migrate to work in the towns as compared to women, 93 per cent of whom live in the rural areas, where poverty is acute and 30 per cent of rural households are female-headed (Mbaya, 2002, p. 8). The continuing scale of male labour migration is indicated by the 2010 MDHS. In rural areas in the 0–19 age group the proportion of males is higher, but after that there are more females.

This suggests a younger population, predominantly male, who tend to migrate later on for employment in urban areas (NSO and ICF Macro, 2011, pp. 10–11).

Women are typically excluded from the formal economy and their contribution in the informal sector – subsistence farming – and their domestic role is marginalised and has a lower perceived value to society (Kishindo, 2004; Tango International, 2004, p. 2; for the situation in general see James, 1994). This is again rooted in a long history of the transformation of labour roles by colonisation and neoliberal policies, with men benefiting in terms of the diversification of labour opportunities. On the one hand, there is horizontal segregation, whereby men spend more time in the labour market, undertaking greater salaried work, including casual, part-time and *ganyu* work (short-term rural labour) (Wodon and Beegle, 2006, p. 103). Typically, rural households mitigate food insecurity resulting from shortfalls in their own maize production through *ganyu* labour – short-term wage-earning opportunities on other farms – in order to purchase maize (Alwang, 1990; Pearce et al., 1996, cited in Ellis et al., 2003, p. 1497). Although women engage in wage labour, smallholder farming, fishing and informal sector work, their opportunities are constrained by limited access to land, capital, credit, technology, deep-rooted cultural practices and high illiteracy levels, as the Programme Officer at WFP highlights (GoM, 2000, 5.6). Where women are engaged in wage labour they may be under pressure from their husbands to cease work on marriage, as the Programme Manager at the Story Workshop considers (see also Luciano, 2006, p. 4):

> There are men who are working, they marry a woman who is working they make that woman stop working. They will tell them 'Stop working, I earn enough.' Jobs are difficult to find so it may take some time before she gets one. Sometimes there are women who try to become economically independent, but they are frustrated: they get loans from these micro loans [but] they find that the man consumes the capital, brings the business down, so the woman will still be dependent on them.

On the other hand, there is a vertical segregation, whereby women tend to be concentrated in the lower tiers of a given profession. Women who are employed in the formal sector typically earn less on average than men: in 2006, the median monthly wage for women was 78 MK compared with 124 for men (GoM, 2006, p. 33). Women's earnings from *ganyu* labour are on average two-thirds those of men, and they are often paid in kind with food or clothing (Tango International, 2004, p. 6; Pinter, 2004). Employment in the informal sector has long been an important source of livelihood for many women and is fundamental to the economy, as is the situation in similar countries. And yet, it is typically not fully recognised, it is not well-developed and is often insecure (GoM, 2000, 5.6).

Furthermore, the majority of women are not in a position to access the necessary resources to start up their own businesses and often need their husband's approval to access credit and for legal transactions (Tango International, 2004, pp. 6–7; Pinter, 2004; Spring, 1995, p. 22). As the Chairperson of COWLHA in 2007 identifies, the limited access of women to credit is exacerbated if they are HIV-positive. Typically, the larger the value of the loan, the smaller the likelihood that the recipient is a woman (GoM, 2006, p. 33). Formal credit lending institutions require collateral or that the loan is for investing in cash crops. For example the Malawi Rural Finance Company (MRFC) and the Malawi Union of Savings and Credit (MUSCCO) provide seasonal agricultural loans based on the size of the land holdings. Women's lack of access to and control of resources, including land and other collateral, restricts their access to credit and loans. Although the Promotion of Micro Enterprises for Rural Women (PMERW) was established as a credit programme for poor rural women with land holdings of less than half a hectare, it still favours relatively rich households. Women also have fewer informal credit opportunities; they tend to access to smaller loans with higher interest rates and are liable to property grabbing exceeding the value of the loan if they fail to repay. Women tend to join informal neighbourhood and women's savings groups or keep their money in a safe place. A woman volunteer in the Credit Room of the African Women Food Farmers Initiative (AWFFI) bank in Jali, Zomba District, explains how the scheme helps women with start-up funds of 5000 to 10,000 MK for small businesses, including trading second-hand clothes, buying small fish, making doughnuts and trading groceries. The women in the community struggle to pay the 15 per cent interest on these loans and the volunteer explains that they have faced challenges ensuring that the loans are repaid and there is a committee of women to ensure that they do.

Commercial sex

Gendered inequalities in wealth that are inextricably linked to the gendered distribution of land, gendered agriculture and labour opportunities, were widely reported by the key informants, focus group discussions and interviewees as being a major contributing factor to the spread of HIV. In the context of limited alternative opportunities, it was widely reported throughout the research that women are economically dependent on men and exchange sex to access support from men. 'Commercial sex' comes in a whole plethora of guises, as the City AIDS Coordinator highlights, including going to a lodge or maybe a guesthouse selling sex, or going to women's homes and even paying them 'in kind'. In Karonga the situation is more acute because of the greater situations of dependency resulting from the patrilineal system of land inheritance. As the Reverend of the Anglican Church reports, married women have no control over the resources in the home and 'for their own security... [try] to get any other income anywhere'. It is a relatively lucrative industry and the clientele basis is maintained, in spite of high unemployment levels. As research by Kishindo in Zomba in 1992 suggests, bar girls who engaged in sex work earned a reasonable wage compared with formal employment. The minimum monthly wage at the time was 52.2 MK, while the bar girls were paid 21.50 MK a month from the bar and for each act of sexual intercourse they could expect to earn 10 MK within the municipality and 5 MK outside it (cited in Forster, 2000, p. 7). Women's bodies become commoditised: Sandra and Patricia at Pokani Omoyo Support Group, for example, reflect how sex workers around Kasowa in Karonga District proclaim that 'God gave me my "sister" [vagina] to make me money', charging as little as 20 MK (US$0.12) for a 'short time'. Several of the support groups report that families sometimes encourage their daughters to bring men to their homes. Women can earn more for sex without a condom: in 2011 sex workers at one of the bars in Zomba City charged between 700 and 1000 MK (US$4–6) for sex with a condom and 5000 MK (US$30) without a condom, justifying the higher price because they are risking their lives. As a WFP HIV Programme Officer highlights, 'Women would do anything when they are poor. Most of them would risk having sexual intercourse just to get funds or just to get food.' However, as Campbell's (2003) work in South Africa reveals, women engaged in more formal 'sex work' or 'prostitution' are not the most at risk. The informal discussions with women in the bars suggest that they are more likely than other groups to adopt a professional attitude towards using condoms to look after their bodies as a resource.

As elsewhere across the continent, risky sexual environments have emerged near the major roads, rural industries (including tea, coffee and tobacco plantations), on the lake and areas of small-scale trading where there are periodic absences and an influx of traders (Ngwira et al.,

2001, p. 8). Across Zomba and Karonga Districts women exchange sex with men who migrate to work in the area. In both districts, there is a daily movement of traders to the markets and, as already discussed, the migration of fishermen, who bring their boats and equipment with them and are relatively very rich in the new society. Male migration was widely reported as a key factor in spreading HIV by the key informants and focus group discussions (see also Anglewicz and Kohler, 2009, p. 73; PSI/Malawi, 2006, p. 17; NSO Malawi and ORC Macro, 2005, p. 201; Kaler, 2001, pp. 529–56; Chimbiri, 2007, p. 1103). As HIV is transmitted through interpersonal sexual relations, the spread of the HIV virus follows movements of people (Decosas et al., 1995; Webb, 1997, p. 13). This is a global phenomenon and the structural factors underscore the HIV–migration nexus. 'Circular migration' (Lurie, 2000, p. 3) has been linked to HIV risk in Malawi (see Mtika, 2007; Chirwa, 1998). The Zomba City AIDS Coordinator highlights the risky environments associated with the central prison, Kobi Barracks, the police colleges, the university, the Ministry of Agriculture, National Statistics Office and City Council. This was a key issue that was raised by the key-informant interviews and focus group discussions across the district. During focus group discussion with One Voice Support Group in Nkolokosa, the men consider the implications:

> Eric reflects that 'women they are easily carried away by strange men that come to work here'. Henry interjects that these are lumberjacks and Majidu adds it is also the soldiers – 'The women think the soldiers will give them lots of money so they easily suggest themselves to the soldiers.'

Traditional Authority T. A. Mulumbe explains, for example, that Nkolokosa is surrounded by two army barracks on both sides and the soldiers spend their free time with women in their area, who are attracted to the money the soldiers have. In Zomba City sex work peaks with the pay day at the end of the month.

In contrast, in Karonga sex work in the *Boma* is sustained by constant flow of people and capital. As the Reverend of the Anglican Church reflects, with all the economic activity there is a constant flow of disposable income and lots of transactional sex. During the observations at bars in the *Boma* there was a constant energy around the bars and night-clubs that stood in stark contrast to the peaks in clientele at the end of the month in Zomba. Karonga *Boma* is an important transit hub situated on the main M1 road along the lakeshore connecting the rest of Malawi with Tanzania through the Songwe border and Zambia through neigh-bouring Chitipa. As the District Coordinator for CHRR reported, and I observed, truck drivers would come and stay at the guest houses around the main roundabout, parking their trucks all along the adjoining roads. It has long been recognised across the continent that long-distance truck drivers are a 'high-risk group' (on Botswana see MacDonald, 1996, p. 1331). Traders would also come from Zambia and Tanzania. The estab-lishment of mines across Karonga District and, most notably, uranium and coal at the Kayelekera mine (until February 2014) 40 km west of Karonga Municipality attracted workers from all over Malawi, the con-tinent and the world, as the District Coordinator for CHRR reports. The Reverend of the Anglican Church explains that Kayelekera pays dispro-portionately high wages, so even the lower-paid jobs at the mine provide men with considerable spending power to indulge in luxuries, includ-ing paying for sex while they are away from their families at home. For example, Nbande Support Group, situated along the Karonga–Chitipa road, report how the Chinese contractors working on building the road to the mine through their area on the road have sex with local girls. Luhango Support Group in Karonga *Boma* (Centre) and Mwenitete Sup-port Group along the lakeshore report how women increasingly move away from their areas to housing around the mine to engage in sex work. The District AIDS Coordinator and the support groups report how the workers have sex on credit until they get paid at the end of the month. When the workers have free time from work many travel to Karonga *Boma* to spend their wages. The District Coordinator for CHRR and the Reverend of the Anglican Church report that the employees drink in the bars and pay for sex workers because there are few bars around the mine itself. Across the district I witnessed mine workers who were negotiat-ing with bar tenders to locate women to pay for sex. Sex workers also travel down from Tanzania to work in the bars in Karonga, although the District AIDS Coordinator reports that they are coming in reduced num-bers as compared to the past. The women in the support groups would often mention women from outside coming to their areas and engaging in sex work as a major contributing factor to the spread of HIV. They would reflect that men in their area would be attracted to the exotic outsiders.

Entrepreneurial women

Despite the pervasive poverty and food insecurity, people are surviving and others are flourishing. Of interest here is how some people exchange sex as a means for upward social mobility. Verheijen (2011, pp. 120–1) uses birth statistics and informal discussions to show how in Mudzi, in Balaka District in southern Malawi, unprotected sexual intercourse peaks not just during times of scarcity but also after harvest, when 'women seize the opportunity to access extra money – which men have pockets of after selling their harvest'. This was supported by the findings in Karonga District. George and Patrick of Kaporo Support Group reflect that women in their area engage in sex to fulfil their material desires for fashion and other luxuries. Henry from Kulirwa Support Group suggests that: 'When the man cannot provide everything for the family, the wife searches for a rich man who can provide for her needs.' The South African men working with the contractor on the Chilumba to Chiweta road between 2000 and 2005 paid up to 40,000 MK (US$270) for one night of sex and many women used this money to buy iron sheets for the roofs of their houses – literally securing the future of their families. Women are not simply the 'passive victims of the cultural expectation that a supportive relationship entails sex', as Verheijen considers, 'women can play an active, at times manipulative, role in enforcing that their sexual relationships entailed material benefit' (2011, p. 120).

In the context of limited employment opportunities, it was widely reported how women, and to a lesser extent men, have sex with their employers in order to secure work and receive bonuses. Shah (2002) considers how transactional sex is being incorporated into short-term rural labour (*ganyu*) contracts. The women from Makunganya Village Support Group also discuss how tea estate workers in their area only receive a salary of 2800 MK (US$17) per month so they seduce the boss for a 1000 MK (US$6) bonus. Anna of Nsondole Support Group reports that women in the Nsondole area have sex with the foremen on the local road projects to get employment with them. The HIV Coordinator at BLM in Zomba reveals how the survey companies pay exceptionally high wages at 9000 MK (US$55) per day, and women will have sex with their employer to get this work, and if they refuse the employer's continued demands for sex then they risk losing their employment.

Women may also decide to exchange sexual services for commercial advantages. In Zomba City the Chairperson of St Charles Lwangwa Parish Home-Based Care Support Group reports that there are numerous bottle stores and cheap housing where prostitutes reside. In addition, at markets such as the Mpondabwino market women brew *Kachasu* beer, which they sell for 100 MK for a small bottle and 500 MK for a big bottle. They charge their customers between 100 and 150 MK for sex. This is considered particularly cheap, but the women know that they will make money from sleeping with lots of men. Similarly, several of the focus group discussions with the support groups report how young women selling small products such as the *Mandasi* buns only charge 20 MK per bun and can earn considerably more from engaging in transactional sex. Women traders have sex with their customers to ensure they were satisfied and to earn extra money. T. A. Mulumbe explains how women brewing *Kachasu* in Nkolokosa sell one beer for 20 MK. Some soldiers pay 500 MK for a cup and tell the women to keep the change and later want sex for the change. It was widely reported during the interviews, focus group discussions and informal discussions across Karonga District that women are also considered to be 'entrepreneurial'. As a Technical Advisor to the 'Women, Girls and HIV/AIDS – Programme and Plan of Action' explains:

> Should they engage into business, most people they have contact in their businesses is men. Usually men ask for sexual favours to support them in that. I will give an example of the border: nowadays most women go to Tanzania or South Africa, when they are asked for customs sometimes they are charged so exorbitantly they cannot afford to pay, so the customs people they will ask 'Let me just sleep with you then you will have to pay nothing.'

Patrick from Kaporo Support Group also reports how women traders from their area travel to Tanzania to buy clothes to sell and have sex with the salesmen to get better deals. Women also have sex with *cargo* (bicycle taxis) riders, minibus drivers and the *matola* (open-back truck) drivers to take goods to market at reduced rate or for free, especially in context of fuel shortages.

Sugar daddies

Similar to the situation across Sub-Saharan Africa, there is the tendency for young girls across to have older 'sugar daddies' in order to access 'the three Cs – cell phones, cars and cash', as the Head of Policy Support and Development at NAC and the Strategic Manager of the Youth Alert! Programme report (see also Rankin et al., 2005, pp. 12–13; Bracher et al., 2003, p. 212; for the case of Tanzania see Silberschmidt and Rasch, 2001). The Reverend of the Anglican Church reports how in the areas of his congregations north of Karonga up to the Songwe border, working men are chasing young girls because they are 'passionate about them'. 'Where lots of areas are socially developed, young girls are competing in terms of dress. They want money and the people with money are older men who are already sexually experienced. So more girls are infected than boys.' As is the situation in general, the Population and Health Specialist at the World Bank reports that it is believed that older men offer greater financial security, are well established and sensible. Age asymmetry in sexual relationships puts younger girls at heightened risk of HIV infection. Older men are more likely to be infected and prevalence is highest among men aged 30–34 at 20 per cent. Women are more likely to become infected at a younger age: girls aged 15–19 are nine times more likely to be infected than boys of the same age (NSO Malawi and ORC Macro, 2005, p. 230; see also GoM, 2005, 3.1.2, 2006; Rankin et al., 2005, p. 6). The high infectivity rates of older men are rooted in gendered structures. Where men often migrate for work this increases the likelihood that they will engage in premarital sex. As is explored in chapter 4, masculinity is associated with having multiple sexual partners, older men tend to have had more premarital sexual partners and this may include bar girls and sex workers. Older men may have sex with young girls by preference as they are perceived to be infection-free, or because of the belief that sexual intercourse with virgins can cure HIV, as representatives of the World Bank, Department for International Development (DfID) and the HIV Section at the Ministry of Education report (see also Bracher et al., 2003, p. 212).

Attitudes are changing – beliefs are emerging that wealthier, older, migrant men are more likely to be infected with HIV. Interviews conducted by Fielder (2005, p. 18) with girls in the Southern Region reveal their perception that forcing girls to marry men whose morals are not known is a contributing factor to the HIV epidemic. However, there are no laws against men marrying younger girls, as the HIV Programme Officer at UNFPA highlights. Section 22 (8) of the Malawi Constitution (GoM, 1994) outlines only that the state shall 'discourage marriage between persons where either of them is under the age of fifteen years, but it is not prohibited'. Whereas for persons between the age of 15 and 18 years, section 22 (7) states that 'a marriage shall only be entered into with the consent of their parents or guardians'. The Law Commission conducted a review of the laws on marriage and divorce in June 2006 with proposals to prohibit marriage and sex with young girls but these were met with opposition, as the Law Commissioner explains:

Quite a sizeable number of our community are saying not *discourage*, that is not strong enough, you must say *prohibit*. But as [the other representatives of the Law Commission] will tell you, you have got problems there, what do you mean prohibit? Criminalise is that what you want to say? You want to criminalise sex between two consenting children who are each 17 for example, or 15 say – your prisons will be full.

The Chief Law Reform Officer at the Law Commission explains that there is a proposal to increase the age of marriage and to introduce penalties for the parents who give consent to marriages where their children are under age. The media is playing a role in discouraging the age asymmetry of sexual relationships. One article, for example, reports how a 14-year-old girl married an older fishmonger, depicting her as envious of her former classmates going to school (Karim, 2006, p. 4).

However, it is widely reported that the practice of engaging in sex for upward social mobility extends beyond young girls and sugar daddies. George and Patrick of Kaporo Support Group reflect that women in their area engage in sex to fulfil their material desires for fashion and other luxuries. The Chairperson of Mawo ndi Anthu CBO in Ntala village explains how:

> There are lots of soldiers living in the Airwe barracks: the soldiers have the money to coax women within the village. The soldiers are married but engage in extra-marital affairs and it becomes like a habit for women. Traditionally women are perceived to be 'home idle' and when they go to the pubs it is a way for them to become 'modernised' – [they] want to say that 'my husband is a soldier'.

Moreover, with increasing numbers of affluent women in recent years, there are reports that men also find sugar mummies to access certain luxuries. During the interviews and informal discussions it was widely reported how older woman entice young men to their homes for sex, paying them in cash or in kind for their services. The HIV Coordinator at BLM suggests that wealthy women in Zomba pay for sex because they are busy working and they do not want to marry because they fear a husband would expect them to stay at home as a housewife. The owner of a bar in Zomba City and one of his bartenders reported in an informal discussion how sugar mummies come to that bar. The owner explains how women might buy a couple of ciders but are not there to drink; they watch the young men, sit with their keys in their hands ready to leave. They are after 3, 4, 5, 6 hot adolescents. The bartender reflects on an incident when he was enticed by a sugar mummy himself; 'She did not want to use condoms, they dress you, feed you, look after you and do not want to use condoms. They pay lots – perhaps 10,000 kwacha, pay your rent – but give you a tough time – follow you, constantly call you up to ask where you are.'

The associating of upward social mobility with HIV risk is indicated in the MDHS: HIV prevalence is greater with increasing wealth, from 8 per cent in the lowest wealth quintile to 15 per cent among those in the highest quintile. And there is a gendered dimension: women in the highest wealth quintile are almost twice as likely to be HIV-positive as men in the highest wealth quintile (20 per cent and 11 per cent respectively) (NSO and ICF Macro, 2011, pp. 198–9).

Conclusions

Gendered poverty is a form of structural violence in that women are the traditional dependants and, as a result, they disproportionately experience HIV risk, preventing them from achieving their full potential. This chapter explores the nuances of these structures to contribute to a better understanding of why the current interventions are not working. Economic and cultural structures tend towards gendered inequalities in land distribution (both in terms of the customary and modern systems of land inheritance), agriculture and food security and labour opportunities. Although this is a global phenomenon, in the world's poorest countries the situation is most acute. This chapter has highlighted how this violence is deeply entrenched in traditional cultural norms and has been transformed over time through colonialism and neoliberalism.

And yet, despite the pervasive structural inequalities and the limited opportunities available, this social injustice is not experienced passively. The analysis exposes how these dynamics manifest themselves in different ways and, in the absence of an effective response to poverty and gender inequality, the seemingly 'powerless' navigate the situations of gendered inequality and dependency. The analysis has identified a number of cultural practices associated with land inheritance that have developed, which serve to secure the extended family system and preserve the status quo. Women traditionally ensure their husbands are satisfied sexually and persevere in order to maintain their marriages. In the context of gender inequalities in agriculture and food distribution, women preserve the status quo by public displays whereby they ensure the husband is well fed (known as '*mkomia*') and yet behind the scenes subtly rebel through 'salt-testing' during food preparation. This connects with James Scott's work (1990) on the weapons of the weak' that sheds light on the discrepancies between the 'public' performances of compliance to the established order (the public transcript) and the subtle ways in which people rebel behind the scenes (the 'hidden tran-script'). Where HIV has become normalised as an inescapable fact of life, risk-taking in sex is a key strategy to bring about immediate security and, in some cases, for upward social mobility. This is especially the case for women who are disproportionately poor. Transactional sex is a vital survival strategy in terms of accessing food (including the phenomenon of 'fish-for-sex') and cash. For some women and men, sex is also employed as a means for upward social mobility including through 'sugar daddies' and 'sugar mummies'.

This contributes to exposing some aspects of what is missing from the picture in the framing of the virus in development and security terms and the dominant neoliberal 'one-size-fits-all' policy response. Technological fixes (including a vaccine, ARVs and condoms) are an important part of the response but they are not sufficient. These gendered structures are rooted in a long history and this requires long-term commitment to the more fundamental task of addressing these underlying structures, as opposed to an emergency response. This is clearly a much harder task – but it is of fundamental importance; if it is not tackled, the incremental responses at best manage the situation and at worst exacerbate the problem. It is vital to recognise these are not permanent relations of violence. HIV risk is not simply experienced – people engage in risk-taking as a means of control and security within their lives to access employment, money and food, and to flourish. Strategies to eliminate these practices through imposing behaviour change from the top down are problematic because these are key safety nets.

The next chapter complements these findings by moving beyond the focus on poverty to examine the gendered ways in which life is valued.

4
Sex for Well-being
The Gendered Value of Life

The preceding chapter examined gendered poverty as a form of structural violence and the concern here is to extend the analysis to understand the gendered ways in which life is valued. This is crucial because, as established in chapter 1, health interventions are predicated on western neoliberal conceptualisations of responsible, rational individuals (see Flynn, 2006, p. 83; Beck-Gernsheim, 2000, p. 123; Beck, 1992, p. 135). And yet, knowledge does not tend to result in behaviour change. The intricacies of the gendered ways in which life is valued and the impact upon HIV risk are particularly obscured by responses that are based on 'best practice' in other contexts. The value of life is not necessarily visible or measurable. As opposed to the emphasis on a top-down response, understanding how people value life requires local-level expertise.

It is well established in the feminist literature that the ways in which the identities of men and women are constructed and their lives are valued in all societies is inextricably linked to gendered division of labour. Traditionally in Malawi men have a productive role in the public sphere and women have a reproductive role in the private sphere, assuming responsibility for the caring for the family (see also MHRC, 2005, p. 26). As is the situation in general, the contributions of men are typically more highly valued and privileged in society than female ones, and this underscores a gendered hierarchy whereby women are inferior to men. Despite the multiple roles women have, their value is rooted in their reproductive role (see Oakley, 2005, pp. 74, 109; James, 1994, p. 174). In Malawi, women typically are considered as second-class citizens, as the Head of the Women Lawyer's Association (WLA) reflects. This begins from the different ways in which the birth of boys and girls is celebrated, as a woman, Mzimba, interviewed by the NGO Women's Voice expresses:

> When a boy is born there is *nthugururu* [ululation] in the room where the child is born. The attendants are too happy because he is the owner of the land [king]. When a girl is born there is only informa- tion. A girl's birth does not go with *nthugururu* ... and they say only that '*mwanakazi munyithu wobabbika*' [our fellow woman is born]. (Women's Voice, 2000, cited in MHRC, 2006)

It is argued that this is a form of structural violence in the sense that the social categorisation along gender lines of how the lives of men and women are valued underscores HIV risk. This is rooted in a long history of colonisation and neoliberalism, which has an enduring legacy for valuing life in contemporary Malawi. And yet this social injustice is not experienced passively. People navigate these structures to bring value and meaning to their lives and this can heighten HIV risk.

In order to make this argument, this chapter questions the gendered ways in which the lives of men and women are valued and the ramifi- cations this has for HIV risk. First, reproduction is fundamental to the gendered ways men and women are valued in society. This has partic- ular implications for women's HIV risk because of the primacy of their reproductive role. Second, sexualised rituals and traditional counselling prepare men and women for their reproductive roles and enhancing sexual fulfilment in marriage forms a crucial part of cultural traditions of different ethnic groups. Third, marriage customs posit men as dom- inant heads of households and as a result men's lives take priority and they tend to wield greater powers with respect to decision-making on a whole range of issues, including sexual reproductive health. Fourth, risk-taking in sex is used to reaffirm gendered identities, escape from gender-based roles and as part of pleasure, particularly for men.

The centrality of reproduction

The reproduction of life is fundamental to gendered ways in which the lives of men and women are valued. Historically the power and prosper- ity of an ethnic group is linked to reproduction because the larger the population, the more land it can cultivate and the greater its political power. This has an enduring legacy in contemporary Malawi. It is widely reported that children are considered a status symbol and traditionally families are large (see Wolf, 2004, p. 46; MHRC, 2006, p. 13). The identities of men and women are constructed around their ability to reproduce. As the Senior Programme Manager of PSI's *Packachere* Programme considers:

> The belief is when you get married the best thing that people would want to see is the wife conceiving, then you must have a baby, that means that then it is a complete family. The woman is on the receiving end; she isn't even to choose who the man should be.

The focus group discussions and informal discussions in both Zomba and Karonga Districts revealed how men tend to take pride in the number of children they have. There is a Christian basis for the importance of men having many children; in the psalms it says 'blessed is a man with a river of children'. Among the Sena in the Southern Region, according to tradition, the bride and bridegroom must have sex before their wedding and the marriage counsellors (*ankhoswe*) inspect the cloth that is used to clean the penis to see if it sticks together because this is believed demonstrate that the man will have children (Fielder, 2005, p. 15).

The traditional value of reproduction has a particular bearing on women because of their gender-based reproductive role. The multitude of ways that women contribute to society is not fully acknowledged and the popular perception is that women's reproductive role is central to their value, status and identity in society (see also Anderson, 2012; James, 1994). As Moser (1991, p. 8) explores for the situation more generally, women fulfil 'triple roles' that are vital to the family, community and society. As the focus group discussions, interviews and informal discussions reveal, the domestic role of women includes responsibilities for the health, education and well-being of the family (I. Phiri, 1997, p. 36). Women also have a productive role, particularly in the agricultural sector where they account for 70 per cent of full-time farmers. Many women provide a secondary income to support their family and, where greater numbers of households are female-headed, they increasingly provide the primary income (GoM, 2000, 1.4; UN, 2004a). Women also have an informal political role in the community, particularly in the absence of adequate state provision of housing and basic services – a role that is under further pressure from HIV. Motherhood is central to a woman's identity and this is rooted in the gendered construction of the female body for its reproductive role. This has a different bearing on women in the matrilineal and patrilineal areas, as the focus group discussions revealed. Isabel Phiri explains that for the Chewa in the Central Region, 'As the root of the lineage, the woman was seen as a sacred vessel of life. She was responsible for the continuation of the community. Thus the community's future and destiny was decisively dependent on her.' As a result, Phiri highlights how 'being barren is considered the greatest misfortune that could happen to a woman' (1997, pp. 36–7; see also Manda and Meyer, 2005, p. 453). Among the ethnic groups in the Northern Region women are under pressure to bear children to extend the husband's lineage. For example, in the focus group discussions with Nbande Support Group Michael (of the Nkonde ethnic group) expresses the view that women have a duty in the community to 'give birth, making the population grow'. The children belong to the husband's family as considered in the preceding chapter. With social pressure on women across Malawi to bear many children from a young age, the majority have their first pregnancies in their early teens and by the age of 19, 60 per cent have had at least one child (Panos and UN, 2000; Tango International, 2004, p. 8).

Reproduction and HIV risk

The value placed on reproduction heightens the particular biological risk to women of HIV infection. During the focus group discussion with the women of One Voice Support Group in Nkolokosa they echo a broader recognition among women that pregnancy heightens HIV risk because of the strain on their bodies. Across Sub-Saharan Africa there are patterns of early marriage and childbearing at a young age, or premarital sex and late marriage (Zabin and Kiragu, 1998). Earlier sexual debut is associated with higher prevalence: prevalence among women who had their sexual debut when they were aged younger than 15 is higher (18 per cent) than among women who had a later debut (15 per cent or lower) (NSO Malawi and ORC Macro, 2005, pp. 235–6). Younger girls are at heightened risk because their reproductive systems are immature and provide less of a barrier to infection. It is often not until a girl reaches her late teens or early twenties that the mucous membrane changes from a thin, single layer of cells to a thick, multilayer wall. Young girls have a higher risk of infection during pregnancy and sexual intercourse where there is vaginal trauma and bleeding, including forced sex or the loss of virginity, because blood is the most effective carrier of the virus (NAC, 2003, p. 17; for the situation in general see Quinn and Overbaugh, 2005, p. 1583; Laga et al., 2001, pp. 931–4; Reid and Bailey, 1992). High levels of progesterone could increase susceptibility to HIV infection, including through increases in the number of target cells and the suppression of the immune responses, but these mechanisms remain poorly defined (Quinn and Overbaugh,

2005, p. 1583). Moreover, the tendency to have closely spaced births does not allow the body to recover in terms of health and nutrition. Although postpartum abstinence is practised for two to three months by some ethnic groups, this is not sufficient time for the body to recover. Zulu reveals that the purpose is to safeguard the man's health: the end of postpartum bleeding is traditionally believed to indicate that the woman's reproductive system has 'cooled down' and that she has been cleansed of the dangerous birth-related fluids (Zulu, 2001, pp. 474, 477). As the Population and Health Specialist at the World Bank reflects, women may experience abuse if they refuse to resume sexual inter-course before the end of the abstinence period. On the other hand, as McIntyre (2005) considers, 'AIDS is becoming the leading cause of maternal death in some African settings.' HIV heightens women's risk of complications during and after birth, particularly haemorrhage or infec-tions after caesarean sections (McIntyre, 2005, p. 131; see also Zabin and Kiragu, 1998). The available statistics do not necessarily capture the extent of the association of HIV with maternal mortality because AIDS-related deaths may be attributed to factors that are not included in the criteria for being recorded as 'maternal mortality' (Hogan et al., 2010).

The reproductive role of women is at odds with the neoliberal behaviour change interventions that champion abstinence or using con-doms. As for the case in general, having children means women have to put themselves at risk of HIV infection (Doyal, 1994). As the Prod-uct Manager for HIV Prevention at PSI/Malawi explains, condoms were initially perceived to be 'unnatural' and were widely rejected for being negatively associated with population control: people 'would always look at something that controls their ability to have kids with a lot of suspicion and negativity' (see also Lwanda, 2005, p. 116–17; Kaler, 2004, pp. 105–15).[1] As the Behaviour Surveillance Research Coordina-tor at FHI proposes, women are at particular risk because 'in a marriage situation you will have to procreate and you cannot procreate with a condom'. If the husband is known to be engaging in extra-marital affairs, women cannot use condoms because of the necessity to bear more children, as the Population and Health Specialist at the World Bank reflects. In addition, during pregnancy women continue to have the burden of balancing multiple tasks, as the Senior Programme Man-ager of PSI's *Packachere* Programme reflects. Despite campaigns for the husband to assist his wife during pregnancy, the wife tends to be solely responsible for all the domestic tasks, especially in the rural areas. This depletes the energy and nutrition levels of women where they do not have the time to eat properly, increasing susceptibility to HIV, as the representative of the World Bank highlights.

Extra-marital sex to conceive

Where the family is considered incomplete without children, women may be under particular pressure to engage in extra-marital sex in order to conceive if the couple fail to bear children (Muula and Mtfutso-Bengo, 2004, p. 485; GoM, 2003, 6.1). As is the reported situation across Sub-Saharan Africa, fertility is more highly valued than concerns about restricting female sexuality to marriage and the risks of contracting HIV or other STIs (see Caldwell, 2000, p. 120; Bond and Dover, 1997). It was widely reported by the key informants in 2007 that the wife might engage in extra-marital sex with either another member of the family, a friend of the husband, a traditional practitioner or a hired man known as the '*fisi*' (hyena) in order to increase the likelihood that she conceives. Traditional Authority Mulumbe explains that in Nkolokosa in Zomba *fisi* is conducted as a secret arrangement between the husband and wife, who either hire someone or ask a friend who has lots of children. This can heighten the risk to women of contracting HIV because the serostatus of the man she has sex with may not be known; he could be HIV-positive and, in situations where the *fisi* is hired, it is likely that he has had unprotected sex with many partners. As the Director of Planning, Research and Evaluation at the Department for Nutrition, HIV and AIDS considers:

> So this man if he is [HIV] positive ... he is used in several families, he will sleep with the woman, tomorrow he is in that house and so on. So this kind of behaviour promotes infection because he might even get some infections from the women themselves and then it will spread.

Although *fisi* is not practised in the patrilineal system in Karonga, there are other traditional practices, including 'sister inheritance' as considered in the preceding chapter. David of Lughano Support Group explains how in some situations, 'When the family want a child and is failing to have one the wife goes somewhere and the husband goes somewhere to have a child. But sometimes the one who is successful then stays with the one who gives them a child.' Typically the husbands are the ones who make the decisions about having children as the head of the family. Men do not want to be stigmatised for not having children and they are not the ones who have to endure pregnancy and its implications.

The majority of women are not in a position to refuse to engage in extra-marital sex in order to conceive because of the pressure from society to have children. It becomes a choice between a potential death associated with the onset of AIDS and the certain 'social death' of being shunned for not bearing children. As the Principal Documentation Officer at the Ombudsman's Office highlights:

> If you are not able to have your own children, some people would say 'Hey this one he is married but cannot have any children.' So it is like the talk of the town. So some people would want to run away from that to say 'now they should think I have a child', yet they know that the child biologically is not theirs. But that as well is what is causing the spread of HIV because if the person involved is HIV-positive then obviously they will infect the woman and the man as well.

Although the Chairperson of COWLHA recognises in 2011 how this situation has relaxed in recent years, there is still pressure on the couple to bear children: 'When people get married, people give them some time, some months, then one year and if it goes beyond one year, then people start talking "what is happening?"' As the informal discussions in Zomba and Karonga reveal, couples are faced with the dilemma that, for the sake of appearance, it is better for the family to have children, even if they are not their own.

Marriage as a girl's 'best option in life'

Associated with the importance of reproduction, marriage is central to a woman's identity. The family provides the foundations for society and Section 13 (i) of the Constitution seeks to 'recognise and protect the family as a fundamental and vital social unit' (GoM, 1994). Although the family as a social unit is undergoing change, its importance remains paramount and there is social pressure to found and maintain their families (Chimbiri, 2007, p. 1102; on the situation more generally see Ahsan and Ahsan, 2004, pp. 95–7; Clark, 2004, p. 149). The family provides a means for society to control its members, for example through socialising children as to how to behave, and this has a particular bearing on women because they have a gender-based role in the family for reproducing, caring and nurturing. The family also provides its members with identity, social status and emotional security (see MHRC, 2006, p. 14).

It is widely believed that marriage is a girl's 'best option in life' and there is financial and social pressure on even the most educated girls to marry. Girls also marry early to avoid premarital sex and because they want to begin having children. Pressure to marry has increased with the escalating HIV threat and people choose marriage as a means of safeguarding against HIV infection (Reniers, 2003, 2005). The Programme Officer at UNAIDS explains that when women are married 'they are a "Mrs", they are respectable people in society' (see also Wolf, 2004, p. 46). The Technical Advisor to the WGHPPA and the National Coordinator of MANERELA consider how women are socially conditioned to want to marry, be successful in their marriage and persevere (also reported in Banda, 2005, p. 188; Chimgwede, 2004a; Bracher et al., 2003, p. 208). The MHRC reports that 'culturally women do not marry but get married', therefore women are not in a position to make decisions about marriage and only have the ability to try to attract a man who will propose to her (2006, p. 15). As the Strategic Manager of the Youth Alert! Programme reveals, 'if they have a chance to be proposed to they would rather keep that affair because they feel that it is going to take a long time for them to be proposed again'. As the Head of AGREDS outlines: 'Some are educated but sometimes they fall into the same, they say "ah, I am ageing, I am not married" and they just go into [marriage with] any man that comes their way.' Women who are not married are subjected to gossip and shame. The Programme Officer at UNAIDS reports that people question 'What is wrong with you?' Verheijen (2011, p. 117) in her research on Mudzi in Balaka, southern Malawi, considers how women stay with men who do not necessarily substantially support them financially, or who are lazy or promiscuous, because of the strength of the desire to be in a relationship. Such is the power of the social norms that 'many of them continued giving birth to children of different fathers, hoping the latest man would stay with them – which often he did not' (see also Van den Borne, 2005).

Women are not in a position to leave a marriage, even if it places them at heightened risk of HIV infection. There is extensive social pressure to be successful in marriage and persevere, as considered in chapter 3. Girls are taught how to be a good wife during their initiations and through the example set by their mother while they are growing up. Divorce or separation can bring shame to the entire family because, as the key informants and focus group discussions widely report, the popular perception would be that they have failed in marriage and are a social outcast (see also Fielder, 2000, p. 38; for the situation across East and Southern Africa see Caldwell and Caldwell, 1993, p. 839). The Gender Programme Manager at CIDA explains that if a woman leaves 'it will look like she is abandoning a husband'. According to the Head of Policy Support and Development at the NAC you may be perceived as being promiscuous.

There is a social pressure for couples to persevere in a marriage and, as the interviews and focus group discussions widely consider, this is even in situations that place the woman at heightened risk of HIV infection. The focus group discussion with the women of Tikondane Support Group, for example, consider how HIV can be a 'stumbling block' in the family:

> Magret explains that 'when us women go for testing and are found positive (the husband negative) they leave us'. She goes on to explain that 'when the husband is positive we live with him because we are told to persevere'. And when both are found positive 'Some men think it is the woman who infected them and divorce her. Some accept us.'

Couples have a responsibility to one another to persevere in times of sickness as the Chief Law Reform Officer at the Law Commission reflects: 'you have to take care of him or her, whether she has AIDS or whatever disease'. Marriage is a lifetime agreement and as the Law Commissioner at the Law Commission reports 'the whole society will shun you' if you divorce your husband, because of the belief in the commitment to 'till death do us part'.

Sexual initiations and cultural identity

Closely associated with the gender-based roles of men and women, sexualised rituals and traditional counselling throughout their lives prepare them for their reproductive roles and enhancing sexual fulfilment in marriage forms a crucial part of cultural traditions of different ethnic groups (Bryceson and Fonseca, 2006, p. 1659). Traditionally, initiation (*Chinamwali*) ceremonies for young boys and girls symbolise the transition to adulthood and include rituals to demonstrate that they have come of age (Skinner et al., 2013; Munthali and Zulu, 2007).

Within the *Nyau* cult of the Chewa in the Central Region there has been the rise of secret societies in recent decades, including the *Gule Wamkulu* ('big dance') of masked men in animal skins (*Zirombo* or monsters) – a fraternity of men initiated into the group (Bryceson and Fonseca, 2006, p. 1659). The initiates are taught about sex but also to respect their wives and not to beat them. After the initiation they are told to have sex to demonstrate their transition to adulthood. There is social pressure for boys to join the fraternity and those who are not initiated may be threatened or beaten up (Munthali and Zulu,

2007, p. 8). Among the Yao and Lomwe in the Southern Region *Jando* (circumcision) traditionally serves as a rite of passage into adulthood for males. It is commonly practised and the MDHS reveals that in 2010, the majority of Yao in Malawi are circumcised (87 per cent) and 29 per cent of the Lomwe. Of circumcised men, 70 per cent underwent the procedure between the ages of 5 and 13 (NSO and ICF Macro, 2011, p. 182). As part of the initiation ceremony the community holds the *Manganje* dance. I conducted a participant-observation of the dance in Makungnya Village in Zomba District in July 2011:

> At that time there were ceremonies occurring in the Yao communities across the District. The surrounding community join in to watch and join in the dancing and singing while drums are played and *Chipembere* dancers (a fraternity of older men who have already been circumcised) blow whistles and stand and smoke in the centre of the dance in displays of their masculinity. The boys are then lined up and the audience watches as the *Chipembere* dance to the drums and the initiates are taken away to have the *Jando* performed.

Male circumcision is identified as a factor contributing to lower risk of HIV transmission (WHO and UNAIDS, 2007). In Zomba the practice is widely perceived as a major contributing factor to HIV infection among young men because of the reported use of a single blade for the ceremony. Prior to the ceremony in Makungnya Village, the Group Village Headman Mkanda explained that in the past a single razor blade would be used for *Jando* but now the villages have been educated not to because of the HIV risk. However, it was widely reported by the support groups and during individual interviews that a major reason for the spread of HIV in their area was the continued use of a single razor blade during the ceremony. During the focus group discussion with the men of One Voice Support Group:

> Majidu explains that 'There is no close supervision because to visit *Jando* is not easy', to which the other men indicate their agreement, and he continues, 'if you have not been circumcised then you are not supposed to go to *Jando'*.

The Chairpersons for Ulumba Support Group and Chikonde Support Group also report that the boys are told after their initiations that they should test their manhood without a condom so that they 'can feel the heat' and want to practise what they have learned. The *Protecting the*

Next Generation study reveals boys who have been circumcised are more likely to be sexually experienced: 37 per cent of circumcised boys aged 12–14 ever had sex as compared to 16 per cent of uncircumcised boys (cited in Munthali and Zulu, 2007, p. 13).

Conversely, girls are taught during their initiations that if they engage in premarital sex they could die of AIDS-related illness for being immoral. Fielder reports how the girls in the initiations in southern Malawi sing the song:

Mtsikana woyendayenda,	The moving [promiscuous] girl,
anafera panjira,	she died on the way,
mwana wachigololo,	the fornicious child
anafera pa njira.	died on the road. (Fielder, 2005, p. 30)

It is reported that girls are instructed during *Kusasa Fumbi* (cleansing the dust), *Kuchotsa Fumbi* (removing the dust) and *Kutaya Mafuta* (spilling the oil) not to refuse sex with their husbands (Skinner et al., 2013, p. 298). Munthali and Zulu (2007, p. 14) highlight that there are mixed messages: girls are taught to abstain from sex before marriage to avoid pregnancy, while boys are encouraged to have sex. This is problematic because men tend to be the ones to initiate sex.

In preparation for marriage, girls in the Southern Region undergo *Chinamwali* (an initiation) to learn how to satisfy their husbands. Among some ethnic groups, including the Chewa and Yao, this involves a sexual initiation where they learn sex techniques, including different positions to assume to give variety to sex, and how they should 'dance' by shaking and swerving their waists. Fielder reports that during the Christianised *Chinamwali* in the south-east the girls learn how to lengthen their labia minora and they sing '*Mayi zinthu zanga za nyekulira*' (Mother, my things [labia minora] are assisting me in sex) (Fielder, 2000, p. 38; see also Bagnol, 2008). The girls demonstrate different sexual dances while singing '*Mr Nyundo, kubedi kuja mumatotani kukada? Ndimangotere!*' (Mr Nyundo, on your bed, when it is dark, what do I do? I just do this!) (Fielder, 2005, pp. 13, 32–8). To complete their rite of passage, the initiates have sexual intercourse with a masked man symbolising 'the hyena' (*fisi*) during a ritual called *Kusasa Fumbi* or *Kuchotsa Fumbi* ('shaking the dust' or 'clearing the dust'). This can place the young girls at risk of HIV infection because the *fisi* has sexual intercourse with all the girls, a condom is not used and, where his identity is secret, it is not known how many other women he has slept with, under what circumstances, and his HIV status is unknown. Typically, condoms are not used because the ritual requires the exchange of sexual fluids, as the representatives of the Women, Girls and HIV/AIDS Programme and Malawi Network of Religious Leaders Living with HIV/AIDS (MANERELA) reflect (see also MHRC, 2006, pp. 2, 32; Jangale, 2006, p. 12; Muula and Mtfutso-Bengo, 2004, p. 485).

It has been widely reported in the press and by the key informants that in Nsanje District 'widow cleansing' (*Kulowakufa*) is practised; this is where women have sex to appease their deceased husband's spirits, typically with his brother or a hired 'death cleanser' (MHRC, 2006, p. 5; GoM, 2003, 5.4.1, 2005, 3.1.1; Lwanda, 2005, p. 124; Muula and Mfutso-Bengo, 2004, p. 485; for the situation in Phalombe District see Kornfield and Namete, 1997). This practice can expose women to HIV infection because, as the Technical Advisor to the Women, Girls and HIV/AIDS – Programme and Plan of Action explains, 'You do not know this hired man, how many other women he has had sex with and whether he is positive or not.... If the man has HIV it will mean that it will go round and round and round in the community.' The interviews and focus group discussions also revealed other cultural sexual practices beyond those included in the government policies that put women at risk. The Technical Advisor to the Women, Girls and HIV/AIDS – Programme and Plan of Action notes the practice of 'the blanket of the chief', whereby a young virgin is identified by the chief to sleep with a visiting chief as a symbol of the highest respect. The Gender Programme Manager at CIDA identifies that in the Northern Region, 'when they are installing the chief, then all visiting chiefs or village heads are given rooms with middle-aged women or girls just to entertain them'.

Although people with greater levels of education may be able to refuse to partake in sexual cultural practices, the majority cannot because of cultural norms. Representatives of the World Food Programme (WFP), the Catholic Church and NAPHAM reflect that it is socially accepted that the female body is under male control. The representatives of DfID and NAPHAM consider how, where there are strong beliefs in witchcraft, many women fear that if they refuse to participate then they might die, get sick, get very thin, develop sores all over their body, their legs might swell up or disaster will fall upon their whole family (see also Saur et al., 2005, p. 44). Condoms are not used because, as the representatives of the WGHPPA, MANERELA and DfID report, these rituals require the exchange of sexual fluids. It was widely reported by the key informants that condoms would act as a barrier between the two bodies engaging in the ritual, which 'dilutes the rite' and 'nullifies the whole purpose of that ceremony'.

Interventions that aim to address these cultural sexual rituals are problematic because they are fundamental to the cultural values of young men and young women. Cultural gendered structures normalise these rituals. Although people may recognise that certain behaviours may increase their susceptibility to HIV infection, as Verheijen (2011, p. 126) considers, social networks are fundamental support structures for survival and adherence to gender-based norms is essential to being accepted as part of the local community. Young boys and girls do not have the power to refuse to participate, especially those who lack education and live in rural areas. The village elders arrange the initiation ceremonies, the entire community participates and refusal would be disrespectful. It was widely reported during the focus group discussions, individual interviews and informal discussions in Zomba that 'You can refuse to send your children but it is the norm to send them.' There is a cultural expectation on young boys to partake in the tradition and those who have been circumcised are envied by those who have not yet been circumcised. It is associated with masculinity and afterwards boys are encouraged to have sex (Munthali and Zulu, 2007, p. 8). People who refuse to partake in cultural practices are seen as stubborn. Similarly, in Thyolo these people are labelled as *alukhu* (people who eat using the back of the hand); they are not part of society and those who have been initiated refuse to associate with them (Skinner et al., 2013, pp. 298–9; Munthali and Zulu, 2007, p. 6). As the Principal Documentation Officer at the Ombudsman and Strategic Manager of the Youth Alert Programme explain, a girl who has not completed the rite of passage may be shunned by her peers, considered ineligible for marriage and stigmatised (see also Fielder, 2005, p. 19). As the National Coordinator of the Malawi Network of Religious Leaders Living with HIV and AIDS (MANERELA) considers, 'culturally you are human being because you have gone through the rites of passage of your culture' and it is not easy to refuse 'unless you have gone beyond the imagination of your cultural set-up'. In addition, it is widely believed that if the initiates do not perform the ritual, a curse may fall on their family (Muula and Mtfutso-Bengo, 2004, p. 485).

In some areas such as Nkolokosa the support groups reported during the focus group discussions that *Kusasa Fumbi* has stopped. In other areas, several of the Traditional Authorities in the Zomba District claimed that these practices are no longer performed, but this was contradicted by the focus group discussions with the support groups for PLHIV in those areas. For example, prior to meeting with the

Makunganya Village Support Group I interviewed the Group Village Headman Mkanda, who claimed that in his area they abolished *Kusasa Fumbi* three or four years before, despite local resistance, because of HIV. During the focus group discussion with the women they were asked what cultural practices put people at risk in their area:

> Lucy identifies '*Kusasa Fumbi*'. I interrupt the discussion to query where they were talking about: 'But you do not have *Kusasa Fumbi* here?' The women unanimously confirm that '*Kusasa Fumbi* we have here.' I reflect that 'the Group Village Headman had said earlier that day it was abolished'. Lucy explains that 'the chief cannot tell you it is happening but it is'. To which I ask 'How do you know it is happening?' Mercy explains that 'It happens in secret.' Lucy continues that 'We know it is happening because people change their behaviours.' Mercy reflects that 'The girls are told during their initiations not to say this is happening to people.' Lucy adds 'The father tells his daughter not to say anything.'

However aspects of *Chinamawali* are focused on protecting young people from HIV infection. Munthali and Zulu (2007) argue that they can be used as a platform for addressing HIV. The Group Village Headman Mkanda had explained how the villagers sing songs teaching them about HIV during the dance and during the dance I attended they sang, 'AIDS is a killer, you have to take care of your movements, if you do not take care you will catch the virus.'

Men as the head of the family

Associated with the gendered division of labour, marriage customs posit men as dominant heads of households. Women's contributions to society, although vital, are less valued than men's contributions. As a result, as Andrew of Mwenitete Support Group in Karonga District explains, 'Men take priority. We say a man is the "*mutu wa banja*" [head of the family] – so he can do anything.' Men marry on more favourable terms, while women are dependent on men to access resources, including land and its produce. Therefore men dominate in decision-making on a whole range of issues, including with respect to sexual reproductive health.

Prioritising the lives of males over females

Men take priority in terms of their health and education, especially in families with limited resources. Where there are typically limited resources in the household, priority is accorded to the health of the males in the family because they are the breadwinners. It was widely observed and reported in the interviews and focus group discussions that women tend to be responsible for taking care of the family's health. Fran of Lupembe Support Group reflects that 'When everyone is sick it is the mother who is the guardian and the father just comes in time to see the patients.' Lucy of Kaporo Support Group considers how 'because they are close to the children and when the child is sick and wants to go to the hospital then men give excuse by saying "it is your child"'. This was also reported during the focus group discussions with men, as for example in the focus group discussion with the men of Nbande Support Group focus group discussions:

> Michael explains, 'it is a rule that women should take the children to hospital, unless it is a serious problem – then the husband can escort'. To which James adds, 'when pregnant they visit ANC [antenatal clinic] but we are home relaxing'. The other men laugh.

Although women frequent health services for their children's health, they typically lack access for themselves, which perpetuates their low health status and compounds their risk of HIV infection. The Head of the Society for the Advancement of Women considers how, even when a woman is sick, 'she would not be the first one to go to the hospital, she would rather take the husband to the hospital and the child and then later on she remembers she is also sick'. Women are also at risk of infection from HIV-positive patients under their care, as the Gender Network National Coordinator at Action Aid and the Head of the Home Based Care Unit at the Roman Catholic Church reflect. Traditionally, the husband does not share in the burden of caring, even when the wife is sick. The Advocacy Officer at NAPHAM reports that as HIV increasingly affects adult women, grandmothers and young girls are obliged to take on the burden (Ngwira et al., 2001, p. 11). In addition, women tend to live in rural areas and lack access to health care facilities, as the Programme Officer at UNAIDS considers. As a result, women may not access Voluntary Counselling and Testing for HIV, receive early detection and treatment of STIs or use contraceptives (Ministry of Health and Population and NAC, n.d., p. 21). The interviews, focus group discussions and observations also reveal the tendency for the men to eat first and be fed the most nutritious food, as considered in the preceding chapter.

As the education of children is a heavy financial burden upon families and often they cannot afford to educate all their children, decisions on education are partially related to the family's 'investment strategy' for its own future. The perceived costs and benefits of education for sons and daughters differ substantially. The Programmes Coordinator at Malawi CARER considers how the sons have a future gender-based role as the wage earners and their education takes priority, whereas the daughters will raise a family, which is believed to solely benefit from experience in assisting the mother and informal education, including initiation. The family bears the costs of educating the daughter but do not perceive it to benefit them. Particularly in the north, families are dissuaded from educating girls because of the patrilineal marriage system. Investing in the girl child's education is seen as a 'waste of resources' because they will marry and join her husband's family, as the focus group discussions also reveal when they discuss who takes priority in terms of education in the family. As the men of Nbande Support Group in northern Karonga explain 'they say a girl is supposed to be looking for a house and they encourage her to get married for *lobola* [bride price]'. Mary of Kapora Support Group also in northern Karonga considers that the belief in her area is that 'if a man is educated he can assist the relatives but a girl will help their husband and girls can be impregnated'. In addition, the opportunity costs of educating girls are higher because they provide the family with an additional source of household labour, helping their mother with childcare, household chores and farm work. Until the daughter is married the family wants to benefit from her unpaid labour in the home and agriculture. For example, as the women of Lupembe Support Group in Karonga consider:

> Edna, Jane and Mercy discuss how in their area 'men take priority in terms of education' and Jane explains that 'women are not given the chance to go to school here. Lots of schools have two sessions in the morning and afternoon, but for women to attend in the afternoon is not easy because they are doing house chores.'

These domestic tasks disrupt schooling for girls, leading to irregular attendance, and limits on their time to do homework. As a result girls may perform poorly in examinations and frequent absenteeism may eventually result in failure or dropout. This burden is exacerbated by HIV because girls may have to take on extra burdens of caring when their parents get infected (GoM, 2005, 3.2.1, 2006; Burton, 2005; Jamieson, 2004). There is a gender imbalance in levels of education, especially in terms of enrolment and performance. Government statistics reveal that in 2005 the literacy rate for males aged 15 and over was 75.8 per cent, while for females it was 52.4 per cent. In rural areas 33.4 per cent of women have received no education (Blackden and Wodon, 2006; MHRC, 2005, p. vii). As a result of the marginalisation of women from education and information, negotiating for safer sex is not on the agenda, as the key informants widely report.

Decision-makers and decision-takers

Men are the heads of the family and tend to wield greater powers with respect to decision-making on a whole range of issues, whereas women tend to be the decision-takers – as the key-informant interviews and focus group discussions widely report. This is supported by the MDHS (2004), which reveals that 'for 65 percent or more of married women their husbands make decisions for their wives' healthcare, and large and daily household purchases.... The only one of these decisions that a majority of women make on their own is the type of food to cook daily' (NSO Malawi and ORC Macro, 2005, p. 44). Women prevail in decisions on some domestic chores because, as the fieldwork reveals, they are popularly considered to be 'the mother of the home' and understand the family's needs. The subordinate position of women in their relationships is exacerbated by the tendency for young girls to marry older men, because of the intersection of age and gender hierarchy. As the Population and Health Specialist at the World Bank suggests, young girls will not necessarily know what to negotiate and it is likely the man will already work while they will not.

Women are socially conditioned throughout their lives to be submissive to men, especially to their husbands, and this is particularly entrenched in the rural areas, as considered extensively by the key informants and focus group discussions. Women are socialised into being obedient to their father, uncles, husband, brothers or guardians (Mbweza et al., 2008, p. 16; Lwanda, 2005, p. 89; Munthali et al., 2004, p. 4; NAC, 2003, p. 17; GoM, 2003, 5.2.1). The Head of the Society for the Advancement of Women explains that the gendered structures mean 'that women have less power, they are not capable, they cannot think for themselves, somebody has to think for them so this now is why women are vulnerable even to HIV'. The Gender Specialist with CIDA explains how they grow up 'seeing their mother just saying yes to their father, thinking that a woman must listen to a man [and] with the mentality that a man is more powerful than a woman'.

In society more generally, men tend to be the ones in leadership positions. The Programme Officer at NICE suggests that this creates the impression that 'women always have to be submissive and they cannot project their own views'. The subordination of women is normalised during initiation trainings and within schools. For example, in the Southern Region the *Chilangizo* initiation ceremony for girls who are about to get married 'revolves around the submission of the wife in the family' (Fielder, 2005, p. 15). Schools perpetuate the marginalised status of women through gender stereotyping within teaching and learning materials, and the way teachers and pupils interact (Kachiwanda, n.d., p. 11). School textbooks, for example, present a distorted representation that enhances the positive male image and negative female image. As the Programme Officer for UNAIDS questions, 'if you look at a book, how is a girl depicted in the story: Is she seen as a mother, is she seen as a wife, or is she seen as somebody who can contribute to society, someone who has got brains to do something, be a doctor, be a nurse, be a pilot, be a lawyer?' As a result, male contributions to society are typically more highly valued and women tend to have an inferior social status, as the Head of the Women Lawyers Association expresses. The interviewees reported that typically men are the 'decision-makers' and women are the 'decision-takers'. The traditional leaders are overwhelmingly men, being selected from the former leader's nephews, and where women are traditional leaders they do not have the same powers as their male counterparts (Banda, 2005, p. 9). Although women have important decision-making roles in the community, for example in matrilineal areas women elders discuss potential candidates for the traditional leader, these roles institutionalise their subordination (Aguillar and Aguillar, 1999).

The subordinate position of women was entrenched during Banda's rule in order to consolidate his political power – despite the popular image that was being presented that he was active in changing the position of women in the country. Political legitimacy relied upon the manipulation of culture to consolidate the president's power and create a disciplined population (Forster, 1994, p. 477; Chirwa, 2001, pp. 11, 17). Hierarchy was central and the status of women was seen in traditional terms, under male guardianship and with strictly enforced gender roles. As Forster (1994, p. 491) outlines:

Malawians were constantly reminded that the mbumba [women] could expect to remain under the guardianship of all *nkoswe* – male members of a Chewa family [the guardian of the family, usually a maternal uncle or eldest brother]...with Banda even declaring himself to be the '*Nkoswe* No.1'.

The rise of nationalism gave previously marginalised groups, including women, an opportunity to participate but this did not equate to their empowerment. Women were not fairly represented, with only one female minister in the first cabinet in 1964 and fewer than five female MPs in the national assembly up to the early 1970s. Within the Women's League, founded by Banda in September 1958, the women were instructed, at times compelled, to dance and sing songs that praised and supported Banda in everything. In 1985 Chitukuko cha Amayi m'Malawi (CCAM, Organisation for the Advancement of Women in Malawi) was established to promote the socio-economic welfare of women; it is criticised, however, because it was 'designed to coerce women into submission and loyalty to the party' and their labour was used in the organisation's gardens, without pay (Chirwa, 2001, pp. 4, 9, 12–14; McCracken, 1998, pp. 238, 241; Ngulube-Chinoko, 1995, p. 95). The marginalisation of women's political participation continued under President Bakili Muluzi.

The lack of decision-making power that women have more generally has important ramifications for women's control over their own health and sexual reproductive health. According to the MDHS (2004) only 23.6 per cent of women who lack decision-making capabilities in their relationship (who do not have the final say on any issues) use a modern method of contraception. In comparison, 30.3 per cent of women who have a greater level of decision-making power in the relationship (who have the final say in five decisions) are reported as using a modern method of contraception (NSO Malawi and ORC Macro, 2005, p. 78).[2] It was widely reported by the interviewees and focus group discussions that men tend to control access to health services, the medicines women take, the timing and spacing of children, and the use of birth control and condoms. The majority of women lack the necessary power to assert their own needs and desires, even though many of these issues more directly affect women than men (GoM, 2005, 3.1.1; CILIC, 2007, p. 6). As the Programme Officer for UNAIDS reports, 'If my husband says "I want to have kids" and I am not ready to have kids, I will be forced to have kids.' The female body is under male guardianship and this was entrenched by the rhetoric of the Banda government that women were under the guardianship of all *nkoswe* (the male guardians of the Chewa family) (Forster, 1994, p. 491). Men may not allow their wife to access HIV treatment to conceal the HIV status of the family. Furthermore, men are targeted for antiretroviral (ARV) programmes through their employers, and several key informants in offices in Lilongwe report how some colleagues may hide the treatment at work or share the medication with their wife without explaining what the drugs are for.

Gender-based cultural scripts justify why men prevail in decisions concerning sexual relations, as Mbweza et al. (2008, p. 16) consider, and these include: that 'men naturally have greater sexual desires than women'; 'men propose to women'; and 'the husband has the power'. Women also mentioned that 'the woman has to obey when the man wants sex' and that 'a wife who initiates sex is looked upon as a prostitute' (2008, p. 16). Women cannot protect themselves from HIV infection in situations where they are not in a position to negotiate the terms of their sexual encounters (Doyal, 1994, p. 14). The Strategic Manager of the Youth Alert! Programme reports that: 'Most of the time the decision to indulge in a sexual activity is [made] by the man.' As a result the most popular family planning method is by injection because women can use it covertly. As the Product Manager for HIV Prevention at PSI/Malawi explains 'The majority of men do not support this idea of family planning so it is easy for the woman to go to the clinic to get injected and then the man doesn't know.'

The situation of course differs between families and it is important to recognise that in many respects marriage is a symbiotic relationship, with male and female roles complementing and reinforcing one another. As Andrew of Mwenitete Support Group considers, a 'good' *mama* (woman/mother) is 'one who follows the man's rules and regulations – being faithful to the man and caring for both sides of the relatives' while a 'good' *dada* (man/father) 'follows the rules of wife – being faithful to the wife, caring for the children in dressing and feeding'. Similarly when the women of Lupembe Support Group consider the qualities of a 'good' *mama,* Doris reports that she, listens to her husband, Edna explains that she is 'sharing ideas with the husband and [they are] loving each other' and Grace adds that both are mutually respectful.

In general, reproductive health programmes typically exclude men (Blanc, 2001, pp. 189–213). In Malawi, there are few services that specifically target men, and few programmes that build their social skills and gender sensitivity (IPPF et al., 2006, p. 4). The Executive Director of MACRO reflects that health clinics are considered to be places where women go and, as a result, men are hesitant to use them. This is not 'family planning' but 'individual planning' because it only involves one partner. It undermines male control of female reproductive health and sexuality and can leave them suspicious of reproductive health services. The Strategic Manager of PSI's Youth Alert! Programme highlights that women do not have the power to negotiate the terms of their sexual encounters or educate their partners based on the information they receive because they are in a subordinate position. The Principal Documentation Officer at the Ombudsman's Office, when reflecting on the staff training on HIV at their office, explains that for some of the women they could not go home and explain to their husbands that they should use of condoms during sex, because their husbands would just say: 'Do you think you are more knowledgeable than I?' As a result these women 'continue suffering even though they know the dos and don'ts'. In addition, men become suspicious of covert use of contraceptives by women and fear the loss of control over decisions to use them. However, there is potential for including men in sexual reproductive health programmes and services. The Programme Officer for HIV at the WFP suggests that the importance of including men is recognised and is gradually being addressed, for example through getting couples to visit antenatal clinics together (FHI, 2004). And yet, as the interviews and focus group discussions in Karonga in the Northern Region reveal, this is problematic in polygamous marriages because the family does not confirm to western norms.

As considered in chapter 1, the focus of behaviour change strategies is often on women as the 'moral guardians' who are responsible for controlling their own and their partner's behaviour. They tend to be the first to know their HIV status in the family because they are tested when they visit antenatal clinics as part of Prevention of Mother-to-Child Transmission initiatives. Esmy and Julita of One Voice Support Group in Nkolokosa explain how it leads to problems in the family because when they are tested first their husbands blame them for bringing the virus into the house. And yet this focus obscures differences and inequalities of gender that mean that women typically are not in a position to negotiate for safer sex because of their subordinate position in general and in their sexual relationships specifically. This is rooted in gendered structures whereby the productive role of men is more highly valued than the reproductive role of women – explored in the preceding chapter. Furthermore, it ignores the role that men play in sexual reproductive health and serves to absolve them of direct responsibility (see Blanc, 2001, p. 169; Gupta, 2005; Kalipeni and Zulu, 1993; see also Gutmann, 2007 on Mexico). It has long been recognised that men must be included in HIV policy initiatives (see Bujra, 2002) and development more broadly: men are marginalised within gender and development policy.

Ultimately, the success women have in negotiating for safer sex depends on how responsive their male partners are, as the Principal

Documentation Officer at the Ombudsman expresses (J. Thomas, 2005, p. 45; Zulu and Chepngeno, 2003, p. 248; Bankole and Singh, 1998, p. 22). However, there is a lack of discussion between partners about contraceptives: the MDHS (2004) reveals that 27.5 per cent of currently married women with knowledge of a contraceptive method had never discussed family planning in the past year (NSO Malawi and ORC Macro, 2005, p. 91). There is a culturally normalised distance between men and women which acts as a barrier to communication: they rarely shake hands and, at social functions, including funerals for example, they sit on different sides. As is the situation in general, masculinity is socially constructed to be associated with appearances of power, which inhibits the scope for men to discuss sexual matters with their partner and health service workers: men want to appear strong, confident and self-reliant (Agadjanian, 2002, p. 195; Blanc, 2001, p. 199). As a result, men may not seek treatment for STIs, including HIV, and this can put their partner at risk.

Sex for well-being

Risk-taking in sex is used to reaffirm gendered identities and escape from gendered roles. Male personhood is closely associated with having multiple sexual partners. Where men have the gender-based role of the breadwinner they use sex as a means of escapism, especially in the context of the global economic crisis. Risk-taking in sex is part of the pursuit of well-being and forms part of social gatherings for both men and women.

'Real' men and sex for male personhood

Polygamy has long been regarded a 'symbol of prestige for men': having many wives and children suggests the man is wealthy and also creates a pool of cheap labour (MHRC, 2006, p. 13). The practice was widespread in Karonga District, where the Tumbuka and Nkonde ethnic groups are dominant. In accordance with gender-based norms, having multiple sexual partners is considered to be a sign of masculinity, as the Chairperson of Tisamukarane Support Group reflects (for the situation among the Baganda see Rwabukwali et al., 1994), and the men are the breadwinners and have to migrate for work (GoM, 2005, 3.1.1; Bracher et al., 2003, p. 212–13; for the situation in general see Bujra, 2002, p. 632). Kaler reports that a discourse has emerged among some men that refusing to use condoms and being HIV-positive are a testament to the number of sexual partners one has had and engaging in risky behaviour, and cites a journal record where one man states:

> I have never tried to use [condoms]. I have slept with many girls and if it is the cause of AIDS then I already have it because the girls with which I had been having sex, gathering them all could fill a *Yanu-Yanu* bus. (2003, pp. 359–62)

Having many sexual partners, engaging in risky sex and not using condoms are all associated with masculinity. Barker and Ricardo consider how being HIV-positive is deemed among some men to be a 'badge of honour' (2006, p. 2; see also Kaler, 2003, p. 359). Mary of Kaporo Support Group reflects: 'Imagine, people here know I am HIV-positive but still more they propose me, they say "please, I love you and I am ready to get your viruses".' Gloria of Mwentitete talks of how 'men are at risk because if we tell them that we are positive they do not care and continue having sex with us without using condoms'. This was a situation that was also reported by several women through informal discussions. The preference for sex without condoms among men is evident in extensive reports from the key informants and focus group discussions that many men will pay more for sex with sex workers who do not use condoms (see also Rankin et al., 2005, p. 12; Forster, 2000, p. 7). Jane of Kapora Support Group explains how in the bottlestores in their area prostitutes charge 200 MK with a condom, 500 MK 'plain'.

Crisis of male personhood and sex for escapism

In the twentieth century, wage labour became increasingly fundamental to men's identity. Marriage is linked to wage-earning capacity, as James Ferguson (2013, p. 228) considers for the case more generally, to be in a position to pay *lobola* and to be able to support family as the breadwinner, in accordance with pervasive gender norms. In Malawi the focus group discussions universally report how the husband has a gender-based responsibility to take care of the entire family and to provide all the needs of the household in terms of building the home and finding money in order to buy clothes, soap and food. However male personhood across Southern Africa is in crisis because, in recent decades, there has been mass unemployment – even in countries that have experienced economic growth such as South Africa since the mid-1970s (J. Ferguson, 2013, p. 230; Seekings and Nattrass, 2005).

Within the context of economic crisis, with increasing cost and scarcity of food and fuel coupled with rising unemployment, men increasingly struggle to fulfil their gender-based role as breadwinner. Where men migrate for work it changes patterns of sexual behaviour (for the situation in South Africa see Marks, 2002). This is against a backdrop of a long history of colonialism and neoliberalism. Male migration was intensified under British colonial rule as a result of the implementation of a 'hut tax', appropriation of arable lands and the control of agricultural prices, which made it difficult to maintain a living on rural lands (on Côte d'Ivoire see Etienne, 1997). Rural impoverishment was exacerbated in post-colonial Malawi, fuelled by SAPs in particular (Craddock, 2006, pp. 156–7, Tango International, 2004, p. 6; Forster, 2000, pp. 1–19; Whiteside and Carr, 1997; Davidson, 1993, pp. 409–1). Men migrated to the gold mines in South Africa and sex workers congregated around the camps. In recent years, it is common for men to have separate urban residences while their wives reside in the rural areas.

Men do not have the same options of support that women do. As the preceding chapter considers, the subordinate position of women means that they are the traditional dependants. The majority of women are relatively poor within the family unit and are financially dependent upon their husbands for their own and their children's survival, especially in the rural areas where poverty is more acute. Women have a number of safety nets within the extended family as a result of that dependence, including cultural practices such as wife inheritance. Women also exchange sex as a survival strategy and for upward social mobility. Furthermore, support from development projects is typically targeted at traditional dependants: women, children, elderly people and the sick – not men, who should be the breadwinners (J. Ferguson, 2013, p. 233). A male accountant in Zomba highlighted how small loans are available to start up small businesses, for example selling baked goods, but men widely report that there are not reasonable loans available for them to start businesses. Men seek to build up relationships of dependence (J. Ferguson, 2013, p. 231); for example, those in influential positions with NGOs mobilise their positions to strengthen their networks of patronage.

Pressure on men as the head of the household is a global phenomenon. In contexts such as Malawi it is more extreme in its implications because this is one of the poorest countries in the world and people have the tightest margins for survival. The pressure on men to be strong and support the family contributes to low life expectancy among men, particularly in the cities where they migrate to find work. Men on average die younger than women: life expectancy at birth is 48.3 for males and 51.4 for females. The crude death rate per 1000 is higher for males (11.2) than females (9.7) (NSO, 2010a, p. 35). The situation is worse in the south where HIV prevalence is highest. In Karonga District in the north, male and female life expectancy is almost equal (at 53.0 and 56.0). The disparities are most acute in Zomba City, where life expectancy for males is 7.4 years less than women, at 48.6 and 56 respectively (NSO, 2010a, pp. 31–4). The *Population and Housing Census 2008, Analytical Report on Gender* highlights that for the population aged 45 years and above there are 32 per cent more females than males, suggesting that this is perhaps a result of biological advantage and the effects of lifestyle, including having multiple sexual partners, alcohol consumption and smoking (NSO, 2010a, p. 8). Men are stressed and in part this frustration is rooted in the loss of capacity to fulfil the gendered role of breadwinner – especially in recent years with the financial crisis – and there is a sense of failure and resentment towards wives for engaging in exchanging sex to meet basic needs of the family (Bryceson and Fonseca, 2006, pp. 1661–2).

Norms of masculinity are at odds with protecting one's own sexual reproductive health. It was widely reported in the focus group discussions, key-informant interviews and the press that men do not get tested and join support groups in the same numbers as women. Knowing one's status is fundamental to living a longer life.

Sex as part of social gatherings

Furthermore, as Bryceson and Fonseca highlight, 'sex is seen as not only enjoyable, natural and necessary for survival but as a vital activity for creative self-expression ... sex can be compensatory, a pleasurable escape from the reality of lives availed of little other physical gratification' (2006, p. 1660). It was widely reported during the focus group discussions that sex is an integral part of social gatherings for men and women, including political, cultural, religious, family and social gatherings that are held at night. Sex plays a fundamental part during cultural ceremonies, including traditional dances, religious ceremonies and funerals. These dances include the *Vimbudza, Viwoda, Malipenga, Indingala, Ifibweng* and *Ndolo* in Karonga and the *Chinamwali* and *Manganje* in Zomba. Funerals are among the most important social activities and in Karonga the Nkonde funerals can last a month (especially for prominent members of the community) (see KDA, 2008, p. 24). The members of several support groups in Karonga and Zomba Districts report that churches in their area (including the Last Church, Fellowship Church, Pentecostal Church and National Church) encourage overnight prayers that last as long as a week and people have sex as part of these functions. Pokani Omoyo and Kaporo Support Groups also report that when a girl is married in Karonga the parents organise a group of people to visit her new home (a practice known *Vihulo* in Nkonde or *Vibwayira* in Chitumbuka), where the group travel at night and consume alcohol, and people engage in riskier sex. Lydia of Talandira Support Group reports how people also have sex at the overnight video shows at Namididi market in Zomba. When people drink at the *Virabu* beer markets in Karonga and the *Kaschasu* beer markets in Zomba they may engage in sex and forget to use condoms when they are drunk.

Conclusions

The neoliberal model for development is predicated on productivism and life is expected from the rational individual for whom the policy response to HIV was designed. However, it does not capture other aspects of the ways in which life is valued and people bring value to their lives. When we begin to interrogate the value of life in Malawi it is apparent that life is valued in accordance with gendered norms and this is linked to the gender division of labour. On the one hand, women are second-class citizens with limited autonomy and status within the household. On the other hand, men are under pressure to fulfil their gender-based roles as the breadwinners in the context of the economic crisis. This is a form of structural violence in the sense that social categorisation along gender lines heightens the risk of HIV infection.

The centrality of reproduction to the gendered ways in which men and women are valued has a particular bearing on the risk to women of HIV infection because of their gender-based reproductive role. This is fundamentally at odds with neoliberal interventions that champion abstaining from sex, being faithful or using condoms. Pregnancy heightens the risk to women and abstaining from sex or using condoms is not an option. Children are central to the family and women may be under pressure to have extra marital sex if the couple fails to bear children. Ultimately, bearing children is considered central to a woman's identity and they may face a choice between potential death from HIV and the certain 'social death' of being shunned for not bearing children. Women cannot ensure that their husbands are faithful where marriage is central to a woman's identity and women are not in a position to leave a marriage, even if it places them at risk of HIV infection. Furthermore, sexualised rituals and traditional counselling for men and women throughout their lives that prepare them for their reproductive roles and enhance sexual fulfilment in marriage form a crucial part of cultural traditions of different ethnic groups. Cultural gendered structures and pervasive tradition normalise these rituals and the majority of women do not have the power to refuse to participate, especially those who lack education and live in rural areas. The interviewees suggest that condoms are not used because the rituals require the exchange of sexual fluids.

Marriage customs posit men as dominant heads of households and, as a result, men's lives take priority in terms of their health and education, especially in families with limited resources. Men marry on more favourable terms and tend to wield greater powers with respect to decision-making on a whole range of issues, including with respect to sexual reproductive health. Risk-taking in sex is used to reaffirm gendered identities, escape from gendered roles and for pleasure. This is particularly the case for men. Male personhood is closely associated with sexual conquest: having multiple sexual partners. Where men have the gender-based role of the breadwinner they use sex as a means of escapism. In the context of mass unemployment and the recent economic crisis, men increasingly struggle to fulfil this role and, as James Ferguson argues, this leads to a crisis of personhood (2013, pp. 230–8). Men and even some women use sex outside marriage as a means of escapism. In addition, within the context of poverty and limited opportunities, people tend to take a short-term view and have a limited sense of self-worth. Risk-taking in sex is part of social gatherings for both men and women.

In a context of entrenched poverty and limited alternatives, engaging in risk-taking in sex becomes a strategy for bringing value and meaning to life for both men and women. Although the literature on survival sex has been long established, the analysis here also emphasises how sex is also a strategy for broader personal security. Sex is fundamental to the identities of men and women. Sex is also an important part of reaffirming gendered identity and escaping from gendered roles. Although these behaviours exacerbate the spread of the virus, strategies to eliminate them are problematic because these are fundamental to social identity and well-being. This understanding leads to more fundamental questions about what empowerment is. As chapter 5 considers, it extends beyond political empowerment to encompass essential cognitive and psychological elements. A critical dimension of understanding empowerment is to understand how life is valued and how, in particular, this is extremely gendered.

5
Gender on the Agenda?
Empowerment

As chapters 3 and 4 explore, gender as structural violence underscores the spread of HIV and places women disproportionately at risk of infection. Where the virus spreads along the gender 'fault lines of society' (Baylies, 2004, p. 7), it exposes the gendered structures and provides the space to challenge them. Questions of empowerment emerge onto the agenda because these structures can no longer be accepted as the status quo. They are violent; they spread HIV, which reduces life expectancy and undermines human capabilities. Gender has long been recognised as a crucial aspect of the global response to HIV and there have been widespread calls for women to be empowered (UNAIDS, 2010, p. 12; USAID Malawi, 2008, p. 70; Nath, 2004). The UN Special Session on HIV/AIDS in 2001 commits African governments to 'empower women to have more control over and decide freely and responsibility on matters related to their sexuality to increase their ability to protect themselves from HIV infection' (2001, p. 9). The notion of 'empowerment' is widely espoused in western development agendas more generally because it appeals to donor-driven preoccupations with sustainability, and yet it does not necessarily bring about meaningful social change (Parpart et al., 2002, p. 3).

Understanding how power operates in gendered ways is fundamental to conceptualising what 'empowerment' is. The analysis in the preceding chapters contributes to de-invisibilising gender as structural violence, focusing on gendered poverty and the gendered ways in which life is valued. Power operating through gender as a form of structural violence is deeply embedded, hard to discern and accepted as the norm – as a result there is inertia and resistance to the deconstruction or transformation of the structures of inequalities.

Therefore, as Stromquist (1995) argues, empowerment is not purely a political or economic task but also has cognitive and psychological aspects. Cognitive empowerment includes critically understanding one's own reality and the ability to challenge disempowerment (Davis, 2008, p. 116). Psychological empowerment encompasses having a sense of self-worth, self-esteem and courage in order to challenge your own internalised oppression through exploring and taking risks beyond your normal capacity (Trevithick, 2005, p. 211). More broadly, it will be argued here that a critical dimension of understanding empowerment is to understand how life is valued and how, in particular, this is extremely gendered.

This chapter critiques the ways in which empowerment is being addressed in Malawi. It argues that these are limited with respect to engaging with gender as structural violence. First, the analysis considers political empowerment. Drawing upon Moser et al. (2004) and Beall and Davila (1994) it is argued that, despite some good intentions, efforts suffer from policy evaporation, resistance, invisibilisation and sectorisation. Second, it examines female condoms and microbicides as empowerment technologies. It is argued that although these offer valuable ways for women to circumvent patriarchal structures, they do not address the gendered structures of poverty and gendered norms of how life is valued. Third, it analyses economic empowerment through social protection, which has been hailed as an 'innovative' solution to gendered poverty. However, these schemes face challenges in scaling up beyond the short-term pilot schemes and entrench some of the gendered structures that underscore HIV risk in the first place. Fourth, it considers education for empowerment. Although education is a cornerstone of broader empowerment and a crucial part of cognitive empowerment, it is insufficient. In the context of gendered poverty, there are limited employment opportunities and oppressive gendered norms remain embedded within the education system. Finally, this chapter considers the role of initiatives that aim at psychological empowerment in terms of valuing people's lives and their contributions to society. These include the establishment of support groups for PLHIV and activities that enhance the capacity of women and their communities as actors in their own empowerment. And yet, despite the appeal of empowering people to solve their own problems, as Swidler and Watkins (2009) have argued, people are often empowered only so far as to be able to navigate and compete for aid resources, thus entrenching existing inequalities of power and the structural violence they reproduce.

Political empowerment: Gender on the agenda?

Gender issues have emerged onto the policy agenda with respect to gender mainstreaming more generally and the HIV response specifically. As elsewhere across the continent, the shift to multi-party democracy in Malawi in 1994 created the space for gender issues to enter onto the political agenda. The Constitution enshrines gender equality and establishes that women have the right 'to full and equal protection by the law, and have the right not to be discriminated against on the basis of their gender or marital status' (GoM, 1994, Section 13a, 24/1). Moreover, there has been pressure from the 'top down' on the government to respond to the subordination of women. Malawi has ratified a number of international declarations and conventions, including the Convention on the Elimination of All Forms of Discrimination Against Women (CEDAW) (1979) in 1987, the Women in Development Strategy (1993) and the Fourth World Conference on Women in Beijing (1995). The Malawi National Gender Policy 'takes cognizance of these UN Conventions and aims at harmonising them with the national policies and laws' (GoM, 2000, 1.10). It seeks to mainstream gender in the national development process to enhance the participation of women and men, girls and boys for sustainable and equitable development for poverty eradication. It recognises that gender is a cross-cutting issue and identifies critical gender concerns in key priority areas. Specifically, the importance of the gendered dimensions of HIV is highlighted and how '[w]omen are at a greater risk because of their disadvantaged and subordinate positions' (GoM, 2000, 3.1, 5.0, 5.2). The National HIV/AIDS Policy 2003–8 pledges to 'protect the rights of women to have control over and to decide responsibly, free of discrimination or coercive violence, on matters related to their sexuality, including sexual and reproductive health' (GoM, 2003, 1.2–1.4). It highlights that poverty is a major driver of the pandemic and that poverty is gendered, which means that women are disproportionately vulnerable to being infected (2003, 5.2.2). Furthermore, the Women, Girls and HIV/AIDS – Programme and Plan of Action (WGHPPA) 2005–10 recognises that addressing gender is essential to an effective response to the epidemic. The Technical Advisor to the WGHPPA highlights that the national response to HIV 'has gender concerns as one of the principles ensuring that all HIV initiatives actually take on board issues of gender'.

There is a necessity to enact gender mainstreaming because, as Moser (2005, pp. 580–4) highlights, Malawi is dependent on aid for 40 per cent of its budget and the donors push for gender mainstreaming. And yet, despite the formulation of gender policies on paper, they have a limited impact in practice. DfID has been particularly influential because it provides the largest bilateral aid programme; its policies and strategies are formulated in the London office and driven by interests of the UK rather than those of Malawi. As Moser et al. (2004) identify in the framework they developed for auditing DfID's gender mainstreaming strategy in Malawi, the good policy intentions vis-à-vis gender suffer from 'policy evaporation', 'resistance' and 'invisibilisation'. Policy evaporation occurs when 'good policy intentions fail to be followed through in practice'. Resistance is 'when effective mechanisms block gender mainstreaming, with opposition essentially "political" and based on gender power relations, rather than on technocratic procedural constraints'. Invisibilisation refers to the process whereby 'monitoring and evaluation procedures fail to document what is occurring on the ground' (Moser et al., 2004, p. v). Furthermore, gender issues suffer from what Beall and Davila (1994) conceptualise as 'sectorisation': where they are treated separate from mainstream issues or sectors, which results in gender being confined to discrete projects and marginalised within under-financed and poorly resourced institutions such as the Ministry of Gender (on the implications for the Farm Input Subsidy Programme see Chinyamunyamu, 2014, pp. 114–18).

First, although gender is included as 'cross-cutting' in the HIV policy response it suffers from policy evaporation because it is not incorporated into gender-specific programmes, objectives or activities – as is the case for gender mainstreaming more broadly (see Eerdewijk, 2014, p. 1; Moser et al., 2004, p. v). Although the National HIV/AIDS Policy (GoM, 2003) recognises gender, Bezner Kerr and Mkandawire (2012, p. 264) argue that 'there is an ironic conjugation between a broad policy that foregrounds structural conditions, and the specific policy strategies that espouse targeting specific groups defined on the basis of risk characteristics'. Moreover, an HIV specialist at CIDA contends in 2007 that the gender response is little more than rhetoric. The tendency has been to enact short-term, superficial gender policies that focus on gender neutrality and gender balance. This fails to engage with how gender as structural violence underscores the particular precarity of women's lives. The consultations in 2011 reveal that in more recent years there is increasing emphasis on empowering women at the community level. There are some public displays of action: the National Coordinator of the WGHPPA highlighted in 2011 a number of individual incidences where they take action, for example their support to mothers in taking their daughters back when they had been married off for debt repayment (*Kupimbira*). However, despite some steps forward, the response to the epidemic and the particular risk to women is limited.

Second, there is resistance to addressing gender issues because of the deeply entrenched patriarchy within the political systems. Women are not equally represented in government and issues affecting women are marginalised in policy making. Ngwira et al. (2003) and Semu et al. (2005) argue that there is a lack of political will at various institutional levels. On the one hand, men dominate in decision-making and tend to ward off any challenges to the status quo that might threaten their power. Despite the shifts towards democracy, in 2005 only 27 per cent of MPs were women (F. Phiri, 2005). The entrenched resistance was indicated throughout the research by men engaged in policy making and implementation, particularly in informal comments outside of the formal interview or consultation. Some would even begin by apologising because they appreciate that this is what my research is interested in, but explain that it is something that the international donors and NGOs bring in but it is not a priority for Malawi. On the other hand, although female representation had almost reached what Dahlerup (1988) defines as the 'Critical Mass' of 30 per cent for the effective representation of women, the Programme Officer for the National Initiative for Civic Education highlights that there is still resistance to putting issues that affect women on the agenda. Women MPs do not always act in the best interests of women because they are under pressure to toe partisan lines (UN, 2004a). For example, women MPs overturned the proposal for the appointment of Malawi's first female Inspector General of Police, Mary Nangwale (F. Phiri, 2005). The Advocacy Officer at NAPHAM, the Head of the Society for the Advancement of Women and the Head of the WLA consider how pervasive traditionalism maintains patriarchal structures that place women at particular risk of HIV transmission, for example polygamy (see Chimgwede, 2004b). Rather than making polygamy illegal, the government instead pledges in the National HIV/AIDS Policy to 'promote and encourage monogamous marriages' (GoM, 2003, 6.1.2). The Malawi Law Commission (2006) recommended that polygamy should be abolished, in line with commitments to the CEDAW (1987) and the African Protocol on the Rights of Women. However, as the Senior Assistant to the Chief State Advocate/Human Rights Coordinator at the Ministry of Justice and Constitutional Affairs explains, should the bill be presented before Parliament 'it would be very interesting to see how [they] would react to the idea that polygamy should be abolished'.

Third, gender issues suffer from invisibilisation because the monitoring and evaluation is ineffective, which Moser et al. (2004, p. 2) consider results in inaccurate and inadequate information on gender-related impacts and outcomes. There have been some advances in gender monitoring and evaluation in Malawi, as the Population and Health Specialist at the World Bank reflects in 2007: the mid-term evaluation of the government's Strategic Plan includes a gender assessment and there has been a push for monitoring disaggregated by gender within the NAC framework to encourage organisations to implement an effective response to the gendered dimensions of HIV/AIDS. Despite this, however, in 2007 there was still no monitoring and evaluation system for the WGHPPA (2005–10) because it was not included in the project document for NAC funding. This contributed to the suspension of funding from December 2006, and in 2007 the Ministry was trying to get NAC approval to include a monitoring and evaluation element. As a result, when asked about the impact, the Technical Advisor for the WGHPPA revealed that they could not measure the impact the programme has on reducing gender-related risk. In addition, it was widely reported by the key informants that the tendency is for monitoring and evaluation to be conducted at the end and this does not feed back into the programmes. The Senior Programme Manager for PSI's *Packachere* Programme reflects that the effectiveness of the programmes at the grassroots is limited because of the tendency to apply a philosophy of 'best practice' based on a body of information on 'what works' in other countries rather than evidence from the Malawi context.

Finally, gender issues also suffer from 'sectorisation'. Crucially, there is a lack of capacity of the Ministry of Women and Child Development, which is the national machinery for all gender-related issues. As White (2007, p. 8) considers, the Ministry is one of the least powerful and has limited influence on the national agenda, although the Minister does sit in Cabinet. It is greatly understaffed with a high senior staff turnover and has limited funds. Taking the budget allocation for the financial year 2006/7, of 804.5 million MK (which equated to approximately £3.2 million at the time) 11 million MK went to the Ministry of Health, 9.1 million MK went to the Ministry of Education and only 131,000 MK went to the Ministry of Women and Child Development (White, 2007, p. 8). Although there was a 152 per cent increase in funding to the Ministry of Women and Child Development over the period 2006/7 to 2007/8, the absolute increase in the allocation was 191,000 MK, which is small compared with the increases for the Ministries of Education and Health (5.3 million MK and 2.2 million MK respectively)

(GoM, n.d., 6.2). The National Gender Policy has not filtered down to the district level, as the Technical Advisor to the WGHPPA within the Ministry of Gender considers in 2007. Furthermore, gender 'focal points' have been established across the organisations engaged in the response but the Senior Programme Manager of PSI's *Packachere* Programme is critical, arguing that 'not much is being done on the ground, apart from many meetings, people discussing what should we do, not much to have the intended impact'.

More specifically, the capacity of the Ministry of Gender to implement the WGHPPA is limited as the interviews with the Technical Advisor to the Programme in July 2007 and the National Coordinator in June 2011 highlight. For the first year, the WGHPPA was funded through the NAC but this was suspended in December 2006 after six months, due to reports of mismanagement. In July 2007 there was only one Technical Advisor working on the programme who was responsible for coordinating it across the country. As Eerdewijk (2014) considers regarding the situation in general, gender is sectorised in the sense that it is treated more as an individual than an institutional affair. Typically, responsibility for delivery is left to this one individual (usually female) who ends up with an insurmountable task. In the office of the Technical Advisor in 2007 she had a single filing cabinet, which was largely empty, save for a copy of the WGHPPA itself. On my second visit to follow up on our interview, I interrupted her work and it transpired that, rather than coordinating the national policy, she was translating documents such as the Constitution into Chichewa. From 2008, the WGHPPA was funded by the Flemish International Cooperation Agency (FICA) but the money was only sufficient to cover just 4 of Malawi's 28 districts: Nsanje in the south, Mangochi in the centre, Ntcheu in the west and Chitipa in the north. In the other 24 districts the programme was reliant on the existing funding and falls within the remit of the District Community Development Officers. In 2011, the National Coordinator reflects that this leaves little incentive for reporting on progress. He explains that they make quarterly monitoring and evaluation visits to the four districts they work in. Since 2009 the aim was to include all 28 districts but this did not happen. He explains that 'the problem is with them reporting to us. We are supposed to receive a report from all other districts but they get no funding so there is no incentive to report to us.' With the end of the WGHPPA in 2010, the Ministry was still awaiting a funding extension in June 2011 to conduct activities that year.

Clearly well-designed, well-meaning policy interventions do not work when confronted with local political realities of under-capacity and chronic funding shortages. Moreover, gender as structural violence permeates the policy response, as considered in chapter 1.

Empowerment technologies: Female condoms and microbicides

Within the dominant neoliberal policy response to HIV there has been an emphasis on 'technological fixes', as considered in chapter 1. With regard to addressing the particular risk to women, there have been important advances in prevention technologies including the female condom and microbicides. These have long been hailed as a major breakthrough to 'empower' women with more control over their bodies, helping them negotiate protection with their partners, promoting healthy behaviours, and increasing self-efficacy and sexual confidence and autonomy (see Gollub, 2000). In Malawi the female condom was piloted by UNFPA in 2007 and *Chisango* at PSI was launching the female condom that year so as to specifically target women. The female condom is considered 'empowering' because women can control its use as they are the ones who wear it. As the Executive Director of MACRO highlights, 'it would give the power to the woman to say "if you don't put on your own condom, I will put on my condom" '. The Programme Officer for UNAIDS and the Product Manager for *Chisango* explain how the female condom is promoted as being easy to use, discreet, that women can insert it in advance of sexual intercourse, it does not interrupt sexual activity and men may not know it is being used. The UNFPA Condom Programming Officer, who is responsible for promoting female condoms through the Ministry of Health Reproductive Health Unit, outlines that:

> The woman actually has the possibility of wearing a female condom 8 hours before sexual intercourse. So even if the male counterpart is refusing to use a condom, what most women have done is just insert the female condom anyway and negotiate condom use much later on. And once it is well lubricated and there is no interruption in the sexual intercourse the men don't have problems in using female condoms. Because they [women] can use it in advance, because they can make the decision on their own, they are more empowered in that sense.

Representatives of UNFPA, *Chisango* and MACRO report that more women are requesting female condoms; women prefer them to the male condom; and men like them because they do not have to wear a condom. It was also widely reported in the focus group discussions with women in the support groups in 2011 that 'if men are refusing we are given female condoms to protect ourselves'.

However, there are challenges. Female condoms are expensive, in short supply and there is only very limited knowledge and awareness of them. It was also widely reported that there is the considerable barrier of affordability to overcome. The female condom is three to four times more expensive than the male condom. The Product Manager for HIV Prevention at PSI/Malawi explains that 'the donors find it easier to support a male condoms programme because they buy them at a cheaper price than they do for the female condoms'. The MDHS (2004) reports that knowledge of the male condom is 89.9 per cent for women and 95.8 per cent for men, while knowledge of the female condom is comparatively very low at 53.6 per cent for women and 56.4 per cent for men (NSO Malawi and ORC Macro, 2005, pp. 70–1). The National Coordinator for Coalition of Women Living with HIV/AIDS (COWLHA) reflects in 2011 that: 'If you go to a supermarket, you go to a till, you find a male condom you can pick it up. But you will not find a female condom anywhere unless you go to a good hospital (not any hospital).'

Despite claims that WLHIV are embracing the condoms, the Programme Officer for UNAIDS and the Product Manager for *Chisango* report that women have experienced difficulty using the female condoms, women fear that it will disappear in the vagina, there is stigma associated with women accessing the condoms and men object to them. The Product Manager for HIV Prevention at PSI/Malawi reports, 'people get shocked when they see it, they say "oh wow, this is huge" and some people say it makes noise'. There were reports that the female condoms distributed in Mangochi (in Central Malawi) were worn by women as bracelets. As the National Coordinator for COWLHA reflects:

> In Mangochi people were taking them – you know it has a big ring that can become a bangle – you will find people wearing a bangle like that and they are beautiful you know. Very beautiful. So that was a misuse because they did not know how to use it. Just from the look of it they think that it cannot fit inside so there is need for awareness on how to use a female condom.

The observations and informal discussions in Zomba and Karonga in 2011 revealed how inflated condoms are being used to make balls. Moreover, there persists a negative social attitude towards condoms in general and this is especially the case for female condoms. Condoms are viewed as 'unnatural' and taboo even in HIV-positive families (UNDP, 2003, p. 18). Crucially there are pervasive barriers to women actually using them – as explored for condoms more generally in chapter 1. Despite these negative reactions, the Condom Programming Officer at UNFPA proposes that there are fewer barriers to the female condom as a result of the lessons learnt from the previous social marketing of the male condom. The Product Manager for HIV Prevention at PSI/Malawi explains, before the social marketing of the female condom began, that 'we should find a better environment than maybe we had when we just started with the male condoms. People are generally more receptive to the whole idea of condoms.' To overcome the stigma against women accessing condoms, there are initiatives to distribute female condoms through hair salons, as was the case in Zambia and Zimbabwe. The owner of a hair salon in Zomba explained in 2011 how women would come to buy the condoms from her while getting their hair done.

The development of female microbicides is also under way, including gels, creams, films or suppositories that can be applied inside the vagina or rectum to protect against STIs including HIV. Research trials have been conducted in Malawi by the Johns Hopkins Project programme since 2005 and over 100 women were using them by July 2006 (Chikoko, 2006, p. 3). In July 2010 CAPRISA announced results of a proof-of-concept trial of microbicides with 1 per cent Tenofovir Gel, which prevents mother-to-child transmission and protects against Simian Immunodeficiency Virus in trials on monkeys. One dose of the gel is inserted up to 12 hours before sex and a second dose as soon as possible within 12 hours after sex. Participants who had greater adherence to using the gels (indicated through the number of applicators that were empty when returned) had lower incidence (CAPRISA, 2010). However, microbicides are still only in the research phase and at present an effective microbicide is not available. As the Condom Programming Officer at UNFPA explains, there are problems that would arise concerning who would distribute and fund microbicides. Microbicides are also potentially problematic because of the belief that 'dry sex' is more pleasurable. However, Zierler (1994, p. 566) suggests that if the microbicides can be mixed with drying agents then their use can be consistent with cultural sexual practices.

Structural violence permeates the global policy response with respect to the female condom. Peters et al. (2013) analyse the AIDS policies of 16 agencies and reveal how the female condom is normalised for sex workers. They highlight that 'none of the 16 policy papers analyzed make a serious attempt to insist on a programme of action to make female condoms universally accessible, that is: to all sexually active women'. They argue that 'The gender-stereotyped AIDS policy discourse at the global level negates women's agency in sexuality and her sexual rights. This in turn might have limited the scale-up of programmes that would make female condoms universally accessible.'

Of particular concern here is that, although these technologies offer important opportunities for women, they are not sufficient. They offer means for women to circumvent the gender structures of power but do not instigate wider social changes vis-à-vis the structures of poverty and gendered norms with respect to how the lives of women and men are valued. As Baird et al. (2012) argue in their work on cash transfers in Malawi, structural interventions beyond those directly targeting sexual behaviour are a fundamental part of addressing HIV risk.

Economic empowerment: Social protection

The intersection of inequalities of poverty and gender heightens the particular risk to women of HIV and therefore improving women's low socio-economic status is a central aspect of an effective response. Financial opportunities are necessary to break the cycle of dependency on sex to bring about short-term security and the commoditisation of life and the body. Social protection schemes that protect and promote livelihoods have been widely espoused as an effective policy framework for addressing extreme poverty and vulnerability more generally across Sub-Saharan Africa (see Commission for Africa, 2005; Devereux and Sabates-Wheeler, 2004). There has been the expansion of existing income transfer schemes and new social protection schemes in East and Southern Africa, including Malawi and Tanzania (see Niño-Zarazúa et al., 2011, p. 163). The Malawi government has established a national-level Social Protection Steering Committee and a Social Protection Technical Committee, with commitments to more staff and resources, including a percentage of the annual budget for social protection (Schubert and Huijbregts, 2006, p. 5). These schemes have been hailed as an 'innovative' solution to HIV through incentivising behaviour change and there have been promising reports from the piloting in Malawi and Tanzania of cash transfer programmes for school girls. Yates (2010) considers how these schemes have the potential to overcome some of the financial, social and cultural barriers to accessing prevention, treatment, care and support. Baird et al. (2010) suggest that the provision of school fees and cash transfers to current schoolgirls and recent dropouts through the Zomba cash transfer programmes not only improves attendance but may also reduce teen pregnancy, early marriage and self-reported sexual activity (see also World Bank, 2010).

Given the extensive support from the World Bank, other international development actors and academics, it is proposed that the role of these cash transfer programmes in global health will continue to expand. However, Niño-Zarazúa et al. (2011) propose that there are three key determinants for future direction – political support, financial viability and institutional capacity. They argue that, despite the promise of social protection, these are short-term pilots with limited reach and weak institutionalisation; there is a reluctance to take them up in the longer term and they reflect donor priorities. In the wake of the food, fuel and financial crises, people tend to revert to older models of social protection, including subsidised inputs and in-kind emergency assistance (see also Hickey, 2008). Similarly the UNAIDS *Report on a Global Epidemic* (2013, p. 12) highlights that:

> Structural approaches, including cash transfers, vouchers and food and nutrition support, show potentially promising results as a possible strategy to reduce vulnerability to HIV infection faced by girls and young women. While these new approaches have proven effective in trials, they have not yet led to a measurable and sustained decline in new infections at the population level, in large measure due to the failure to bring these strategies to scale.

Niño-Zarazúa et al. (2011) argue that it is necessary to 'get the politics right': national governments need to be involved and donors need to better understand the politics. Moreover, the concern here is the need to address the wider socio-economic context, including the intersection of poverty with health and gender that has been exposed in the preceding chapters.

Harman (2011) warns that, despite the short-term appeal of these approaches, there should be greater caution. She argues that 'buying behaviour' through conditional cash transfers serves as a form of 'biopolitical control' – these neoliberal 'innovations' that govern risk are an extension of the pervasive marketisation of global health to the individual and their bodies. This links to the discussion of risk in chapter 1, which recognises that risk cannot be governed through top-down donor policies dictating what constitutes so-called 'good' and 'moral' behaviour. Although these schemes address some aspects of gendered poverty, they ignore the broader gendered inequalities. They focus on the economic empowerment of women, emphasising their role in reproduction and ignoring, for example, how people engage in sex for self-worth, including sexual satisfaction and escapism (see also Harman, 2011, p. 881). As chapter 4 considers, men have the pressure of their gender-based roles as the breadwinners in a context where it is increasingly difficult to fulfil their responsibilities, and thus financial and employment opportunities are also essential for men. The small loans that are available tend to only be sufficient for young girls to start up a small business, for example selling baked goods, but men widely report that there are not reasonable loans available for them to start businesses. The focus on addressing poverty is vital but, as Nattrass (2009) argues, this obscures the deeper contextual social and behavioural factors. At a more fundamental level, real social change necessitates engaging more effectively with gender as structural violence.

Cognitive empowerment: Education for empowerment

Education has long been considered as integral to empowerment more generally (see Heward, 1999, p. 4). Education for All (EFA) was launched in 1990 to bring the benefits of education to 'every citizen in every society' and commitments to education are included within the MDGs. The education of women and girls is widely highlighted as essential, including as a crucial part of empowering them to take greater control of their reproductive health. It is a fundamental part of cognitive empowerment, for people to be able to understand their reality and challenge their disempowerment.

It is widely reported by the key informants that where women are marginalised from education they lack the confidence and power to confront the pervasive gendered structures to negotiate for safer sex. The WGHPPA outlines how women in general tend to have 'inadequate life skills' (GoM, 2005, 3.1.4) and the Head of AGREDS suggests that this is especially the case for rural women because of their low levels of education. The Director of Planning, Research and Evaluation at the Department for Nutrition, HIV and AIDS reflects that a few women who are informed and educated may be able to negotiate for safer sex, but the majority are illiterate, especially in the rural areas. The Product Manager for PSI's *Chisango* Condom Programme suggests that more women need to be educated so that they can be empowered to be more assertive in order to be able to discuss sex, insist on condoms and negotiate their sexual relationships (for the situation in general see Grown et al., 2005, p. 542). The MDHS (2004) highlights that, with increased education, a higher percentage of women believe that if a husband has an STI, then his wife is justified in either refusing to have sex with him or proposing condom use (NSO Malawi and ORC Macro, 2005, p. 197).

Furthermore, it is proposed that women need to be educated in order for them to be able to have to have the capacity to understand, defend and promote their rights (Tango International, 2004, p. 5). Although there are laws that protect women, the majority are not aware of their legal rights because of their lack of education. The IPPF et al. *Report Card* highlights that where supportive legislation exists, public awareness of rights under the law is low, and reporting of breach of rights is even lower (IPPF et al., 2006, p. 2). Many women, for example, do not know they can leave a marital union or they are not informed about their property rights and processes, including how to buy and register land, claim ownership or contest land rights. As the National Coordinator of MANERELA considers, the courts are in a position to be able to grant divorce but 'many local women will not access the courts because of their levels of understanding'. Women tend to have a greater knowledge of the traditional legal system as opposed to the modern legal system. For example, all villagers are aware of the role of chiefs in dispute resolution and women were found in a study by WLSA (2000, p. 35) to use chiefs more than police and courts. The Advocacy Officer for NAPHAM considers the way in which women seek justice is very different to how the justice system should work. In addition, the focus group discussions, interviews and informal discussions revealed that the majority of women are not aware of existence and role of the NGOs in their villages (see also WLSA, 2000, p. 35).

However, although schools should provide a safe environment for young people to learn and develop, they are gendered spaces of violence. As Maluwa-Banda (2003, p. 3) and Leach (2003) consider in their work on Malawi, Zimbabwe and Ghana, violence against women is normalised within schools. Burton's report on *Suffering at School: Results of the Malawi Gender-based Violence in Schools Survey* reveals that it is where most violence against children occurs, with pupils being physically, emotionally or sexually victimised: 1 per cent of forced sex, 57 per cent of incidents of sexual touching and 54 per cent of bullying occurred within the school environment (2005, p. 34). In particular, gender violence is widespread. There is an awareness of it but it is accepted as a part of everyday school life and a 'normal' feature of adolescent relationships (Leach, 2003, p. 386). Twenty per cent of teachers reported that they are aware of teachers who entice students into 'love relationships'. Of those who reported awareness of such incidents, 74 per cent knew of these incidents happening at their school (Burton, 2005, pp. x–xi; for a specific study of Chiradzulu District see Chanika, 2003). High levels of bullying are tolerated. Girls are those most likely to be bullied and most often experience unwanted sexual touching or forced sex from their classmates and teachers. For example, classmates were identified as the perpetrators by 61 per cent of children experiencing sexual touching (Burton, 2005, pp. 27, 37).

> Almost one third of all children reported that teachers at their school demanded sex from children in return for good grades. The majority of children 13 years and younger knew someone personally, or knew of an actual case where this had happened, while one third of older children could think of an actual incident. (2005, pp. x, 13)

Furthermore, gender as structural violence permeates the education system, playing a fundamental role in social conditioning of gendered norms. The education system, as in other parts of Africa, was imported to Malawi by missionaries during colonialism and was built upon a narrow nineteenth-century European gender ideology. The schooling of girls was focused on domesticity to educate them to be more suitable wives, expanding only to enable them to become more fitting companions (Thompson, 2005, p. 576; Davidson, 1993, p. 409; for the situation in Sierra Leone see Leach, 2007). Although it is no longer government policy that girls have to study home economics and needlework and boys have to study woodwork and technical drawing, a gender division persists. Girls are educated and trained to fulfil a gender-based domestic role as a mother and a wife, while boys are encouraged to aspire to wage-earning, high-status jobs. As the Programme Officer for UNAIDS reflects, female images in textbooks depend upon the stereotyped role of women in the home (see also Hyde, 1999; Semu and Binauli, 1997, p. 88; Ngulube-Chinoko, 1995, p. 92).

Although education is a fundamental aspect of social change and development, on its own it is insufficient. The 2010 MDHS reveals that HIV prevalence is highest for women with secondary education and above:

> By education, HIV prevalence in Malawi is highest among respondents with more than a secondary education and those with no education (14 and 13 percent, respectively). The same pattern is seen among men; 12 percent of men with more than a secondary education and 11 percent of men with no education are infected with HIV. However, among women, the pattern differs. Women with a

secondary education and more than a secondary education have the highest HIV prevalence at 16 percent for both groups. (NSO and ICF Macro, 2011, p. 199)

As considered in chapter 1, while there is almost universal understanding of HIV in Malawi this does not tend to result in behaviour change. Pervasive gender roles and relations mean that even women with greater levels of education may not be able to take greater control of their reproductive health. Where a few women are more educated they might be able to question the negative cultural aspects and their subordinate position to some extent. However, where the cultural norms are so deeply embedded, including within the education system, it is still difficult for even the more educated and empowered women to overcome them. With pervasive taboos and stigma surrounding HIV, sex and death, a report from CILIC (2007, p. 7) reveals 'women are generally discouraged by moral assumptions of guilt, shame and blame by the community', and this is also the case for people with higher education. As the Executive Director of MACRO identifies, 'people's knowledge is there but for people to change their behaviour that is the biggest hurdle which is there'. In the context of the economic crisis and soaring unemployment levels people (and women in particular) lack the opportunities to use these qualifications and may engage in risk-taking in sex for survival, upward social mobility and well-being, as considered in chapters 3 and 4.

Psychological empowerment: Valuing lives and contributions to society

At a much more fundamental level, psychological empowerment encompasses having a sense of self-worth, self-esteem and courage in order to challenge the oppressive patriarchal structures. As part of psychological empowerment, people's lives and their contributions to society must be valued. As J. Ferguson (2013, p. 238) concludes, it is fundamental to 'find ways to restore value in people (not only their labour), and to build a new dispensation within which people truly count, once again, as the most precious form of wealth'. This includes valuing the ways in which men and women contribute to society – in ways within and beyond their gendered roles. As chapter 3 considers, women are typically excluded from the formal economy and their broader contributions to society are marginalised and perceived to be of less value to society (for the situation in general see James, 1994). A gender analysis recognises the previously ignored and yet crucial role of women in security and development, dispelling the protector/protected myth, that women are the objects of security and development with little control over conditions of their protection (Seckinelgin et al., 2010, p. 516; Tickner, 1992, pp. 28, 58–9; Elshtain, 1987). Women have essential, yet often ignored, roles as mothers, wives, providers, farmers and caregivers, providing the very basis for survival in families and communities. Furthermore, women and girls bear the brunt of the immediate impact of the virus at individual, family and community levels: they take on the burden of care for the infected, particularly where there is an absence of adequate state provision. As considered in chapter 1, women tend to be targeted by family planning and behaviour change programmes, based on their perceived gender-based reproductive role in the family. The National Coordinator of COWLHA highlights their Home-Based Care Programme in Mwanza to support WLHIV to look after chronically ill PLHIV:

> They know how to handle this person because they have gone through it themselves. They know what to talk about, they know how to ease that person, they know where to touch, they know when to come and what the person is going to answer or what the person is hiding...because they have insider knowledge. And the good thing about them is that those women are now role models in those villages.

Moreover, people must be recognised and valued as actors in their own empowerment. As an Advocacy Officer at NAPHAM highlights, the focus should be to 'build their capacity, give them the skills that they need and they will be the best agents of change'. The donor programmes aim at sustainability through 'empowering' villagers (particularly women) to solve their own problems.

Across Malawi, PLHIV were encouraged to form CBOs and support groups. NAPHAM was established in 1993 by a group of PLHIV. It has played a key role in registering support groups for PLHIV and undertaking trainings to mobilise collective action to enhance the health and well-being of the group (for the situation in general see also Nguyen, 2010; Campbell, 2003, p. 3). In the absence of a more effective response, local support groups offer one of the most immediate means by which communities have sought to expose the contingency of destructive social dynamics and their effects on Malawians. By mobilising 'technologies of the self' (Foucault, 1988), support groups interrogate actors' feelings of worthlessness so as to promote behavioural and cognitive change on an individual and collective basis. The Assistant Programme Manager reported how NAPHAM had been rolled out to all districts in 2011 and that this has an important impact on PLHIV: 'People are able to cope, live longer and encourage each other. In discussions with focus groups that is what they say, that the activities are having an impact.' NAPHAM was established in Zomba in February 2011 and there was an opportunity for participant observation of the first training sessions. I observed NAPHAM's training sessions on 'positive living' that were being undertaken in Zomba in July 2011. These encouraged participants to value their own lives, advised them on ways to deal with the stigma they face in their communities and encouraged them to prioritise their own health through adhering to their drug regime, drinking adequate water and eating a nutritionally balanced diet. There were high expectations among the newly established support groups in the district. Nanchegwa Support Group in Zomba District had particularly high levels of male membership and several participants expressed how joining the group has been a positive experience because they support and encourage each other. The Assistant Programme Manager at NAPHAM highlights in particular how the network contributes to:

> empowering women, giving them information so they can make informed decisions about having children and the consequences. Training them as leaders of support groups to facilitate discussions in the importance of having children and PMTCT [prevention of mother-to-child transmission]. How to cope with the stigma and discrimination, access and adherence to drugs. We identify their potential to provide support to the group and select representatives to be trained to provide information to the rest of the group.

The participant observations and focus group discussions with the support groups revealed how they contribute to empowering WLHIV to talk about sex and their own sexual behaviour, as chapter 2 considers. WLHIV are becoming politicised and are rising up to tackle the issues that affect them because they need services and options for themselves and their children. Reflecting a popular sentiment among WLHIV in the focus group discussions, Mercy from Makungnya Village Support Group reflects that women go for HIV testing and to access ARVs because of the concern that when they die their children will be orphaned. There are many strategies that women are using in activist organisations across the world to combat HIV. As the Acting Programmes Manager at the MANET+ recognises:

> [Women] know they are vulnerable to HIV infection hence some of them are very aggressive [regarding] preventative measures.... They want them, they want these programmes and they participate in HIV prevention programmes by engaging themselves in income-generating activities, by wanting to have their own husbands, by wanting to have adequate education that will make them get employment.

A plethora of women's associations, networks and NGOs have been established. NAPHAM seeks to enable women to identify and advocate on issues that are affecting them, supporting women in small-scale businesses by providing them with small loans and training. The Coalition of Women Living with HIV and AIDS (COWLHA) was launched in 2006 to address the intersection of violence against women and HIV, and to actively advocate for women's rights for WLHIV. The HIV Advisor at DfID reports that these networks provide support to women 'to start income-generating activities ranging from fishing to inter-cropping, embroidery, handicrafts which they sell and they use that to buy drugs for themselves or they use that to send each other's children to school'.

Furthermore, men and wider communities must be included in initiatives for broader social change to provide the enabling environment for positive empowerment outcomes for women (Bujra, 2002; Gutmann, 2007; Mane and Aggleton, 2001; Baylies and Bujra, 2000). As the analysis in the preceding chapters revealed, HIV risk is determined by the behaviour of both sexual partners and gender is constructed by both men and women within their communities. As the Principal Documentation Officer at the Ombudsman's Office highlights, the success women have in negotiating condom use depends on how responsive their male partners are. Men must be included in order to bring about positive empowerment outcomes (see Gupta, 2005; Blanc, 2001, p. 169; Kalipeni and Zulu, 1993; see also Gutmann, 2007 on Mexico). Men often control the couple's sexual reproductive health and it tends to be their risky sexual behaviour that puts women at risk: men are the perpetrators of gender-based violence; cultural practices favour men; where men migrate to work they are at heightened risk of contracting HIV and other STIs; and men do not seek treatment when they have early signs of STIs. And yet it has also long been recognised that men have typically been excluded in terms of the response at the local level (see Kalipeni and

Zulu, 1993). The HIV/AIDS Advisor at DfID identifies in 2007 the trend to target women and girls, 'but the issue was that not enough information was targeted at young men ... they also have to be informed'. Often, as chapter 2 explores, it is men who are resistant to joining support groups and lack a voice when it comes to discussing their own sexual behaviour. This was of particular resonance at a time when the government was formulating the Gender and HIV Programme to guide the response once the then current Women, Girls and HIV/AIDS Programme concluded in 2012.

The National Coordinator for COWLHA has utilised the Stepping Stones approach to develop dialogue within the family, which she explains 'is a methodology that promotes communication, awareness, openness in people'. Reflecting on the approach in 2011, which they had undertaken in Machinga, Kasungu and Ntcheu she explains:

> When they go back home it will be improved because it has been discussed in that group. So communication in the family – it is also [about issues] like sex, sexuality, communication in how to use the finances in the family, communication in child bearing – people will just see that they are pregnant without knowing when they want to have a child or when not. A woman will just see a man making love to her without communicating 'I want to do it now' and if they are positive they cannot say 'no' or they cannot say 'let's use a condom'.

Banda (2014) reports that the approach enables men and women to collectively decide about issues of sex and sexuality and it leads to self-reporting of reduced cases of intimate partner violence. The approach is also complemented by the Society Tackling AIDS through Rights (STAR) initiative, which COWLHA was adopting in Dowa. The National Coordinator explains:

> We just bring the community together, they just sit down, we don't give them a topic, we just let them talk about anything but you find that by the end of the day they bring out issues. And we just put in a facilitator there to just direct things if they are going on well or not. Our aim is to bring in HIV issues so by doing this we have seen that people can talk freely about HIV transmission, prevention, what they have to do about sex has come out. Men and women discussing together. So what we have seen is where we are just in two weeks' discussion that the whole village wanted to test for HIV, that issue of knowing your HIV status came out and they said 'Why don't we

all know about our status, so that we know about how we live in the village?' so they asked us to bring an organisation to come to the whole village, so we did that and that was out of the whole project of that. So because this was a good initiative we told the donors that we really have to do this because if everybody wants to test and they know their status it is going to be good for the whole village.

It is important to have a degree of caution because, as Swidler and Watkins (2009) consider, although local people are becoming 'empowered' by these projects, it is not in the way that was intended. When NAPHAM was establishing itself in Zomba in 2011, the women of Makunganya Village Support Group talked of their resistance to joining because they were disillusioned by the endless promises from NGOs and donors that fail to materialise. There were concerns when the funds failed to materialise for the third week of NAPHAM trainings. In contrast, NAPHAM has been operating in Karonga District since 2008, with a total of 54 registered support groups in 2011. The participant observation of the NAPHAM Executive Meeting in August 2011 (where the support groups were reporting their progress), the individual interviews with the support group representatives at the meeting and the focus group discussions with 11 of the groups revealed that, despite expectations, these CBOs and support groups have received few resources and are seldom, if ever, visited – especially those in more remote areas (see also Swidler and Watkins, 2009). The 'pass-on-projects', which sought to give goats to the support groups that they could rear and then 'pass on' the young to other groups, was ill-conceived and there were widespread reports that the goats died in transit, never had kids, do not produce milk and the support group members were not sufficiently trained to rear them.

People are empowered by these initiatives to become competitive, rational, neoliberal individuals. In his work on West Africa, Nguyen (2010, p. 177) highlights the 'logic of triage' (the process of determining the most important people or things), which includes the 'bundling' of services for PLHIV. Villagers, local NGO workers and volunteers learn what the 'hoops' are, how best to navigate them and how to mobilise these projects to their own ends – playing the system (Swidler and Watkins, 2009, p. 1183; see also Sparke, 2012; Bird-David, 1983, 1990). A number of representatives of different organisations engaged in the response informally reflected on the growth of 'professional aid recipients'. Observation of NGO visits on several occasions to the support groups for PLHIV in Zomba and Karonga revealed how people mobilise their HIV-positive status to access assistance from NGOs and international donors, including the financial and food incentives to attend training sessions because these conform to donor preoccupations with sustainability. The competition for aid can pitch communities against one another and dismantle local survival strategies. In one case, in Karonga District, the representatives of the NGO outlined that the group was competing with other potential recipient groups for the limited resources available and they assessed how well the people in the support group had memorised the lessons of previous trainings. This is reportedly the situation in other areas across Sub-Saharan Africa. Boesten's (2011) work in Tanzania, for example, reveals how PLHIV strategically navigate the AIDS industry to obtain the aid they need to survive, and this creates tension and conflict between communities. Furthermore, women's organisations tend to be dominated by a small clique of women, whose power derives from the powerful men to whom they are married; these women tend to protect their own positions of power and restrict the advancement of other women (for the situation in general see Ampofo et al., 2004, p. 702).

The neoliberal policy response to HIV does not reflect on its own impact, including the way in which people experience empowerment strategies and how interventions institutionalise particular relations and actors (Seckinelglin, 2008, p. 1). As de Bruijn and van Dijk consider, policy intervention norms of 'carrying capacity' and 'sustainability' have a bias towards stability and normal situations, 'producing at best irrelevant and at worst damaging results for the survival strategies of the populations in the short as well as the long term' (1999, p. 6). Of course, it is important to recognise that the research for this book was not outside the power games. During my own fieldwork people attended meetings with me who were not HIV-positive but were presenting themselves as HIV-positive in the hope that there would be some financial benefit for their attendance. In one case in Zomba District two entire villages had come to meet us because our local contact had misinformed the village head that we were from an NGO.

Conclusions

Gender and empowerment have long been on the international agenda with respect to responding to the HIV pandemic. However, the ways in which empowerment is being addressed in Malawi are limited with respect to engaging with gender as structural violence. Although the policy response in Malawi pays lip-service to 'gender mainstreaming' and 'the gender dynamics of HIV', this often equates to little more than rhetoric. These policies serve to appease donor demands in a country that is dependent on donor aid. Despite some good policy intentions that aim at women's political empowerment, these policies suffer from policy evaporation, resistance, invisibilisation and sectorisation (Moser et al., 2004, p. v; Beall and Davila, 1994). In practice, they do not adequately respond to those aspects of women's lived experiences that heighten their risk.

Empowerment technologies, such as female condoms and microbicides, are important aspects of the response to HIV, including the particular risk to women. Women need a range of better tools and technologies so they can choose those which are the most effective for them to protect their own bodies from infection. And yet, the preceding chapters have considered some of the deeper structural inequalities that underscore risk and these act as pervasive barriers to women actually using such tools. These technological fixes can serve to circumvent the patriarchal structures but they do not address the gendered structures of poverty and gendered norms of how life is valued. These require structural interventions beyond those targeting sexual behaviour.

In this respect, economic empowerment through social protection has been hailed as an 'innovative' solution to gendered poverty. The aim is to enhance women's livelihood security through schemes such as the cash transfer initiatives. However, these schemes face challenges in scaling up beyond the short-term pilot schemes and entrench some of the gendered structures that underscore HIV risk in the first place. Furthermore, education for empowerment is fundamental, including for cognitive empowerment, but it is insufficient. In the context of gendered poverty, there are limited employment opportunities and the education system itself is a gendered space of violence.

Initiatives such as the establishment of support groups for PLHIV and activities that enhance the capacity of PLHIV and their communities as actors in their own empowerment aim at psychological empowerment in terms of valuing people's lives and their contributions to society. WLHIV in particular are being politicised and are rising up to tackle the issues that affect them; they cannot afford to wait because they need services and options for themselves and their children. Women are using activist organisations across the world to combat HIV and it is argued that people, including WLHIV, have been and are being agents for change in their own lives. However, such activities tend to exacerbate the gendered structures that underscore risk in the first place. Moreover, despite the appeal of empowering people to solve their own problems, as Swidler and Watkins (2009) argue, people are mainly empowered to navigate and compete for aid resources.

There are no quick 'fixes' to the deeply entrenched structural violence that underscores the gender context of HIV risk. This makes addressing these gender structures unattractive to governments, donors, NGOs and other stakeholders engaged in the response, as they endeavour to produce measurable solutions. It requires a level of commitment that extends beyond the typically short-term visions of these actors. Moreover, the policy response needs to reflect on its own impact, including the way in which people experience empowerment strategies and how interventions institutionalise particular relations and actors.

Conclusion

Gender Social Justice

On 6 July 2014 Malawi marked 50 years of independence from the former colonial power, the UK. President Peter Mutharika reflects in his Presidential Speech that there is much to celebrate. He highlights 'we are celebrating that we have not only attained 50 years of independence but also 50 years of peace, stability, progress and prosperity'. He reflects that 'The country has also continued to be an island of peace in Africa' (Malawi News Agency, 2014). And yet, it is fundamental to recognise that although contemporary Malawi has not experienced mass violence such as war, conflict, genocide and apartheid that has plagued many other African countries, it is not a country at peace in the broadest sense. As Galtung (1969) propounds, 'positive peace', and thus meaningful social justice, encompasses more than the absence of personal violence; it requires the absence of structural violence.

This book began by focusing on what will follow the MDGs in 2015 and how this presents an opportunity to critically reflect on development more broadly. The case of Malawi is a vital one to reflect on precisely because it is one of the least developed and most aid-dependent countries in the world. It has some of the world's worst development indicators for a non-conflict country and many of the challenges it faces in terms of development are not new. Moreover, there is a gender dimension because it is women who disproportionately experience under-development and HIV (see UN, 2004a). It is well established that it is necessary to engage with gender-based violence because it is pervasive. As the Intimate Partner Violence Survey (Pelser et al., 2005) reveals, one-third of women have experienced physical abuse, one-tenth have experienced sexual abuse and half have experienced some form of abuse. However, these figures only scratch the surface of gender as violence.

Narrow conceptualisations of violence obscure the entrenched, every-day experiences of structural violence (see Scheper-Hughes, 1993). As Kelly (1988, p. 95) considers, gender-based violence is a part of a 'con-tinuum of violence' that extends from direct violence (in the sense of domestic violence) to structural violence. It is vital to harness the lan-guage of 'violence' because that is precisely what it is. Gender impacts on longevity and the quality of life in terms of broader psychological and physical well-being. The concern here has been how it underscores HIV risk in particular. The challenge for advancing gender social jus-tice is that, where violence permeates the very structures of society, it is obscured from view. And yet, although it is harder to address, it is fun-damental to do so. As Farmer et al. consider, 'structural violence remains a high-ranking cause of premature death and disability. We can begin to address this by "resocializing" our understanding of disease distribution and outcome' (2006, p. e449).

Where unequal gender structures are deeply embedded, hard to discern and accepted to be the norm, there is resistance to their decon-struction or transformation. These gender frameworks of power can be challenged by showing that the 'frame' never contained the reality it was supposed to depict (Butler, 2009, pp. 9–10). The gender analysis of HIV risk in this book contributes to the feminist task of de-invisibilising the nuances of gender as structural violence. As Sylvester (2006) consid-ers, the 'feminist gaze' seeks to locate what is missing from the picture; what the frame tries to control or keep out. In this case, what is miss-ing from the picture of Malawi as an 'island of peace'. In drawing attention to this, the book extends beyond the valuable research on gender and HIV risk within conflict situations (see Seckinelgin, 2012a; Seckinelgin et al., 2010) and women's experience of domestic violence (see Price, 2012). It shifts the focus beyond the spectacular to the nor-malised, everyday experiences of the gender dimensions of HIV risk in non-conflict contexts. Although power is deeply embedded in societal structures, its operation can be understood through observing whose interests are furthered by the dominant ideas of the current system and whose interests are harmed. In Malawi, it is women's interests that are harmed by the current system. This is violent because current patriar-chal conditions prevent women in particular from achieving their full potential. Inequitable distribution of resources and social categorisation in accordance with gender norms underscores the spread of HIV and places women at particular risk of infection. Where the virus spreads along the fault lines of society, it highlights the existing social, eco-nomic and cultural patterns of exclusion (Baylies, 2004, p. 71; see also

Seckinelgin, 2008, p. 147). These can no longer be accepted as the status quo – these are inequities in the sense that they are unjust.

The conclusion begins by exploring what this means for de-invisibilising gender as structural violence. The discussion then moves on to consider the challenges for the academy and the policy response for structural change vis-à-vis gender as social justice.

De-invisibilising gender as structural violence

HIV was one of the big 'winners' of the MDGs and AIDS exceptionalism has led to an unprecedented global response to the virus as compared to other health issues. Despite the global attention to the virus, the dominant ways of conceptualising and responding to the pandemic fail to engage with the local level (see also Seckinelgin, 2008, pp. 146–7), including the gender dimensions of people's lived experiences of insecurity and risk. Chapter 1 argues that structural violence permeates the way in which HIV is framed and responded to. The dominant neoliberal 'development' discourse focuses on technocratic and universal initiatives, which, as James Ferguson (1990) considers, obscure the real issues of structural inequalities, including gender and poverty. Similarly, as recognised by the human security discourse, problematising HIV in security terms obscures the levels where insecurity is experienced. It ignores individual women, men and children who are infected or coping with the impact. Although contemporary Malawi has not experienced conflict, the linkages between HIV and (in)security have resonance, particularly in terms of poverty and food security. These are violent and these are gendered. This brings questions of what we can learn about development and insecurity from the local level to the fore, challenging the primacy accorded to medical and scientific expertise. The emergency response to a perceived 'crisis situation' is not compatible with understanding and engaging with the structural violence that underscores risk. This is not a crisis – this is the situation. The pandemic is a 'long-wave event' (Barnett and Prins, 2006) that requires long-term political commitment to respond to the structural inequalities that underscore risk. Furthermore, the dominant neoliberal response legitimises, manages, reinforces and exacerbates the very structures that underscore risk in the first place. The medicalisation of risk focuses on technological fixes (including ARVs and condoms), which, although important, ignore the deeper structures that act as a pervasive barrier to people actually using them. In the absence of a scientific fix, the emphasis is on changing so-called 'risky' behaviours from the top down, based on the model of a male neoliberal, rational individual. The responsibilisation of women obscures the unequal power dynamics in sexual relationships where men tend to be the decision-makers.

These limitations highlight the necessity to better understand and engage with gender as a structural violence because this is undermining the effectiveness of the response. This book draws upon extensive fieldwork to analyse how gendered structures are produced, experienced and responded to at the local level. It has long been recognised in the interdisciplinary scholarship on HIV that inequalities and differences of gender contribute to the spread of the virus. The analysis in chapters 3 and 4 provides a historically situated and culturally contextualised analysis of the specificities of how gender as structural violence permeates Malawian society and underscores risk in a plethora of complex ways. This violence is not static and the findings here reveal some of the complexities of the agency of seemingly 'powerless' Malawians to navigate gender in 'tight corners'.

Chapter 3 identifies how gendered poverty in Malawi is a form of structural violence that exacerbates the spread of HIV. Women disproportionately experience poverty because of structural inequalities in land distribution, agriculture and food security, and employment opportunities. These are rooted in a long history of the pre-colonial period, colonisation and, since independence, in the globalisation of capitalism. And yet, although these structures are deeply entrenched, they are not experienced passively. First, women are disadvantaged by both the customary and modern systems of land inheritance. This has fundamental implications for women's impoverishment because this is a predominantly agrarian economy. A number of cultural practices have developed to maintain the status quo and ensure the security of the extended family system, including wife inheritance (*Chihalo* or *Chilingo*), sister inheritance (*Kuhalira* or *Siyazi)* and marriage for debt repayment (*Kubimbira* or *Kupimbigha*). Women are under pressure to maintain their marriages for their own and the extended family's survival. In accordance with what Pateman (1988) terms the 'sexual contract', women fulfil their husband sexually to sustain their marriage and secure the support that it brings. Women may engage in riskier sexual practices including *nyama-ku-nyama* ('skin-to-skin' ejaculation) to maximise the man's satisfaction. Violence can be considered socially acceptable if the wife denies the husband sexual satisfaction. Women have limited options to leave a marriage that places them at risk of infection and the emphasis is upon persevering in marriage. Second, gendered inequalities permeate agriculture. Although women account for 70 per cent of full-time farmers and bear the brunt of subsistence agriculture, they lack control of the land and its produce. The husband tends to control food resources and, traditionally, as part of maintaining marriage and satisfying men as the breadwinners, men's nutrition takes priority. Women preserve the status quo by public displays whereby they ensure the husband is well fed (known as *mkomia*) and yet, behind the scenes, subtly rebel through 'salt-testing' during food preparation. Where HIV is normalised at the local level, engaging in risky sex provides a fundamental means to meet immediate needs for food, including the exchange of 'fish-for-sex'. Third, women are typically disadvantaged in their labour and business opportunities. Commercial sex is an important strategy for survival and upward social mobility. Women can be 'entrepreneurial' in that they exchange sex for employment opportunities and commercial advantages. Some women find sugar daddies to access the 'three Cs' – cell phones, cars and cash – and, with the increasing numbers of affluent women, some men also find sugar mummies. In the absence of an effective response to poverty and with often limited alternative options, risk-taking provides a fundamental strategy for navigating situations of gendered inequality and dependency to bring about security (see also Watkins, 2004).

The analysis in chapter 4 moves on to explore how gender as structural violence permeates the very way in which life is valued as a result of social categorisation along gender lines. This is crucial to understand because, in accordance with the 'top-down' neoliberal policy response, rational, responsible individuals are expected to act in such a way as to preserve their life, yet, in practice, knowledge does not necessarily result in behaviour change. The life of men and women, and their contributions to society, are valued in gendered ways and this is linked to the gender division of labour. This is a form of structural violence that heightens risk of HIV infection. First, the centrality of reproduction to the gendered ways in which men and women are valued has a particular bearing on the risk to women of infection because of the emphasis on the value to society of their reproductive role. Pregnancy places women at risk, particularly with the pressure to begin conceiving at a young age and to closely space the births. Reproduction is fundamentally at odds with neoliberal interventions that champion abstaining from sex, being faithful or using condoms. Where couples fail to conceive, women may be under pressure to have extra-marital sex in order to conceive and thus to preserve the image of the family. Second, sexualised rituals and traditional counselling for men and women throughout their lives, which prepare them for their reproductive roles and enhance sexual fulfilment in marriage, form a crucial part of cultural traditions of different ethnic groups. Traditionally, *Chinamwali* (initiation) is part of the transition into adulthood for boys and girls and includes sexual rituals to demonstrate their 'coming of age'. These include for example the *Nyau* cult for Chewa boys, *Jando* (circumcision) for Yao boys and *Kusasa Fumbi* or *Kuchotsa Fumbi* ('shaking of the dust' or 'clearing of the dust') for Chewa and Yao girls. Interventions to address these practices can be problematic because they are central to the cultural value of young men and women. Third, marriage customs posit men as dominant heads of households (the *'mutu wa banja'*). As a result, men's lives take priority in terms of their health and education. Men also tend to wield greater powers with respect to decision-making on a whole range of issues, including with respect to sexual reproductive health, and women are socially conditioned to be submissive to men. Fourth, risk-taking in sex is part of well-being. It forms part of reaffirming gendered identities and male personhood is closely associated with having multiple sexual partners. Where men have the gender-based role of the breadwinner, sex can provide a means of escapism, especially in the context of the global economic crisis. In the context of entrenched poverty and limited alternatives, engaging in risk-taking in sex becomes a strategy to bring value and meaning to life for both men and women, including as part of social gatherings.

A more sophisticated understanding of risk acknowledges that it is differentially experienced along what Sanders (2006) conceptualises as a 'continuum' that extends to risk-taking. Although so-called 'risky' sexual behaviours exacerbate the spread of the virus, strategies to eliminate them are problematic because these are fundamental to survival, upward mobility, social identity and well-being. As Bordo argues, 'although many people *are* mystified... often there will be a high degree of consciousness. Often, given the sexism, racism, narcissism of the culture, their personal happiness and economic security may depend on it' (2003, p. 30; see also Lukes, 2005 [1974], p. 150). These understandings help to further highlight why the current interventions are not working.

The gender dynamics of HIV have long attracted attention and this is part of broader commitments to gender mainstreaming and empowerment. Understandings of gender as structural violence raise fundamental questions about what empowerment is. As chapter 5 considers, empowerment extends beyond political and economic empowerment to encompass cognitive and psychological elements (Stromquist, 1995). A critical dimension of understanding empowerment is to account for how life is valued and how this is extremely gendered. Despite the plethora of policies and initiatives that have been developed that pay lip-service to gender as a 'cross-cutting issue' and the 'female face' of HIV, in practice these suffer from policy evaporation (good intentions fail to inform practice); resistance (political mechanisms block gender mainstreaming); invisibilisation (ineffective monitoring and evaluation) and sectorisation (where they are treated separate from mainstream issues or sectors) (see Moser et al., 2004, p. v; Beall and Davila, 1994). Moreover, the gender context of risk cannot simply be 'fixed' through imposing moral behaviour or empowering women from the top down. Technological fixes, including female condoms and microbicides, offer the potential to circumvent some of the gendered power structures but they fail to bring about meaningful social change. Empowerment through social protection has been hailed as the 'innovative' solution to gendered poverty but it faces challenges in scaling up and entrenches some of the gendered structures. Education is important but it is not sufficient. Initiatives such as support groups for PLHIV aim at psychological empowerment in terms of valuing people's lives and their contributions to society. And yet, despite the appeal of empowering people to solve their own problems, as Swidler and Watkins (2009) have argued, people are often empowered only so far as to be able to navigate and compete for aid resources, thus entrenching existing inequalities of power and the structural violence they reproduce. In the absence of a more effective response, women and men navigate the structures of inequalities and maximise what they can gain from the aid that does materialise, especially from the unprecedented level of funds directed towards HIV initiatives.

The challenges for the academy

This work contributes in particular to Global Health scholarship, which is situated at the intersection of science and social sciences. The transboundary challenges of health bring the significance of analyses at multiple levels to the fore, contesting the traditional, disembodied state-centrism of IR. HIV is a global pandemic that is experienced at the local, familial and individual levels. And yet much of the Global Health literature focuses on the global level of governance and obscures other scales, particularly the local level where health is actually *experienced*.[1] Despite a long history of feminist scholarship highlighting the significance of the personal level and the interconnectedness of the global and local (Tickner, 2005; Mohanty, 1991, 2003; Elshtain, 1981), these remain marginalised and under-researched within IR (Parpart, 2011; Young,

2005, p. 1). The IR literature on HIV is criticised for its tendency to speculate from limited evidence and the lack of strong fieldwork studies (see Whiteside and Poku, 2004, p. 215; Barnett and Prins, 2006, p. 360). This book complements the wealth of interdisciplinary literature that highlights the importance of bringing in different scales.[2] It draws upon extensive fieldwork to re-orientate the analysis along the global–local axis by focusing on the micro-level of the politics of health 'from below'. This refocusing is important because viruses spread at the level of the body as a result of interpersonal sexual relations and have ramifications at all levels, from the bodily to the familial, communal, national and the international (see also Anderson, 2012, p. 271; Seckinelgin, 2008, 2012b; Seckinelgin et al., 2010). In so doing, it connects with work in feminist geopolitics that Koch (2011, p. 500) argues challenges the 'masculinist privileging of the "big things" and the disembodied vision that such an approach generally employs' (see Dowler and Sharp, 2001; Secor, 2001; Sharp, 2000). The analysis here situates people's lived experiences and the hierarchical gender relations in everyday lives at the very centre of the analysis. This work asks what we can learn about the gender context of risk from marginalised African perspectives for a more complete approach to understanding of the linkages between gender, peace, security and risk.

The realm of Global Health presents the opportunity to re-imagine security (Thomas, 1989; see also McInnes and Lee, 2006; Feldbaum et al., 2006b). Framing health issues within the discourse of 'security' – securitising the issue – is attractive in both academic and policy terms, as Elbe (2006) highlights, because of the rhetorical power it has to mobilise political support and resources. Human security in particular enables development and rights to be taken more seriously within the realms of IR. This work contributes to the broader feminist task of dispelling the gender silences that continue to persist in the security discourses (Hudson, 2005; Tickner, 1997). As V. Spike Peterson argues, feminist scholars can offer 'critiques of modernity's interlocking systems of domination' and 'speak of moving towards a more just, less terrifying world' (1992, pp. 1–30). Drawing upon the Malawi case highlights how gender as structural violence permeates even seemingly 'peaceful' and 'secure' contexts and underscores risk. Furthermore, this work identifies some of the different forms agency takes within the structural constraints of gender as people endeavour to bring about physical and psychological security.

Research on global health brings questions of what IR can understand from African experiences and perspectives to the fore. Sub-Saharan

Africa is the most impoverished region in the world, where there has been limited progress towards the health-related MDGs and women disproportionately experience poor health, including HIV. This is particularly poignant because the discipline of IR is traditionally dominated by scholarship from North America and Western Europe, and African IR particularly marginalised (see Brown and Harman, 2013; Brown et al., 2009). As Beck considers, the trans-boundary challenges of interdependence and globalisation require a new frame of reference, including analysis of non-western perspectives in order to understand the 'specific refractions and reflections of the global'(1999, pp. 2–3). This challenges the western, masculine metanarratives of security, risk and power that disconnect from local experiences. There is a tendency in political science scholarship to apply western conceptual frameworks, including notions of 'Development' and 'Security', to African cases, rather than understanding the existing conditions in the first place (see Chabal and Daloz, 1999, p. 142). Concepts – including security and risk – are 'given new form' in Africa, and this poses multiple challenges to scholars and practitioners (Brown et al., 2009, p. 263). Among the challenges is to further strengthen the capacity of universities across Sub-Saharan Africa, and this includes addressing the barriers to the development of African feminist scholarship. In their work on English-speaking Sub-Saharan Africa, Ampofo et al. (2004, p. 687) consider how these include the impact of economic and political crisis on funding and institutional support, the shortage of current publications, few available publishing outlets, women's conflicting responsibilities within the universities, the hostile intellectual climate and the patriarchal structures. For the case of Malawi, Isabel Phiri (1996) highlights the barriers to female researchers in her account of her own personal experiences. In addition, fundamental inequities permeate the broader academy. Despite important steps forward, women and academics of Sub-Saharan Africa are marginalised in the disciplines of politics and IR (see the debates raised in Mitchell and Hesli, 2013). African feminist literature remains largely invisible in western feminist discourses, despite playing a key role in repositioning feminism more broadly (Ampofo et al., 2004, pp. 686–8; Chim'modzi, 1994/5, p. 46). Hudson (2005) highlights the vital role of alternative feminist approaches, including those that explore African experiences, to contribute to the feminist task of engendering African IR (see also Parpart, 2011). This book is informed by the scholarship of African women, and particularly Malawian women, including for example, Rachel Banda, Lucy Binauli, Stella Kachiwanda, Stella Ndau, Isabel Phiri, Linda Semu and Seodi White. It also draws extensively upon the lived experiences and perspectives of both women and men to understand the gender context of HIV in Malawi.

The sheer complexity of trans-boundary challenges that health poses requires understandings from interdisciplinary work at the intersection of the sciences and social sciences. It opens up new possibilities for fundamental shifts in how we understand the world.

The challenges for policy

The challenge for the post-2015 agenda is to augment gender social justice. This encompasses freedom from gender as structural violence, as this work on HIV in the Malawi case reveals. Gender inequities in societal structures act as a barrier to effectively responding to the under-lying reasons why populations are at risk. This represents a substantial task. Gender social justice requires a level of commitment that extends beyond the typically short-term visions of many actors. There are no quick 'fixes' for gendered structures that are rooted in a long history of tradition, colonisation and neoliberal development. Moreover, where it is problematic to measure success, this means that addressing these gender structures is unattractive to governments, donors, NGOs and other stakeholders engaged in the response. And yet it is fundamental to do so. For as long as the policy response avoids engaging with these structural factors it will continue to have limited results. If the dominant policy responses simply, manage, reinforce and exacerbate the very structures that create problems in the first place, then this is not true 'value for money'. It is necessary to seriously question what it is that is being measured and how those measures are being developed.

In the twenty-first century there has been emphasis within the inter-national development discourse on the centrality of local ownership, participatory processes and the empowerment of poor and marginalised people. It is widely recognised that development interventions must have greater understanding of the specific economic, political, social, gender and cultural contexts. And yet, despite the rhetoric, neoliberal policies are based on notions of 'best practice' in other contexts, and continue to be disconnected from complexities of people's lived experiences. The empirical work here reveals that the gender context of HIV infection is more complex than 'top-down' interventions aimed at securing women's lives, imposing so-called 'moral' behaviour, giving women rights and empowering women would suggest. Behaviours, needs and perceptions of risk are powerful forces in terms of governing behaviour. An effective and sustainable response must be based on an understanding of the context and be participatory. Local perspectives and understanding are crucial in order to challenge both the tendency to speculate on the basis of limited data and the limitations of the notion that 'one size fits all', which has proven to be ineffective. Hickey (2009) argues that, despite some lip-service and new forms of political analysis and efforts to support 'pro-poor' initiatives, these are limited and the entrenched agenda of liberalism is still based on ideology rather than evidence. It is necessary to speak to local populations in their language and listen to how they perceive their own situation. Moreover, it is about ensuring those perspectives meaningfully inform the policy response and are translated into practice. This is problematic in a broader development context where organisations are ultimately at the mercy of the priority areas of their external funders and have tight time frames for developing initiatives.

Actors engaged in the policy response need to reflect on the implications of the policies being implemented, particularly the potential impact on the structures of inequities and power relations that underscore the spread of HIV. Risk is underscored by deeply entrenched disparities of gender that intersect with wealth and cultural practices. Such disparities and norms force local communities into finding adaptive strategies, which can often distort or subvert the intended outcomes of the initiatives. Policy makers need to account for unique country contexts; otherwise their policies risk being irrelevant and even damaging to the communities for whom they are designed. Considerable work is necessary to overcome the challenges that the policy response itself has engendered. This includes the ways in which people subvert the interventions for their own ends.

Appendix 1: Interviews, Consultations and Focus Groups

Key-informant interviews 2007

Director of Planning, Research and Evaluation, Department of HIV, AIDS and Nutrition (25/07/07)

Advisors on HIV, Ministry of Education (13/07/07)

Technical Advisor to the Women, Girls and HIV/AIDS – Programme and Plan of Action, Ministry of Women and Child Development (13/07/07)

Senior Assistant to the Chief State Advocate/Human Rights Coordinator, Ministry of Justice and Constitutional Affairs (25/07/07)

STI Programme Officer, Ministry of Health Reproductive Health Unit (RHU) (11/07/07)

Head of Home-Based Care Unit, Roman Catholic Church (20/07/07)

Head of Assemblies of God Relief and Development Services (AGREDS), Assemblies of God Church (12/07/07)

Head of Seventh Day Adventist Church, Seventh Day Adventist Church (24/07/07)

Law Commissioner, Law Commission (11/07/07)

Chief Law Reform Officer, Law Commission (11/07/07)

HIV Law Reform Officer, Law Commission (11/07/07)

Deputy Director for Research and Documentation, Malawi Human Rights Commission (MHRC) (12/07/07)

Executive Director, Malawi AIDS Counselling and Resource Organisation (MACRO) (25/07/07)

Head of Policy Support and Development, National AIDS Commission (NAC) (24/07/07)

Programme Officer, National Initiative for Civic Education (NICE) (16/07/07)

Principal Documentation Officer, Ombudsman (23/07/07)

HIV Advisor, Department for International Development (DfID) (27/07/07)

Gender Specialist, Canadian International Development Agency (CIDA) (27/07/07)

HIV Specialist, CIDA (26/07/07)

Population and Health Specialist, World Bank (27/07/07)

Programme Officer, Joint United Nations Programme on HIV/AIDS (UNAIDS) (25/07/07)

Programme Officer – Reproductive Health and HIV, United Nations Children's Fund (UNICEF) (19/07/07)

Programme Analyst – Governance and HIV, United Nations Development Programme (UNDP) (27/07/07)

Programme Officer – HIV, United Nations Population Fund (UNFPA) (19/07/07)

Programme Officer – Gender, UNFPA (17/07/07)
Condom Programming Officer, UNFPA (24/07/07)
Programme Officer – HIV, United Nations World Food Programme (WFP) (23/07/09)
Gender Network National Coordinator, Action Aid (17/07/07)
Behaviour Surveillance Research Coordinator, Family Health International (FHI) (26/07/07)
Senior Programme Manager – *Packachere* Programme, Population Services International (PSI) (20/07/07)
Strategic Manager – Youth Alert! Programme, PSI (20/07/07)
Product Manager HIV for *Chisango* Condoms, PSI (19/07/07)
Programme Manager, Global AIDS Interfaith Alliance (GAIA) (12/07/07)
Programme Assistant, Family Planning Association of Malawi (17/07/07)
Advocacy Officer, National Association for People Living with HIV and AIDS in Malawi (NAPHAM) (12/07/07)
Acting Programmes Manager, Malawi Network of People Living with HIV (MANET+) (24/07/07)
National Coordinator, Malawi Network of Religious Leaders Living with HIV and AIDS (MANERELA) (26/07/07)
Programmes Coordinator, Malawi Center for Advice, Research and Education on Rights (Malawi CARER) (18/07/07)
Head of the HIV Department, Civil Liberties Committee (CILIC) (19/07/07)
Head, Society for the Advancement of Women (SAW) (11/07/07)
Programme Manager, Story Workshop (18/07/07)
Head, Women's Campaign (12/07/07)
Chairperson, Coalition of Women Living with HIV and AIDS (COWLHA) (17/07/07)
Head, Women Lawyers Association (WLA) (16/07/07)

Consultations 2011

Department of HIV, AIDS and Nutrition within the Office of the President and Cabinet (OPC) (17/06/11)
National Coordinator, Women, Girls and HIV/AIDS – Programme and Plan of Action, Ministry of Women and Child Development (17/06/11)
Head of Monitoring and Evaluation, National AIDS Commission (NAC) (16/06/2011)
Programme Coordinator, Malawi Network of AIDS Service Organisations (MANASO), Blantyre (12/07/2011)
Programme Officer for Monitoring and Evaluation (Coordinator for Stigma Survey 2010, Southern Regional Coordinator 2007–9), Malawi Network of People Living with HIV (MANET+) (13/06/11)
Assistant Programme Manager, National Association for People Living with HIV and AIDS (NAPHAM) (16/06/07)
National Coordinator, Coalition of Women and Girls Living with HIV/AIDS (16/06/11)
National Coordinator, Malawi Network of Religious Leaders Living with HIV and AIDS (MANERELA) (13/06/11)

Professor Alister Munthali, Centre for Social Research, Chancellor College, University of Malawi (20/06/2011)

Observations 2011

MANET+ on Community Mobilisation, Mponela
Yankho Support Group at the Zomba Police College, Zomba
NAPHAM trainings on Group Therapy and Child Therapy, Zomba
Malawi Network of AIDS Service Organisations (MANASO) on the Community Scorecard (CSC), Zomba
District Interfaith AIDS Committee on Behaviour Change and Life Skills for the Youth
Youth Rights Stakeholders Meeting in Zomba
NAPHAM Executive Meeting in Karonga
Manganje dance, Makungnya Village, Zomba District [July 2011]
Nsondole Support Group meeting, Zomba

Selected key-informant interviews 2011

Chief Executive, Zomba City Council (23/06/2011)
Zomba City AIDS Coordinator, Zomba City Council (21/06/2011)
Karonga District AIDS Coordinator, Karonga District Assembly (18/08/2011)
Zomba District Coordinator, NAPHAM (28/06/2011)
HIV Coordinator, Banja La Mtsolgolo (BLM), Zomba and Trainer with NAPHAM (28/06/2011)
Paralegal working with Malawi CARER in Zomba (19/07/2011)
Chairman, Nkuba Beach, Lake Chilwa, Zomba (07/07/2011)
Volunteer, Credit Room AWIFF, Jali, Zomba District (18/07/2011)
Chairperson, Tisamukarane Support Group (29/06/2011)
Howard Parker Sharp Health Centre, Domasi Mission (15/07 2011)
Matola driver, Zomba (06/07/2011)
Accountant, Zomba (22/07/2011)
18 Group Village Headmen and Village Headmen, Zomba (June–July 2011)
18 representatives of support groups for PLHIV, Zomba and Karonga (June–August 2011)

Focus group discussions 2011

Tianjane Support Group, Chiseu, Zomba (25/07/2011)
Omodzi Support Group, Nambande, Zomba (26/07/2011)
St Charles Lwanga Home-Based Care, Zomba (27/07/2011)
Nanchenga Support Group, Nanchenga, Zomba (28/07/2011)
Makunganya Village Support Group, Zomba (29/07/2011)
One Voice Support Group Nkolokosa, Zomba (30/07/2011)
Talandira Support Group, Namadi Trading Centre, Zomba (01/08/2011)
Tikondone Support Group, Near Nsondole, Zomba (02/08/2011)
Nsondole Support Group, Zomba (03/08/2011)

Tigwirisani Support Group, St Agnes Catholic Church, Zomba (04/08/2011)
Tukamanerane Support Group, TA Kutamanje, Zomba (05/08/2011)
Chisomo Support Group, Chinawali Anglican Church, Zomba (06/08/2011)
Lughano Support Group, Karonga *Boma*, Karonga (20/08/2011)
Pokani Omoyo Support Group, Kasowa (22/08/2011)
Kapora Support Group, Puse, Karonga (23/08/2011)
Lufiya CBO, Mwenitete, Karonga (24/08/2011)
Nbande Support Group, Nbande, Karonga (25/08/2011)
Lupembe Support Group, Lupembe, Karonga (26/08/2011)
Temwanani Support Group, Nyungwe, Karonga (27/08/2011)
Hangalawe Support Group, Uliwa, Karonga (30/08/2011)
Chigomezgo Support Group, Ngara, Karonga (31/08/2011)
Majaliro Support Group, Chilumba Galizon, Karonga (01/08/2011)
Fuliwira Support Group, Fuliwira, Karonga (02/09/2011)
Chilumba Support Group, Chilumba, Karonga (03/09/2011)

Notes

Introduction: Gendered Risk as Structural Violence

1. Although the importance of recognising the link between HIV and AIDS is acknowledged, 'HIV' is used throughout this volume when referring to HIV/AIDS to allow the argument to be more readily accessible to the reader.
2. Prevalence for 2004 has been adjusted from 14 per cent to 12 per cent (based on adjustments in the mathematical modelling) (see NAC, 2009, p. 1; NSO and ORC Macro, 2005) and decreased slightly to 11 per cent by 2010 (NSO and ICF, 2011, p. 196).
3. For the situation in general see Sen (1990).
4. This was useful as a proxy for HIV incidence at the time this research commenced (prior to the publication of the Malawi Demographic and Health Survey [MDHS] in 2011; see NSO Malawi and ICF Macro, 2011) because where it is likely people have been recently infected, this can indicate new trends in the spread of the virus.
5. For the case of South Africa see Moffett (2006) and Jewkes et al. (2003).
6. For the situation in general see Larner and Le Heron (2005), Larner (2000) and Simon (1995).

1 Framing the Virus: The Policy Response to HIV

1. Feminism is diverse and contested, comprising multiple, overlapping feminisms, but, nonetheless, there are common commitments to understanding gender as socially constructed and as a fundamental form of power. Many feminist scholars propound that gender is distinct from sex, which concerns the biological difference between men and women; feminist post-structuralists contest that sex is socially constructed too. See, for example, Butler (1990, p. 7, 1993, pp. 1–2, 2004, pp. 9–11).
2. Case no.1 01/04/05 – Victim Support Unit, Mulanje – Fieldwork (2006).

2 Methodology

1. This research complied with ESRC ethical guidelines.
2. A Visiting Fellowship with the Centre for Social Research (CSR) had been organised but the university had been on strike since February following the dispute over academic freedom.
3. This research complied with Keele University ethics procedures.

3 Sex for Security: Gendered Poverty

1. The incidence of poverty and ultra-poverty is higher in female-headed house-holds (FHHs): 59 per cent of people living in FHHs are poor, compared with 51 per cent in male-headed households (MHHs). This disparity is partially due to gender-based differences in access to resources and bargaining power. The value of assets in FHHs is half that of MHHs and MHHs are more likely to own productive assets for agricultural activities (GoM, 2006, pp. xx, 33).

4 Sex for Well-being: The Gendered Value of Life

1. In the Democratic Republic of Congo, for example, condoms were suspected of being an imperialist design because they were promoted as a population control technology by western agencies (see Schoepf, 1992). Condom promotion in Botswana came up against the stigmatisation that associated condoms with the start and spread of AIDS (see Allen and Heald, 2004, p. 5).
2. These findings are consistent with research on power and HIV in South Africa (see J. Thomas, 2005, p. 45; MacLean, 2004, p. 148).

Conclusion: Gender Social Justice

1. See for example McInnes and Lee (2012), Harman (2007, 2009, 2010, 2012), Rushton and Williams (2011), Davies (2010), Elbe (2010), Hill (2011), Rushton (2010b), Goeman et al. (2010), Feldbaum et al. (2010), Lee (2003, 2004a, 2004b, 2010).
2. In geography see Kalipeni and Zulu (2012), Koch (2011). In sociology see Flynn (2006, p. 84), Adam and Van Loon (2000, p. 4). In feminism see Tickner (1992, 2005), Mohanty (1991, 2003), Webb (1997).

Bibliography

Adam, B. and J. Van Loon (2000) 'Introduction: Repositioning Risk – The Challenge for Social Theory', in B. Adam, U. Beck and J. Van Loon (eds) *The Risk Society and Beyond: Critical Issues for Social Theory* (London: Sage), 1–31.

Agadjanian, V. (2002) 'Men Talk About "Women's Matters": Gender, Communication, and Contraception in Urban Mozambique', *Gender & Society*, vol. 16, no. 2: 194–215.

Aguillar, M. I. and L. B. Aguillar (1999) 'Women's Organizing Abilities: Two Case Studies of Kenya and Malawi' (Washington, DC: Organizing for Development).

Ahsan, N. and H. Ahsan (2004) 'Foundation of a Family: Importance, Obstacles and Possible Solutions', *Policy Perspectives*, vol. 1, no. 1.

Allen, J. A. V. (2001) 'Poverty as a Form of Violence', *Journal of Human Behavior in the Social Environment*, vol. 4, nos 2–3: 45–59.

Alwang, J. (1999) 'Labour Shortages on Small Landholdings in Malawi: Implications for Policy Reform', *World Development*, vol. 27, no. 8: 1461–75.

Ampofo, A. A., J. N. Beoku-Betts, N. Wairimu and M. Osirim (2004) 'Women's and Gender Studies in English-speaking Sub-Saharan Africa: A Review of Research in the Social Sciences', *Gender & Society*, vol. 18, no. 6: 685–714.

Anderson, E.-L. (2012) 'Infectious Women: Gendered Bodies and HIV in Malawi', *International Feminist Journal of Politics*, vol. 14, no. 2: 267–87.

Anglewicz, P. and H. P. Kohler (2009) 'Over-estimating HIV Infection: The Construction and Accuracy of Subjective Probabilities of HIV Infection in Rural Malawi', *Demographic Research*, vol. 20, no. 6: 65–96.

Anglin, M. K. (1998) 'Feminist Perspectives on Structural Violence', *Identities: Global Studies in Culture and Power*, vol. 5, no. 2: 145–51.

Bagnol, B. (2008) 'Closing the Vagina through the Elongation of the Labia Minora and Use of Vaginal Products to Enhance Eroticism', paper presented at the Third Africa Conference on Sexual Health and Rights, 4–7 February, Abuja, Nigeria.

Baird, S., E. Chirwa, C. McIntosh and B. Özler (2010) 'The Short-term Impacts of a Schooling Conditional Cash Transfer Program on the Sexual Behavior of Young Women', *Health Economics*, vol. 19(suppl.): 55–68.

Baird, S., R. S. Garfein, C. T. McIntosh and B. Özler (2012) 'Effect of a Cash Transfer Programme for Schooling on Prevalence of HIV and Herpes Simplex Type 2 in Malawi: A Cluster Randomised Trial', *The Lancet*, vol. 379, no. 9823: 1320–9.

Banda, A. (2014) 'Stepping Stones: Strategies for Safety', AIDS 2014 – 20th International AIDS Conference, Melbourne, Australia, 20–5 July.

Banda, R. (2005) *Women of the Bible and Culture: Baptist Convention Women in Southern Malawi* (Zomba: Kachere Series).

Bankole, A. and S. Singh (1998) 'Couples' Fertility and Contraceptive Decision-making in Developing Countries: Hearing a Man's Voice', *International Family Planning Perspectives*, vol. 24, no. 1: 15–24.

Barker, G. and C. Ricardo (2006) 'A Key to HIV Prevention: Understanding What Drives Young Men in Africa', *Global AIDS Link*, Nov./Dec., 100.

Barnett, T. (2006) 'A Long-wave Event: HIV/AIDS, Politics, Governance and "Security": Sundering the Intergenerational Bond?', *International Affairs*, vol. 82, no. 2: 297–313.

Barnett, T. and G. Prins (2006) 'HIV/AIDS and Security: Fact, Fiction and Evidence – A Report to UNAIDS', *International Affairs*, vol. 82, no. 2: 359–68.

Baum, B. (2004) 'Feminist Politics of Recognition', *Signs: Journal of Women in Culture and Society*, vol. 29, no. 4: 1073–102.

Baylies, C. (2004) 'Cultural Hazards Facing Young People in the Era of HIV/AIDS: Specificity and Change', in N. K. Poku and A. Whiteside (eds) *The Political Economy of AIDS in Africa* (Aldershot: Ashgate), 71–84.

Baylies, C. and J. Bujra (1995) 'Discourses of Power and Empowerment in the Fight Against HIV/AIDS in Africa', in P. Aggleton, P. Davies and G. Hart (eds) *AIDS: Safety, Sexuality and Risk* (London: Taylor & Francis).

Baylies, C. and J. Bujra (eds) (2000) *AIDS, Sexuality and Gender in Africa: Collective Strategies and Struggles in Tanzania and Zambia* (London: Routledge).

Beall J. and J. Davilla (1994) 'Integrating Gender into Policy for Manufacturing Industry', Working Paper 66, Unit for the Integration of Women (UIW) in Industrial Development at the United Nations Industrial Development Organisation (UNIDO).

Beck, U. (1992) *Risk Society: Towards a New Modernity* (London: Sage).

Beck, U. (1999) *World Risk Society* (Cambridge: Polity).

Beck, U. (2000) *What is Globalization?* (Cambridge: Polity).

Beck-Gernsheim, E. (2000) 'Health and Responsibility: From Social Change to Technological Change and Vice Versa', in B. Adam, U. Beck and J. Van Loon (eds) *The Risk Society and Beyond: Critical Issues for Social Theory* (London: Sage), 122–35.

Bezner Kerr, R. and P. Mkandawire (2012) 'Imaginative Geographies of Gender and HIV/AIDS: Moving beyond Neoliberalism', *GeoJournal*, vol. 77, no. 4: 459–73.

Bird-David N. (1983) 'Wage-gathering: Socio-economic Change and the Case of the Naiken of South India', in P. Robb (ed.) *Rural South Asia: Linkages, Changes and Development* (London: Curzon), 57–86.

Bird-David, N. (1990) 'The Giving Environment: Another Perspective on the Economic System of Gatherer-hunters', *Current Anthropology*, vol. 1, no. 2: 189–96.

Blackden, C. M. and Q. Wodon (2006) 'Introduction', in C. M. Blackden and Q. Wodon (eds) *Gender Time Use and Poverty in Sub-Saharan Africa*. World Bank Working Paper 37 (Washington, DC: World Bank), 1–12.

Blaikie, N. (2000) *Designing Social Research* (Cambridge: Polity).

Blanc, A. K. (2001) 'The Effect of Power in Sexual Relationships on Sexual and Reproductive Health: An Examination of the Evidence', *Studies in Family Planning*, vol. 32, no. 3: 189–213.

Boesten, J. (2011) 'Navigating the AIDS Industry: Being Positive and Poor in Tanzania', *Development and Change*, vol. 42, no. 3: 781–803.

Boesten, J. and N. Poku (2009) 'Introduction: Gender, Inequalities, and HIV/AIDS', in J. Boesten and N. Poku (eds) *Gender and HIV/AIDS: Critical Perspectives From the Developing World* (Farnham: Ashgate), 1–25.

Bond, V. and P. Dover (1997) 'Men, Women and the Trouble with Condoms: Problems Associated with Condom Use by Migrant Workers in Rural Zambia', *Health Transition Review*, vol. 7(suppl. 3): 377–91.

Bordo, S. (2003) *Unbearable Weight: Feminism, Western Culture and the Body* (Berkeley: University of California Press).

Boserup, E. (1970) *Woman's Role in Economic Development* (London: George Allen & Unwin).

Bracher, M., G. Santow and S. C. Watkins (2003) ' "Moving" and Marrying: Modelling HIV Infection among Newly-weds in Malawi', *Demographic Research*, Special Collection, vol. 1, no. 7: 207–46.

Brown, W. (2012) 'A Question of Agency: Africa in International Politics', *Third World Quarterly*, vol. 33, no. 10: 1889–908.

Brown, W. and S. Harman (2013) 'In From the Margins? The Changing Place of Africa in International Relations', *International Affairs*, vol. 89, no. 1: 69–87.

Brown, W., S. Harman, S. Hurt, D. Lee and K. Smith (2009) 'Editorial: New Directions in International Relations and Africa', *The Round Table: Commonwealth Journal of International Affairs*, vol. 98, no. 402: 263–7.

Bryceson, D. F. (1995) *Women Wielding the Hoe: Lessons for Rural Africa for Feminist Theory and Development Practices* (Oxford: Berg).

Bryceson, D. F. and J. Fonseca (2006) 'Risking Death for Survival: Peasant Responses to Hunger and HIV/AIDS in Malawi', *World Development*, vol. 34, no. 8: 1654–66.

Bryceson, D. F., J. Fonseca and J. Kadzadira (2004) 'Social Pathways from the HIV/AIDS Deadlock of Disease, Denial and Desperation in Rural Malawi' (Lilongwe: CARE).

Bryman, A. (1988) *Quantity and Quality in Social Research* (London: Unwin Hyman).

Bryman, A. (2008) *Social Research Methods* (Oxford: Oxford University Press).

Bujra, J. (2002) 'Targeting Men for a Change: AIDS Discourse and Activism in Africa', in F. Cleaver (ed.) *Masculinities Matter! Men, Gender and Development* (Claremont, South Africa: Zed), 209–34.

Burton, P. (2005) *Suffering at School: Results of the Malawi Gender-based Violence in Schools Survey* (Pretoria: CJSD/ISS).

Butegwa, F. (1994) 'Using the African Charter on Human Rights to Secure Women's Access to Land in Africa', in R. Cook (ed.) *Human Rights of Women: National and International Perspectives* (Philadelphia: University of Pennsylvania Press), 495–514.

Butler, J. (1990) *Gender Trouble and the Subversion of Identity* (London: Routledge).

Butler, J. (1993) *Bodies that Matter: On the Discursive Limits of 'Sex'* (London: Routledge).

Butler, J. (2004) *Undoing Gender* (London: Routledge).

Butler, J. (2009) *Frames of War: When Is Life Grievable?* (London: Verso).

Caldwell, J. C. (1997) 'The Impact of the African AIDS Epidemic', *Health Transition Review*, vol. 7(suppl. 2): 169–88.

Caldwell, J. C. (2000) 'Rethinking the African AIDS Epidemic', *Population and Development Review*, vol. 26: 117–35.

Caldwell, J. C. and P. Caldwell (1993) 'The Nature and Limits of Sub-Saharan African AIDS Epidemic: Evidence from Geographic and Other Patterns', *Population and Development Review*, vol. 19, no. 4: 817–48.

Campbell, C. (2003) *Letting Them Die: How HIV/AIDS Prevention Programmes Often Fail* (Cape Town: Double Storey Books Press).

Campbell, C., C. Foulis, S. Maimane and Z. Sibiya (2005) ' "I Have an Evil Child at My House": Stigma and HIV/AIDS Management in a South African Community', *American Journal of Public Health*, vol. 95, no. 5: 808–15.

Capra, F. (1983) *The Turning Point* (New York: Bantam).

CAPRISA (2010) 'Update on Microbicides: Special Session', 18th International AIDS Conference, 18–23 July, Vienna, Austria.

Castaneda, C. (2000) 'Child Organ Stealing Stories: Risk Rumour and Reproductive Technologies', in B. Adam, U. Beck and J. Van Loon (eds) *The Risk Society and Beyond: Critical Issues for Social Theory* (London: Sage), 136–54.

Chabal, P. and J. Daloz (1999) 'The Political Instrumentalization of Disorder', in P. Chabal and J. Daloz, *Africa Works: Disorder as Political Instrument* (Oxford: International African Institute), 141–63.

Chanika, E. (2003) *Male Teacher Sexual Abuse of the Girl Child in the School Context: A Case Study of Primary Schools in Chiradzulu District*. Report by the Civil Liberties Committee submitted to the Commonwealth Education Fund (Lilongwe).

Charlesworth, H. (1994) 'What are "International Women's Rights"?', in R. J. Cook (ed.) *Human Rights of Women: National and International Perspectives* (Philadelphia: University of Pennsylvania Press), 58–84.

Charmes, J. and S. Wieringa (2003) 'Measuring Women's Empowerment: An Assessment of the Gender-related Development Index and the Gender Empowerment Measure', *Journal of Human Development*, vol. 4, no. 3: 419–35.

CHGA (Commission on HIV/AIDS Governance in Africa) (2004) 'Impact of HIV/AIDS on Gender, Orphans and Vulnerable Children', *Discussion Outcomes of CHGA Interactive Cameroon*, www.uneca.org/chga/cameroon_orphans.pdf, accessed 20 June 2009.

Chikoko, R. (2006) 'Over 100 Women in an Anti-AIDS Research Trial', *Malawi News*, 22–28 Jul.

Chilowa, W. (1998) 'The Impact of Agricultural Liberalisation on Food Security in Malawi', *Food Policy*, vol. 23, no. 6: 553–69.

Chilowa, W. and E. W. Chirwa (1997) 'The Impact of SAPs on Social and Human Development in Malawi', in W. Chilowa (ed.) *Bwalo: Forum for Sustainable Social and Human Development in Malawi: Towards Poverty Alleviation*, vol. 1: 39–68 (Zomba: Centre for Social Research).

Chimbiri, A. M. (2007) 'The Condom as an "Intruder" in Marriage: Evidence from Rural Malawi', *Social Science & Medicine*, vol. 64: 1102–15.

Chimgwede, W. (2004a) 'It's Survival of the Fittest', *CFSC Press Review*, Feb.–March.

Chimgwede, W. (2004b) 'Of Polygamy, Women and Children's Rights', *The Malawi Standard*, 4–9 Feb.

Chim'modzi, H. F. (1994/5) 'Addressing African Feminism', *Journal of Humanities*, vol. 8/9.

Chinyamunyamu, B. (2014) 'The Impact of Government Interventions in Agriculture on Women Farmers: The Case of the Malawi Farm Input Subsidy Programme (FISP)', PhD thesis, University of Leeds.

Chirwa, W. C. (1998) 'Aliens and AIDS in Southern Africa: The Malawi–South African Debate', *African Affairs*, vol. 97: 53–79.

Chirwa, W. C. (2001) 'Dancing towards Dictatorship: Political Songs and Popular Culture in Malawi', *Nordic Journal of African Studies*, vol. 10, no. 1: 1–27.

CILIC (Civil Liberties Committee) (2007) *Program Study Final Report*, June (Blantyre, Lilongwe: CILIC).

Clark, S. (2004) 'Early Marriage and HIV Risks in Sub-Saharan Africa', *Studies in Family Planning*, vol. 35, no. 3: 149–60.

Cockburn, C. (2004) 'The Continuum of Violence: A Gender Perspective on War and Peace', in W. Giles and J. Hyndman (eds) *Sites of Violence: Gender and Conflict Zones* (Berkeley: University of California Press), 24–44.

Commission for Africa (2005) *Our Common Interest: Report of the Commission for Africa*, March (Commission for Africa).

Craddock, S. (2006) 'Disease, Social Identity and Risk: Rethinking the Geography of AIDS', *Transactions of the British Institute of Geographers*, New Series, vol. 25, no. 2: 153–68.

Crenshaw, K. (1993) 'Mapping the Margins: Intersectionality, Identity Politics and Violence against Women of Colour', *Stanford Law Review*, vol. 43, no. 6: 1241–79.

Dahlerup, D. (1988) 'From a Small to a Large Minority: Women in Scandinavian Politics', *Scandinavian Political Studies*, vol. 11, no. 4: 275–98.

Davidson, J. (1993) 'Tenacious Women: Clinging to *Banja* Household Production in the Face of Changing Gender Relations in Malawi', *Journal of Southern African Studies*, vol. 19, no. 3: 405–21.

Davies, S. (2010) *The Global Politics of Health* (Cambridge: Polity).

Davis, M. (2008) *The Blackwell Encyclopaedia of Social Work* (Oxford: Blackwell).

de Beauvoir, S. (1953) *The Second Sex*, trans. and ed. by H. M. Parshley, Introduction to the Vintage edition by D. Bair (New York: Vintage Books).

de Bruijn, M. E. and H. J. W. M. Van Dijk (1999) 'Insecurity and Pastoral Development in the Sahel', *Development and Change*, vol. 30: 115–39.

de Waal A. (2010) 'HIV/AIDS and the Challenges of Security and Conflict', *The Lancet*, vol. 375, no. 9708: 22–3.

Dean, M. (1999) *Governmentality: Power and Rule in Modern Society* (London: Sage).

Decosas, J., F. Kane, J. K. Anarfi, K. D. Sodji and H. U. Wagner (1995) 'Migration and AIDS', *The Lancet*, vol. 23, no. 346: 826–8.

Denzin, N. and Y. Lincoln (2000) *Handbook of Qualitative Research* (Thousand Oaks, CA: Sage).

Devereux, S. and R. Sabates-Wheeler (2004) 'Transformative Social Protection', IDS Working Paper 26 (Brighton: Institute of Development Studies).

Douglas, M. (1992) *Risk and Blame: Essays in Cultural Theory* (London: Routledge).

Dowler, L. and J. Sharp (2001) 'A Feminist Geopolitics?', *Space and Polity*, vol. 5, no. 3: 165–76.

Doyal, L. (1994) 'HIV/AIDS Putting Women on the Global Agenda', in L. Doyal, J. Naidoo, and T. Wilton (eds) *AIDS: Setting a Feminist Agenda* (London: Taylor & Francis), 11–29.

Dreyfus, H. and P. Rainbow (1982) *Michel Foucault: Beyond Structuralism and Hermeneutics* (New York: Harvester).

Dzekedzeke, K. and K. Fylkesnes (2004) 'Reducing Uncertainties in HIV Prevalence Estimates: The Case of Zambia', paper presented at the 15th International Conference on AIDS, Bangkok, Thailand, 11–16 July: abstract no. C11478.

Elbe, S. (2003) 'The Security Implications of HIV/AIDS in Southern Africa', in J. J. Hentz and M. Boas (eds) *New and Critical Security and Regionalism: Beyond the Nation State*, (Aldershot: Ashgate).

Elbe, S. (2005) 'HIV/AIDS: The International Security Dimensions', in E. Krahman (ed.) *New Actors and New Issues in International Security* (London: Palgrave), 111–30.

Elbe, S. (2006) 'Should HIV/AIDS be Securitized? The Ethical Dilemmas of Linking HIV/AIDS and Security', *International Studies Quarterly*, vol. 50, no. 1: 119–44.

Elbe, S. (2009) *Virus Alert: Security, Governmentality, and the AIDS Pandemic* (New York: Columbia University Press).

Elbe, S. (2010) *Security and Global Health* (Cambridge: Polity).

Elbe, S. (2012a) 'Let Them Eat Tamiflu: The Global Rise of a Medical Countermeasure', paper presented at the International Studies Association Conference, San Francisco.

Elbe, S. (2012b) 'Bodies as Battlefields: Toward the Medicalization of Insecurity', *International Political Sociology*, vol. 6, no. 3: 320–2.

Ellis, F., M. Kutengule and A. Nyasulu (2003) 'Livelihoods and Rural Poverty Reduction in Malawi', *World Development*, vol. 31, no. 9: 1495–510.

Elshtain, J. B. (1981) *Public Man, Private Woman: Women in Social and Political Thought* (Princeton University Press).

Elshtain, J.B. (1987) *Women and War* (University of Chicago Press).

Enemark, C. (2007) *Disease and Security: Natural Plagues and Biological Weapons in East Asia* (London: Routledge).

Enemark, C. (2009) 'Is Pandemic Flu a Security Threat?', *Survival*, vol. 51, no. 1: 191–214.

Enloe, C. (1989) *Bananas, Beaches and Bases* (London: Pandora).

Etienne, M. (1997) 'Women and Men, Cloth and Colonization: The Transformation of Production–Distribution Relations among the Baulé (Ivory Coast)', in R. Grinker and C. B. Steiner (eds) *Perspectives on Africa: A Reader in Culture, History, and Representation* (Oxford : Blackwell).

Farmer, P. (2004) 'An Anthropology of Structural Violence', *Current Anthropology*, vol. 45, no. 3: 305–17.

Farmer, P. E., B. Nizeye, S. Stulac and S. Keshavjee (2006) 'Structural Violence and Clinical Medicine', *PLoS Medicine*, vol. 3, no. 10: e449.

Farquhar, C. and R. Das (1999) 'Are Focus Groups Suitable for "Sensitive" Topics?', in R. S. Barbour and J. Kitzinger (eds) *Developing Focus Group Research* (London: Sage), 47–63.

Fauci, A. S. (2003) 'HIV and AIDS: 20 Years of Science', *Nature Medicine*, vol. 9, no. 7: 839–43.

Fay, B. (1977) *Social Theory and Political Practice* (London: George Allen & Unwin).

Feldbaum, H., K. Lee and P. Patel (2006a) 'The National Security Implications of HIV/AIDS', *PLoS Medicine*, vol. 3, no. 6: 774–8.

Feldbaum, H., P. Patel, E. Sondorp and K. Lee (2006b) 'Global Health and National Security: The Need for Critical Engagement', *Medicine, Conflict and Survival*, vol. 22, no. 3: 192–8.

Feldbaum, H., K. Lee and J. Michaud (2010) 'Global Health and Foreign Policy', *Epidemiologic Reviews*, vol. 32, no. 1: 82–92.

Feldmeier, H., I. Krantz and G. Poggensee (1994) 'Female Genital Schistosomiasis as a Risk-factor for the Transmission of HIV', *International Journal of STD and AIDS*, vol. 5, no. 5: 368–72.

Ferguson, A. (1994) 'Gendered Science: A Critique of Agricultural Development', *American Anthropologist*, vol. 96, no. 3: 540–52.

Ferguson, A. (2005) 'Water Reform, Gender and HIV Perspectives from Malawi', in L. Whiteford and S. Whiteford (eds) *Globalization, Water and Health: Resource Management in Times of Scarcity* (Oxford: James Currey), 45–66.

Ferguson, J. (1990) *The Anti-Politics Machine: 'Development', Depoliticization and Bureaucratic Power in Lesotho* (Cambridge University Press).

Ferguson, J. (1999) *Expectations of Modernity: Myths and Meanings of Urban Life on the Zambian Copperbelt* (Berkeley: University of California Press).

Ferguson, J. (2013) 'Declarations of Dependence: Labour, Personhood, and Welfare in Southern Africa', *Journal of the Royal Anthropological Institute*, vol. 19: 223–42.

FHI (Family Health International) (2004) Behaviour Surveillance Survey (Lilongwe: Family Health International).

Fielder, R. N. (2000) 'The Place of Religion in the Struggle for the Rights of Girl Children: A Case Study of Experiences of Girls in Initiation Programmes in Rural Communities in Southern Malawi', *Religion in Malawi*, vol. 10: 37–41.

Fielder, R. N. (2005) *Coming of Age: A Christianised Initiation for Women in Southern Malawi* (Zomba: Kachere Series).

Flynn, R. (2006) 'Health and Risk', in G. Mythen and S. Walklate (eds) *Beyond the Risk Society: Critical Reflections on Risk and Human Security* (Maidenhead: Open University Press), 77–95.

Flyvbjerg, B. (2001) *Making Social Science Matter: Why Social Enquiry Fails and How it Can Succeed Again* (Cambridge University Press).

Fontana, A. and J. H. Frey (1994) 'Interviewing: The Art of Science', in N. Denzin and Y. Lincoln (eds) *The Handbook of Qualitative Research* (Thousand Oaks, CA: Sage), 361–76.

Forster, P. G. (1994) 'Culture, Nationalism, and the Invention of Tradition in Malawi', *Journal of Modern African Studies*, vol. 32, no. 3: 477–97.

Forster, P. G. (2000) 'Prostitution in Malawi and the HIV/AIDS Risk', *Nordic Journal of African Studies*, vol. 9, no. 1: 1–19.

Foucault, M. (1988) *Politics, Philosophy, Culture: Interviews and Other Writings, 1977–84*, ed. L. D. Kritzman (London: Routledge).

Frith, H. (2000) 'Focusing on Sex: Using Focus Groups in Sex Research', in K. Plummer (ed.), *Sexualities* (London: Sage), 275–98.

Fraser, N. and L. Nicholson (1989) 'Social Criticism without Philosophy: An Encounter between Feminism and Postmodernism', *Social Text*, vol. 21: 83–104.

Gailey, C. W. (1998) 'Making Kinship in the Wake of History: Gendered Violence and Older Child Adoption', *Identities: Global Studies in Culture and Power*, vol. 5, no. 2: 249–92.

Galtung, J. (1969) 'Violence, Peace, and Peace Research', *Journal of Peace Research*, vol. 6, no. 3: 167–91.

Galtung, J. and T. Høivik (1971) 'Structural and Direct Violence: A Note on Operationalisation', *Journal of Peace Research*, vol. 8, no. 1: 73–6.

García-Calleja, J. M., E. Gouws and P. D. Ghys (2006) 'National Population Based HIV Prevalence Surveys in Sub-Saharan Africa: Results and Implications for HIV and AIDS Estimates', *Sexually Transmitted Infections*, vol. 82(suppl. 3), pp. iii64–iii70.

Garrett, L. (2005) 'The Lessons of HIV/AIDS', *Foreign Affairs*, vol. 64: 4.

Ghosh, J. and E. Kalipeni (2005) 'Women in Chinsapo, Malawi: Vulnerability and Risk to HIV/AIDS', *Journal of Social Aspects of HIV/AIDS*, vol. 2, no. 2: 320–32.

Gillespie, S. R. (2006) *AIDS, Poverty, and Hunger: Challenges and Responses* (Washington, DC: International Food Policy Research Institute).

Glaser, B. and A. Strauss (1967) *The Discovery of Grounded Theory: Strategies for Qualitative Research* (Chicago: Aldine).

Global Coalition on Women and AIDS (2008) 'Educate Girls, Fight AIDS', http://data.unaids.org/GCWA/GCWA_FS_GirlsEducation_Sep05_en.pdf, accessed 20 June 2009 Washington, DC: World Health Organization.

Goeman, L., B. Galichet, D. G. Porignon, P. Hill, N. Hammami, M.-S. E. Elouma, P. Y. Kadama et al. (2010) 'The Response to Flexibility: Country Intervention Choices in the First Four Rounds of the GAVI Health Systems Strengthening Applications', *Health Policy Plan*, vol. 25, no. 4: 292–9.

Gollub, E. L. (2000) 'The Female Condom: Tool for Women's Empowerment', *American Journal of Public Health*, vol. 90, no. 9: 1377.

GoM (Government of Malawi) (1994) The Malawi Constitution (Lilongwe: Government of Malawi).

GoM (Government of Malawi) (2000) National Gender Policy (Lilongwe: Ministry of Women and Child Development).

GoM (Government of Malawi) (2001) *Sexual Reproductive Health Behaviours in Malawi: A Literature Review to Support Situation Analysis for the National Behaviours Change Interventions Strategy on HIV/AIDS and Sexual Reproductive Health* (Lilongwe: National AIDS Commission and Sexual Reproductive Health Unit, Ministry of Health and Population).

GoM (Government of Malawi) (2003) National HIV/AIDS Policy: A Call for Renewed Action (Lilongwe: Office of the President and Cabinet and NAC).

GoM (Government of Malawi) (2005) Women, Girls and HIV/AIDS Programme and National Plan of Action (Lilongwe: GoM).

GoM (Government of Malawi) (2006) *Malawi Poverty and Vulnerability Assessment* (Lilongwe: GoM and World Bank).

GoM (Government of Malawi) (2010) *Malawi HIV and AIDS: Monitoring and Evaluation Report 2008–2009*. UNGASS Country Progress Report (Zomba: NSO).

GoM (Government of Malawi) (n.d.) 'Supplementary Information on the Second Periodic Report of the Republic of Malawi: Implementation of the Convention on the Rights of the Child' (Lilongwe: Government of Malawi).

Graham, H. (ed.) (2000) *Understanding Health Inequalities* (Buckingham: Open University Press).

Graham, H. (2002) 'Building an Interdisciplinary Science of Health Inequalities: The Example of Lifecourse Research', *Social Science & Medicine*, vol. 55: 2005–16.

Grant, R. (1991) 'The Sources of Gender Bias in International Relations', in R. Grant and K. Newland (eds) *Gender and International Relations* (Milton Keynes: Open University Press), 8–25.

Gray, L. and M. Kevane (1999) 'Diminished Access, Diverted Exclusion: Women and Land Tenure in Sub-Saharan Africa', *African Studies Review*, vol. 42, no. 2: 15–39.

Green, M. (2006) 'Representing Poverty and Attacking Representations: Perspectives on Poverty from Social Anthropology', *Journal of Development Studies*, vol. 42, no. 7: 1108–29.

Grown, C., G. R. Gupta and R. Pande (2005) 'Taking Action to Improve Women's Health through Gender Equality and Women's Empowerment', *The Lancet*, vol. 365: 541–3.

Guba, E. G. and Y. S. Lincoln (1994) 'Competing Paradigms in Qualitative Research', in N. Denzin and Y. Lincoln (eds) *Handbook of Qualitative Research* (Thousand Oaks, CA: Sage), 105–17.

Gupta, G. R. (2005) 'How Men's Power over Women Fuels the HIV Epidemic: It Limits Women's Ability to Control Sexual Interactions – Editorials', *British Medical Journal*, vol. 324, no. 7331: 183–4.

Gupta, A. (2012) *Red Tape: Bureaucracy, Structural Violence, and Poverty in India* (Durham, NC: Duke University Press).

Gutmann, M. (2007) *Fixing Men: Sex, Birth Control, and AIDS in Mexico* (Berkeley: University of California Press).

Hammersley, M. (1992) *What's Wrong with Ethnography?* (London: Routledge).

Harding, S. (1986) *The Science Question in Feminism* (Ithaca, NY: Cornell University Press).

Harman, S. (2007) 'The World Bank: Failing the Multi-country AIDS Program (MAP): Failing HIV/AIDS', *Global Governance*, vol. 13, no. 4: 485–92.

Harman, S. (2009a) 'Bottlenecks and Benevolence: How the World Bank is Helping Communities to "Cope" with HIV/AIDS', *Journal of Health Management*, vol. 11, no. 2: 279–313.

Harman, S. (2009b) 'The World Bank and Global Health', in O. Williams and A. Kay (eds) *The Crisis of Global Health Governance: Challenges, Institutions and Political Economy* (Basingstoke: Palgrave), 227–44.

Harman, S. (2010) *The World Bank and HIV/AIDS: Setting a Global Agenda* (Abingdon: Routledge).

Harman, S. (2011) 'Governing Health Risk by Buying Behaviour', *Political Studies*, vol. 59, no. 4: 867–83.

Harman, S. (2012) *Global Health Governance* (Abingdon: Routledge).

Harrigan, J. (2001) *From Dictatorship to Democracy: Economic Policy in Malawi 1964–2000* (Aldershot: Ashgate).

Harvey, D. (2005) *A Brief History of Neoliberalism* (Oxford University Press).

Hawkesworth, M. (1997) 'Confounding Gender', *Signs: Journal of Women in Culture and Society*, vol. 22, no. 3: 649–85.

Hay, C. (2004) 'The Normalizing Role of Rationalist Assumptions in the Institutional Embedding of Neoliberalism', *Economy and Society*, vol. 33, no. 4: 500–27.

Heward, C. (1999) 'Introduction: The New Discourses of Gender, Education and Development', in C. Heward and S. Bunwaree (eds) *Gender, Education and Development: Beyond Access to Empowerment* (London: Zed).

Hickey, S. (2008) 'Conceptualising the Politics of Social Protection in Africa', in A. Barrientos and D. Hulme (eds) *Social Protection for the Poor and the Poorest: Concepts, Policies and Politics* (London: Palgrave), 247–63.

Hickey, S. (2009) 'The Politics of Protecting the Poorest: Moving beyond the "Anti-politics Machine"?', *Political Geography*, vol. 28, no. 8: 473–83.

Hill, P. (2011) 'Understanding Global Health Governance as a Complex Adaptive System', *Global Public Health: An International Journal for Research, Policy and Practice*, vol. 6, no. 6: 593–605.

Hindin, M. J. (2005) 'Women's Autonomy, Status and Nutrition in Zimbabwe, Zambia and Malawi', in USAID (ed.) *A Focus on Gender: Collected Papers on Gender Using DHS Data* (Calverton, MD: ORC Macro), 93–116.

Hirschmann, D. and M. Vaughan (1983) 'Food Production and Income Generation in a Matrilineal Society: Rural Women in Zomba, Malawi', *Journal of Southern African Studies*, vol. 10, no. 1: 86–99.

Hogan M. C., K. J. Foreman, M. Naghavi, S. Y. Ahn, M. Wang, S. M. Makela et al. (2010) 'Maternal Mortality for 181 countries, 1980–2008: A Systematic Analysis of Progress towards Millennium Development Goal 5', *The Lancet*, vol. 375, no. 9726: 1609–23.

Høivik, T. (1977) 'The Demography of Structural Violence', *Journal of Peace Research*, vol. 14, no. 1: 59–73.

Holland, J., C. Ramazanoglu, S. Scott, S. Sharpe and R. Thompson (1991) 'Between Embarrassment and Trust: Young Women and the Diversity of Condom Use', in P. Aggleton, G. Hart and P. Davies (eds) *AIDS: Responses, Interventions and Care* (London: Falmer), 127–48.

Hoogensen, G. and K. Stuvøy (2006) 'Gender, Resistance and Human Security', *Security Dialogue*, vol. 37, no. 2: 207–28.

Hope, R. K. (2001) 'Africa's HIV/AIDS Crisis in Development Context', *International Relations*, 15: 15–36.

Hudson, H. (2005) ' "Doing" Security as Though Humans Matter: A Feminist Perspective on Gender and the Politics of Human Security', *Security Dialogue*, vol. 36, no. 2: 155–74.

Hulme, D. (2007) 'The Making of the Millennium Development Goals: Human Development Meets Results-based Management in an Imperfect World', Brooks World Poverty Institute Working Paper 16 (Manchester: University of Manchester).

Hyde, K. (1999) 'Barriers to Educational Opportunity in Malawi', in S. Erskine and M. Wilson (eds) *Gender Issues in International Education: Beyond Policy and Practice* (London: Falmer), 131–47.

IPPF, UNFPA and the Global Coalition on Women and AIDS (2006) *Report Card: HIV Prevention for Girls and Young Women* (Lilongwe: IPPF, UNFPA and the Global Coalition on Women and AIDS).

James, S. (1994) 'Women's Unwaged Work – The Heart of the Informal Sector', in M. Evans (ed.) *The Woman Question* (London: Sage), 173–7.

Jamieson, P. (2004) 'Sexuality and the Adolescent Girl', *The Chronicle* (Lilongwe), 1–7 Mar.

Jangale, C. (2006) 'On Fighting Gender Imbalance', *The Nation*, 5 Jul., 12.

Jewkes, R. K., J. Levin and L. Penn-Kekana (2003) 'Gender Inequalities, Intimate Partner Violence and HIV Preventative Practices: Findings of a South Africa Cross-sectional Study', *Social Science & Medicine*, vol. 56, no. 1: 125–34.

Kachiwanda, S. (n.d.) 'Gender Disparity in the Acquisition of Literacy in Sub-Saharan Africa: The Case of Malawi' (unpublished), Centre for Language Studies, University of Malawi, Zomba.

Kaler, A. (2001) ' "Many Divorces and Many Spinsters": Marriage as an Invented Tradition in Southern Malawi, 1946–1999', *Journal of Family History*, vol. 26, no. 4: 529–56.

Kaler, A. (2003) ' "My Girlfriend Could Fill a Yanu-Yanu Bus": Rural Malawian Men's Own Claims about Their Sero-status', *Demographic Research*, Special Collection, vol. 1, no. 11: 349–72.

Kaler, A. (2004) 'The Moral Lens of Population Control: Condoms and Controversies in Southern Malawi', *Studies in Family Planning*, vol. 35, no. 2: 105–15.

Kalipeni, E. and E. M. Zulu (1993) 'Gender Differences in Knowledge and Attitudes Toward Modern and Traditional Methods of Child Spacing in Malawi', *Population Research and Policy Review*, vol. 12, no. 2: 103–21.

Kalipeni, E. and L. Zulu (2012) 'HIV and AIDS in Africa: A Geographic Analysis at Multiple Spatial Scale', *GeoJournal*, vol. 74, no. 4: 505–24.

Kalipeni, E., S. Craddock, J. R. Oppong and J. Ghosh (2004) *HIV/AIDS in Africa: Beyond Epidemiology* (Oxford: Blackwell).

Karim, J. (2006) 'Gogo Chalo Malengachanzi Advises against Risky Behaviour', *The Sunday Times*, 9 Jul.: 4.

KDA (Karonga District Assembly) (2008) *Karonga District Socio-Economic Profile 2009–2011* (Karonga: District Assembly).

Kelly, L. (1988) *Surviving Sexual Violence* (Cambridge: Polity).

Kevane, M. (2004) *Women and Development in Africa: How Gender Works* (London: Lynne Rienner).

Kim, S. S. (1984) 'Global Violence and a Just World Order', *Journal of Peace Research*, vol. 21, no. 2: 181–92.

King, N. and C. Horrocks (2010) *Interviews in Qualitative Research* (London: Sage).

Kishindo, P. (2004) 'Customary Land Tenure and the New Land Policy in Malawi', *Journal of African Studies*, vol. 22, no. 2: 213–25.

Kjetland, E. F., G. Poggensee, G. Helling-Giese, J. Richter, A. Sjaastad, L. Chitsulo et al. (1996) 'Female Genital Schistosomiasis Due to Schistosoma Haematobium: Clinical and Parasitological Findings in Women in Rural Malawi', *Acta Tropica*, vol. 62, no. 4: 239–55.

Koch, N. (2011) 'Security and Gendered National Identity in Uzbekistan', *Gender, Place & Culture: A Journal of Feminist Geography*, vol. 18, no. 4: 499–518.

Koopman J. (1995) 'Women in the Rural Economy: Past, Present and Future', in M. J. Hay and S. Stichter (eds) *African Women South of the Sahara* (Harlow: Longman), 3–22.

Kornfield, R. and D. Namete (1997) 'Cultural Practices Related to HIV/AIDS Risk Behaviour: Community Survey in Phalombe, Malawi', STAFH Project 10 (Lilongwe: Support to AIDS and Family Health [STAFH]) Project).

Kydd, J. and A. Hewitt (1986) 'Limits to Recovery – Malawi after 6 Years of Adjustment, 1980 to 1985', *Development and Change*, vol. 17, no. 3: 531–55.

Labonté, R. and M. L. Gagnon (2010) 'Framing Health and Foreign Policy: Lessons for Global Health Diplomacy', *Globalization and Health*, vol. 6: 14.

Laga, M., B. Schwärtlander, E. Pisani, P. S. Sow and M. Caraël (2001) 'To Stem HIV in Africa, Prevent Transmission to Young Women', *AIDS*, vol. 15, no. 7: 931–4.

Langa, J. (2006a) 'Wife Chopper a Known Hooligan', *The Nation*, 2 Nov. http://www.nationmalawi.com/print.asp?articleID=15136, accessed 10 June 2008.

Langa, J. (2006b) 'M'mbelwa's Wife Files for Divorce', *The Nation*, 11 Jul.: 1–2.

Lamer, W. (2000) 'Neo-liberalism: Policy, Ideology, Governmentality', *Studies in Political Economy*, vol. 63: 5–25.

Lamer, W. and R. Le Heron (2005) 'Universities Neo-liberalizing Spaces and Subjectivities: Reinventing New Zealand', *Organization*, vol. 12, no. 6: 843–67.

Leach, F. (2003) 'Learning to be Violent', *Compare*, vol. 33, no. 3: 385–400.

Leach, F. (2007) 'African Girls and Mission Education – New Identities and New Boundaries', paper presented at the Gender and Education Conference, Trinity College Dublin, 28–30 Mar.

Lee, K. (2003) 'The Global Trade and Public Health Nexus: The Role of the World Health Organization', *New Solutions*, vol. 13, no. 1: 61–5.

Lee, K. (2004a) 'The Pit and the Pendulum: Can Globalization take Health Governance Forward?', *Development*, vol. 47, no. 2: 11–17.

Lee, K. (2004b) 'Globalisation: What Is It and How Does It Affect Health?', *Medical Journal of Australia*, vol. 180, no. 4: 156–8.

Lee, K. (2006) 'Avian Influenza: The Threat to Human Security', *Human Security Bulletin*.

Lee, K. (2010) 'How Do We Move Forward on the Social Determinants of Health? The Global Governance Challenges', *Critical Public Health*, vol. 20, no. 1: 5–12.

Lele, U. (1990) 'Structural Adjustment, Agricultural Development and the Poor: Some Lessons from the Malawian Experience', *World Development*, vol. 18, no. 9: 1207–19.

Lemke, T. (2001) 'The Birth of Bio-politics: Michel Foucault's Lecture at the Collège de France on Neo-liberal Governmentality', *Economy and Society*, vol. 30, no. 2: 190–207.

Lewin, S. (2010) 'State of the Epidemic: Strategies for a Cure', paper presented at the 18th International AIDS Conference, 18–23 July, Vienna, Austria.

Linking, A. (1996) 'AIDS as a Development Issue', *Canadian HIV/AIDS Policy and Law Newsletter*, vol. 2, no. 4.

Long, N. (2001) *Development Sociology: Actor-oriented Perspectives* (Abingdon: Routledge).

Lonsdale, J (2000) 'Agency in Tight Corners: Narrative and Initiative in African History', *Journal of African Cultural Studies*, vol. 13, no. 1: 5–16.

Luciano, E. (2006) 'Stalemate on Preventing Domestic Violence', *Malawi News*, 13–19 May: 4.

Lukes, S. (2005 [1974]) *Power: A Radical View*, 2nd edn (London: Macmillan).

Lupton, D. (1994) *Medicine as Culture: Illness, Disease and the Body in Western Societies* (London: Sage).

Lupton, D. (1999) *Risk* (London: Routledge).

Luric, M. (2000) 'Migration and AIDS in Southern Africa: A Review', *Southern Africa Journal of Science*, vol. 96, no. 6: 343–7.

Lwanda, J. (2005) *Politics, Culture and Medicine in Malawi* (Zomba: Kachere Series).

Mabala, R. (2006) 'From HIV Prevention to HIV Protection: Addressing the Vulnerability of Girls and Young Women in Urban Areas', *Environment and Urbanization*, vol. 18, no. 2: 407–32.

MacDonald, D. (1996) 'Transmission of HIV in Botswana', *Social Science & Medicine*, vol. 42, no. 9: 1325–33.

MacLean, R. (2004) 'Partner Violence Elevates the Risk of HIV Infection for South African Women', *International Family Planning Perspectives*, vol. 30, no. 3: 148–9.

MacPherson, E. E., J. Sadalaki, M. Njoloma, V. Nyongopa, L. Nkhwazi, V. Mwapasa et al. (2012) 'Transactional Sex and HIV: Understanding the Gendered Structural Drivers of HIV in Fishing Communities in Southern Malawi', *Journal of International AIDS Society*, vol. 14, no. 15(suppl. 1): 1–9.

Mahoney, J. and G. Goertz (2006) 'A Tale of Two Cultures: Contrasting Quantitative and Qualitative Research', *Political Analysis*, vol. 14: 227–49.

Malawi Law Commission (2006) *Report of the Law Commission on the Review of the Laws on Marriage and Divorce*, June (Lilongwe: Malawi Law Commission).

Malawi News Agency (2014) 'Malawi: President Mutharika Speech During the Golden Jubilee Celebrations', 6 July.

Maluwa-Banda, D. (2003) *Gender Sensitive Educational Policy and Practice: The Case of Malawi*, report submitted to UNESCO's International Bureau of Education (Zomba: University of Malawi).

Maluwa-Banda, D. (2005) 'HIV/AIDS Related Stigma and Discrimination: Overcoming "Them and Us" ', *Religion in Malawi*, vol. 12: 14–18.

Manda, S. and R. Meyer (2005) 'Age at First Marriage in Malawi: A Bayesian Multilevel Analysis Using a Discrete Time-to-event Model', *Journal of the Royal Statistical Society*, vol. 168, no. 2: 439–55.

Mane, P. and P. Aggleton (2001) 'Gender and HIV/AIDS: What Do Men Have to Do With It?', *Current Sociology*, vol. 49, no. 6: 23–37.

Marková, I., P. Linell, M. Grossen and A. Salazar-Orvig (eds) (2007) *Dialogue in Focus Groups: Exploring Socially Shared Knowledge* (London: Equinox).

Marks, S. (2002) 'An Epidemic Waiting to Happen? The Spread of HIV/AIDS in South Africa in Social and Historical Perspective', *Africa Studies*, vol. 61, no. 1: 13–26.

Marmot, M. and R. G. Wilkinson (1999) *Social Determinants of Health*, 2nd edn (Oxford University Press).

Mason, J. (2002) *Qualitative Researching* (Thousand Oaks, CA: Sage).

Mbaya, S. (2002) 'HIV/AIDS and Its Impact on Land Issues in Malawi', paper presented at the FAO/SARPN Workshop on HIV/AIDS and Land, 24–5 June, Shere View Lodge, Pretoria.

Mbweza, E., K. F. Norr and B. McElmurry (2008) 'Couple Decision Making and the Use of Cultural Scripts in Malawi', *Journal of Nursing Scholarship*, vol. 40, no. 1: 12–19.

McCracken, J. (1998) 'Democracy and Nationalism in Historical Perspective: The Case of Malawi', *African Affairs*, vol. 97, no. 387: 231–49.

McFadden, P. (1992) 'Sex, Sexuality and the Problem of AIDS in Africa', in R. Meena (ed.) *Gender in Southern Africa: Conceptual and Theoretical Issues* (Harare: SAPES).

McInnes, C. (2011) 'HIV, AIDS and Conflict in Africa: Why Isn't It (Even) Worse?', *Review of International Studies*, vol. 37, no. 2: 485–509.

McInnes, C. (2006) 'HIV/AIDS and Security', *International Affairs*, vol. 82, no. 2: 315–26.

McInnes, C. and K. Lee (2012) *Global Health and International Relations* (Cambridge: Polity).

McInnes, C. and K. Lee (2006) 'Health, Security and Foreign Policy', *Review of International Studies*, vol. 32, no. 1: 5–23.

McInnes, C. and S. Rushton (2010) 'HIV, AIDS and Security: Where Are We Now?', *International Affairs*, vol. 86, no. 1: 225–45.

McIntyre, J. (2005) 'Maternal Health and HIV', *Reproductive Health Matters*, vol. 13, no. 25: 129–35.

Melesse, T. (2008) 'Human Security and Sexual Health', paper presented at Third Africa Conference on Sexual Health and Rights, 4–7 Feb., Abuja, Nigeria.

Mhone, C. S. (1996) 'Autocracy and AIDS: The Post-Banda Challenge. Country Focus: Malawi', *AIDS Analysis Africa*, vol. 6, no. 5: 16.

MHRC (Malawi Human Rights Commission) (2002) *Investigations Report of a Case on Young Girls (Minors) in Karonga Being Forced to Marry Elderly People in Exchange for Cattle or Repayment for Loans*, December (Lilongwe: MHRC).

MHRC (Malawi Human Rights Commission) (2005) *Gender Based Violence in the Workplace with a Focus on Maternity Leave*, December (Lilongwe: MHRC).

MHRC (Malawi Human Rights Commission) (2006) *Cultural Practices and Human Rights: A Study into Cultural Practices and Their Impact on the Enjoyment of Human Rights, Particularly the Rights of Women and Children in Malawi*, May (Lilongwe: MHRC).

Ministry of Health and Population and the National AIDS Committee (NAC) (n.d.) Social Mobilization Implementation Plan for Working with Six Key Social Groups on Behaviour Change (Lilongwe: Ministry of Health and Population and NAC).

Mitchell, S. M. and V. L. Hesli (2013) 'Women Don't Ask? Women Don't Say No? Bargaining and Service in the Political Science Profession', *PS: Political Science & Politics*, vol. 46, no. 2: 355–69.

Moffett, H. (2006) ' "These Women, They Force Us to Rape Them": Rape as a Narrative of Social Control in Post-Apartheid South Africa', *Journal of Southern African Studies*, vol. 32, no. 1: 129–44.

Mohanty C. T. (1991) 'Under Western Eyes: Feminist Scholarship and Colonial Discourses', in C. T. Mohanty, A. Russo and L. Torres (eds) *Third World Women and the Politics of Feminism* (Indianapolis: Indiana University Press), 51–80.

Mohanty, C. T. (1998) 'Feminist Encounters: Locating the Politics of Experience', in A. Phillips (ed.) *Feminism and Politics* (Oxford University Press), 254–72.

Mohanty, C. T. (2003) ' "Under Western Eyes" Revisited: Feminist Solidarity through Anticapitalist Struggles', *Signs: Journal of Women in Culture and Society*, vol. 28, no. 2: 499–535.

Moser, C. (1989) 'Gender Planning in the Third World: Meeting Practical and Strategic Gender Needs', *World Development*, vol. 17, no. 11: 1799–825.

Moser, C. (1991) 'Gender Planning in the Third World', in R. Grant and K. Newland (eds) *Gender and International Relations* (Milton Keynes: Open University Press), 83–121.

Moser, C. (2005) 'Has Gender Mainstreaming Failed?', *International Feminist Journal of Politics*, vol. 7, no. 4: 576–90.

Moser C., O. M'chanju-Liwewe, A. Moser and N. Ngwira (2004) *DFID Malawi Gender Audit: Evaporated, Invisibilized or Resisted?* (Lilongwe: DfID).

Mowforth, M. (2014) *Violence of Development: Resource Depletion, Environmental Crisis and Human Rights Abuses in Central America* (London: Pluto).

Mtika, M. M. (2007) 'Political Economy, Labor Migration, and the AIDS Epidemic in Rural Malawi', *Social Science & Medicine*, vol. 64, no. 12: 2454–63.

Munthali, A. C. and E. M. Zulu (2007) 'The Timing and Role of Initiation Rites in Preparing Young People for Adolescence and Responsible Sexual and Reproductive Behaviour in Malawi', *African Journal of Reproductive Health*, vol. 11, no. 3: 150–67.

Munthali, A. C., A. Chimbiri and E. M. Zulu (2004) *Adolescent Sexual and Reproductive Health in Malawi: A Synthesis of the Research Evidence*. Alan Guttmacher Institute Occasional Report 15(4).

Muula, A. S. and J. M. Mfutso-Bengo (2004) 'Important but Neglected Ethical and Cultural Considerations in the Fight against HIV/AIDS in Malawi', *Nursing Ethics*, vol. 11, no. 5: 479–88.

MVAC (Malawi Vulnerability Assessment Committee) (2012) *Vulnerability Update Report: Malawi Food Security Outlook: October 2012 to March 2013*, http://www.fews.net/docs/Publications/Malawi_OL_2012_10_Final.pdf, accessed October 2014.

Mwafulirwa, S. (2006a) 'Man Cuts Pregnant Wife's Sex Organs', *Sunday Times*, 9 July.

Mwale, P. N. (2002) 'Where Is the Foundation of African Gender? The Case of Malawi', *Nordic Journal of African Studies*, vol. 11, no. 1: 114–37.

NAC (National AIDS Commission) (2003) *HIV/AIDS in Malawi: Estimates of the Prevalence of Infection and the Implications* (Lilongwe: NAC).

NAC (National AIDS Commission) (2004) *HIV and AIDS Monitoring and Evaluation Report 2004* (Lilongwe: National AIDS Commission).

NAC (National AIDS Commission) (2009) National HIV Prevention Strategy 2009–2013 (Lilongwe: National AIDS Commission).

Namangal, F. (2004) 'Manyuchi Stirs Controversy', *Daily Times*, 9 Sept.

Nath, M. B. (2004) *Gender, HIV and Human Rights: A Training Manual* (Geneva: UNIFEM).

Nattrass, N. (2009) 'Poverty, Sex and HIV', *AIDS and Behaviour*, vol. 13: 833–40.

Nattrass, N., B. Maughan-Brown, J. Seekings and A. Whiteside (2012) 'Poverty, Sexual Behaviour, Gender and HIV Infection among Young Black Men and Women in Cape Town, South Africa', *African Journal of AIDS Research*, vol. 11, no. 4: 307–17.

Navarro, V. and L. Shi (2001) 'The Political Context of Social Inequalities and Health', *Social Science & Medicine*, vol. 52: 481–91.

Ngulube-Chinoko, P. (1995) 'The Experience of Women under the One-party State and in the Political Transition', in M. S. Nzunda and K. R. Ross (eds) *Church, Law and Political Transition in Malawi, 1992–94* (Gweru: Mambo Press), 89–100.

Nguyen, V.-K. (2010) *The Republic of Therapy: Triage and Sovereignty in West Africa's Time of AIDS* (Durham, NC: Duke University Press).

Nguyen, V.-K. and K. Stovel (2004) *The Social Science of HIV/AIDS: A Critical Review and Priorities for Action* (New York: Social Science Research Council Working Group on HIV/AIDS).

Ngwira, N. and E. Mkandawire (2003) *Cost of Gender Disparities in Access to Socioeconomic Services in Malawi* (Blantyre: IPRAD).

Ngwira, N., S. Bota and M. E. Loevinsohn (2001) *HIV/AIDS, Agriculture and Food Security in Malawi: Background to Action* (Lilongwe and The Hague: Regional Network on HIV/AIDS, Rural Livelihoods and Food Security [RENEWAL]).

Ngwira, N., G. Kamchedzera and L. Semu (2003) *Malawi: Strategic Country Gender Assessment* (Lilongwe: World Bank and UNDP).

Niño-Zarazúa, M., A. Barrientos, S. Hickney and D. Hulme (2011) 'Social Protection in Sub-Saharan Africa: Getting the Politics Right', *World Development*, vol. 40, no. 1: 163–76.

Nkawire, M. (2006) 'Thyolo Leaders for Family Planning', *Daily Times*, April.

Nkenza, S. (2000) 'Women in Post-colonial Africa: Between African Men and Western Feminists', in P. Darby (ed.) *At the Edge of International Relations: Post-Colonialism, Gender and Dependency* (London: Continuum).

Nkulembe, D. (2004) 'Women and HIV/AIDS: The Aftermath of Testing Positive', *Daily Times*, 11 Mar.

NSO (National Statistics Office) (2008) *Population and Housing Census 2008, Analytical Report* (Zomba: NSO).

NSO (National Statistics Office) (2010a) *Population and Housing Census 2008, Analytical Report, 4: Gender*, October (Zomba: NSO).

NSO (National Statistics Office) (2010b) *Population and Housing Census 2008, Analytical Report, 3: Migration* (Zomba: NSO).

NSO (National Statistics Office) (2011) *Annual Trade Statistics Report 2010* (Lilongwe: NSO).

NSO and ICF Macro (2011) Malawi Demographic and Health Survey (MDHS), 2010 (Zomba: NSO and ICF Macro).

NSO Malawi and ORC Macro (2005) Malawi Demographic and Health Survey (MDHS), 2004 (Calverton, MD: NSO and ORC Macro).

Ntombela, A. (2008) 'Sexual and Reproductive Health of Women Living with HIV/AIDS', paper presented at the International Community of Women Living with HIV and AIDS, Third Africa Conference on Sexual Health and Rights, 4–7 February, Abuja, Nigeria.

Nussbaum, M. (1992) 'Human Functioning and Social Justice: In Defence of Aristotelian Essentialism', *Political Theory*, vol. 20, no. 2: 202–46.

Nussbaum, M. (2000) *Women and Human Development: The Capabilities Approach* (Cambridge University Press).

Nyirenda, E. (2006) 'Kupimbira Giving Way', *The Nation*, 19 Jul.

Oakley, A. (1986) 'Feminism, Motherhood and Medicine – Who Cares?' in J. Mitchell and A. Oakley (eds) *What Is Feminism?* (Oxford: Blackwell), 127–50.

Oakley, A. (2005) *The Ann Oakley Reader: Gender, Women and Society* (Bristol: Policy Press).

Odotei, I. (1992) 'The Migration of Ghanaian Women in the Canoe Fishing Industry', *Maritime Anthropological Studies*, vol. 5, no. 3: 88–95.

OIG (Office of the Inspector General) (2012) Audit of the Global Fund Grants to the Republic of Malawi, 3 Aug. (Global Fund/OIG).

O'Manique, C. (2005) 'The "Securitisation" of HIV/AIDS in Sub-Saharan Africa: A Critical Feminist Lens', *Policy and Society*, vol. 24, no. 1: 24–47.

Organization of African Unity (2001) Abuja Declaration and Framework for Action for the Fight Against HIV, Tuberculosis, and Other Related Infectious Diseases in Africa (Abuja: OAU).

Orubuloye, I. O. and F. Oguntiniehin (1999) 'Intervention for the Control of STDs, Including HIV among Commercial Sex Workers, Commercial Drivers and Students in Nigeria', in I. O. Orubuloye et al. (eds) *The Continuing HIV/AIDS*

Epidemic in Africa (Canberra: Health Transition Centre/National Centre for Epidemiology and Population Health), pp. 121–9.

Ostergard, R. L. (2002) 'Politics in the Hot Zone: AIDS and the Threat to Africa's Security', *Third World Quarterly*, vol. 23, no. 2: 333–50.

Ostergard, R. L. (2008) 'HIV/AIDS, the Military, and the Future of Africa's Security', in S. Cummings and E. Keller (eds) *HIV/AIDS, Development and the Next Generation in Africa* (Lawrenceville, NJ: Red Sea Press).

Paliani-Kamanga, P. (2004) 'Should Pregnant Women Be Compulsorily Tested for HIV?', *Malawi News*, 20 Feb.

Panos and the UN (2000) *Men and HIV in Malawi* (Lusaka: Panos Southern Africa).

Parpart, B. J. L. (2011) 'Engendering African IR in an Increasingly Insecure World', paper presented at the International Studies Association (ISA) Conference, Montreal, 16–19 March.

Parpart, J., S. Raj and K. Staudt (2002) *Rethinking Empowerment Gender and Development in a Global/local World* (London: Routledge).

Pass, S. (2005) *English Chichewa-Chinyanja Dictionary*, 3rd edn (Zomba: Kachere Series).

Pateman, C. (1988) *The Sexual Contract* (Cambridge: Polity).

Patton, M. (1980) *Qualitative Evaluation Methods* (Beverley Hills, CA: Sage).

Pelser, E., L. Gondwe, C. Mayamba, T. Mhango, W. Phiri and P. Burton (2005) *Intimate Partner Violence: Results from a National Gender-based Violence Survey in Malawi*, December (Zomba: Crime and Justice Statistical Division, National Statistics Office).

Peters, A. J., F. T. van Driel and W. H. Jansen (2013) 'Silencing Women's Sexuality: Global AIDS Policies and the Case of the Female Condom', *Journal of the International AIDS Society*, vol. 16, no. 1: 18452.

Peters, P. E. (1992) 'Against All Odds: Matriliny, Land and Gender in the Shire Highlands', *Critique of Anthropology*, vol. 17, no. 2: 189–210.

Peters, P. E. (2002) 'Bewitching Land: The Role of Land Disputes in Converting Kin to Strangers and in Class Formation in Malawi', *Journal of Southern African Studies*, vol. 28, no. 1: 155–78.

Peterson, A. (1997) 'Risk, Governance and the New Public Health', in A. Peterson and R. Bunton (eds) *Foucault, Health and Medicine* (London: Routledge).

Phiri, F. (2005) 'Challenges 2005–2006: Where are Malawi's Women Legislators Now?', 18 December, http://www.ipsterraviva.net/Africa/print.asp?idnews=465, accessed 10 June 2008.

Phiri, I. (1996) 'Marching, Suspended and Stoned: Christian Women in Malawi 1995', in K. R. Ross (ed.) *God, People and Power in Malawi* (Limbe, Malawi: Assemblies of God Press), 63–106.

Phiri, I. (1997) *Women, Presbyterianism and Patriarchy: Religious Experience of Chewa Women in Central Malawi* (Blantyre: CLAIM-Kachere).

Phiri, K. (1983) 'Some Changes to the Matrilineal Family System among the Chewa of Malawi since the Nineteenth Century', *Journal of African History*, vol. 24, no. 2: 257–74.

Phoenix, A. and P. Pattynama (2006) 'Intersectionality, Editorial', *European Journal of Women's Studies*, vol. 13, no. 3: 187–92.

Pini, B. (2002) 'Focus Groups, Feminist Research and Farm Women: Opportunities for Empowerment in Rural Social Research', *Journal of Rural Studies*, vol. 18, no. 2: 339–51.

Pinter, C. (2004) *Economic Pathways for Malawi's Rural Households* (Report for Care International, Malawi).

Piot, P. and A. M. C. Seck (2001) 'International Responses to the HIV/AIDS Epidemic: Planning for Success', *Bulletin of the WHO*, vol. 79, no. 12: 1106–12.

Poku, N. K. and A. Whiteside (2004) 'Introduction: Africa's HIV/AIDS Crisis', in N. K. Poku and A. Whiteside (eds) *The Political Economy of AIDS in Africa* (Aldershot: Ashgate), xvii–xxii.

Porter, L., L. Hao, D. Bishai, D. Serwadda, M. J. Wawer, T. Lutalo et al. (2004) 'HIV Status and Union Dissolution in Sub-Saharan Africa: The Case of Rakai, Uganda', *Demography*, vol. 41, no. 3: 465–82.

Price, J. M. (2012) *Structural Violence: Hidden Brutality in the Lives of Women* (New York: SUNY Press).

PSI (Population Services International)/Malawi (2006) *PSI/Malawi Project TraC – HIV/AIDS Prevention* (Blantyre : PSI/Malawi).

Quinn, T. C. and J. Overbaugh (2005) 'HIV/AIDS in Women: An Expanding Epidemic', *Science*, vol. 308, no. 5728: 1582–3.

Rankin, S. H., T. Lindgren, W. W. Rankin and J. Ng'Oma (2005) 'Donkey Work: Women, Religion, and HIV/AIDS in Malawi', *Health Care for Women International*, vol. 26, no. 1: 4–16.

Reid, E. and E. Bailey (1992) 'Young Women: Silence, Susceptibility and the HIV Epidemic', UNDP HIV and Development Program Issue Paper, http://www.undp.org/hiv/publications/issues/english/issue12e.htm, accessed 10 June 2008.

Reniers, G. (2003) 'Divorce and Remarriage in Rural Malawi', *Demographic Research*, vol. 1, no. 6: 174–205.

Reniers, G. (2005) 'Marital Strategies for Managing Exposure to HIV in Rural Malawi', paper presented to the Annual Meeting of the Population Association of America, Philadelphia, 31 March–2 April, http://www.malawi.pop.upenn.edu/Level%203/Papers/PDF-files/reniers-2005.pdf, accessed 10 June 2008.

Rhodes, T. (2002) 'The "Risk Environment": A Framework for Understanding and Reducing Drug-related Harm', *International Journal of Drug Policy*, vol. 13: 85–94.

Rivers, K., P. Aggleton, J. Elizondo, G. Hernandez, G. Herrera, P. Mane et al. (1998) 'Gender Relations, Sexual Communication and the Female Condom', *Critical Public Health*, vol. 8, no. 4: 273–90.

Roberts, B. (2002) *Biographical Research* (Buckingham: Open University Press).

Rushton, S. (2010a) 'Framing AIDS: Securitization, Development-ization, Rights-ization', *Global Health Governance*, vol. 4, no. 1: 1–17.

Rushton, S. (2010b) 'AIDS and International Security in the United Nations System', *Health Policy & Planning*, vol. 25, no. 6: 495–504.

Rushton, S. and C. McInnes (2012) 'Health as Soft Power: Medical Interventions for Strategic Ends', paper presented at the Towards an International Political Sociology of Health and Medicine Workshop, Humanitarian and Conflict Response Institute (HCRI), Manchester and Centre for Global Health Policy, Sussex.

Rushton, S. and O. D. Williams (eds) (2011) *Partnerships and Foundations in Global Health Governance* (Basingstoke: Palgrave Macmillan).

Rwabukwali, C. B., D. A. Schumann, H. W. McGrath, C. Carroll-Pankhurst, R. Mukasa, S. Nakayiwa et al. (1994) 'Culture, Sexual Behavior, and Attitudes toward Condom Use among Baganda Women', *Global AIDS Policy*, 70–89.

Sanders, T. (2006) 'Sexuality and Risk', in G. Mythen and S. Walklate (eds) *Beyond the Risk Society: Critical Reflections on Risk and Human Security* (Maidenhead: McGraw-Hill/Open University Press), 96–113.

Saur, M., L. Semu and S. Hauya Ndau (2005) *Nkanza, Listening to People's Voices: A Study of Gender-based Violence, Nkanza in Three Districts of Malawi*, Kachere Series (Balaka, Zomba: Monfort Media).

Scheper-Hughes, N. (1993) *Death without Weeping: The Violence of Everyday Life in Brazil* (Berkeley: University of California Press).

Scheper-Hughes, N. and P. Bourgois (eds) (2004) *Violence in War and Peace: An Anthology* (London: Blackwell).

Schoepf, B. G. (1992) 'AIDS, Sex and Condoms: African Healers and the Reinvention of Tradition in Zaire', in R. Bolton and M. Singer (eds) *Rethinking AIDS Prevention: Cultural Approaches* (Reading: Gordon & Breach), 87–106.

Schoepf, B. G. (2003) 'Uganda: Lessons for AIDS Control in Africa', *Review of African Political Economy*, 98: 553–72.

Schoffeleers, M. (1997) *Religion and the Dramatisation of Life: Spirit Beliefs and Rituals in Southern and Central Malawi* (Blantyre: CLAIM-Kachere).

Schratz, M. and R. Walker (1995) *Research as Social Change: New Opportunities for Qualitative Research* (London: Routledge).

Schubert, B. and M. Huijbregts (2006) 'The Malawi Social Cash Transfer Pilot Scheme: Preliminary Lessons Learned', paper presented at the Conference on Social Protection Initiatives for Children, Women and Families: An Analysis of Recent Experiences, New York, 30–31 October, http://www.unicef.org/socialpolicy/files/The_Malawi_Social_Cash_Transfer_Pilot_Scheme_-_Preliminary_Lessons_Learned.pdf, accessed 10 June 2008.

Scott, J. C. (1990) *Domination and the Art of Resistance: Hidden Transcripts* (London: Yale University Press).

Seckinelgin, H. (2008) *The International Politics of HIV/AIDS: Global Disease – Local Pain* (London: Routledge).

Seckinelgin, H. (2012a) *International Security, Conflict and Gender: HIV/AIDS is Another War* (London: Routledge).

Seckinelgin, H. (2012b) 'The Global Governance of Success in HIV/AIDS Policy: Emergency Action, Everyday Lives and Sen's Capabilities', *Health & Place*, vol. 18, no. 3: 453–60.

Seckinelgin, H. (2013) 'Gender and Masculinities in Conflict Contexts: What Do We Know and How Do We Think About Them?', paper presented at the International Studies Association Conference, San Francisco, 3–6 April.

Seckinelgin, H., J. Bigirumwami and J. Morris (2010) 'Securitization of HIV/AIDS in Context: Gendered Vulnerability in Burundi', *Security Dialogue*, vol. 41, no. 5: 515–35.

Secor, A. J. (2001) 'Toward a Feminist Counter-geopolitics: Gender, Space and Islamist Politics in Istanbul', *Space and Polity*, vol. 5, no. 3: 91–211.

Seekings, J. and N. Nattrass (2005) *Class, Race and Inequality in South Africa* (New Haven, CT: Yale University Press).

Seidman, A. (1981) 'Women and the Development of Enderdevelopment: The African Experience', in R. Daunber and M. Cain (eds) *Women and Technological Change in Developing Countries* (Boulder, CO: Westview Press).

Semu, L. (2002) 'Kamuzu's Mbumba: Malawi Women's Embeddedness to Cultures in the Face of International Political Pressure and Internal Legal Change', *Africa Today*, vol. 49, no. 2: 77–99.

Semu, L. and L. C. Binauli (1997) 'Women's Status in Malawi: A Case for Gendered Development', *Bwalo* (University of Malawi, Centre for Social Research), vol. 1: 85–104.

Semu, L., N. Ngwira and G. Kamchedzera, G. (2005) *Malawi Strategic Gender Country Assessment (SGCA)* (Lilongwe: World Bank/ UNDP).

Sen, A. (1985) *Commodities and Capabilities* (Oxford University Press).

Sen, A. (1990) 'Gender and Cooperative Conflicts', in I. Tinker (ed.) *Persistent Inequalities: Women and World Development* (New York: Oxford University Press).

Sen, A. and M. Nussbaum (eds) (1993) *The Quality of Life* (Oxford: Clarendon Press).

Serour, G. A. (2008) 'New Technologies in Promoting Women's Sexuality', paper presented at the Third Africa Conference on Sexual Health and Rights, 4–7 Feb., Abuja, Nigeria.

Shah, M. K. (2002) *Buying Sex for Three Sweet Potatoes: Participatory Assessment of Adolescent Sexual and Reproductive Health in Makala village, Lilongwe* (Lilongwe: CARE International).

Sharp, J. P. (2000) 'Remasculinising Geo-politics? Comments on Gearo'id O'Tuathail's Critical Geopolitics', *Political Geography*, vol. 19, no. 3: 361–4.

Shiffman, J. and S. Smith (2007) 'Generation of Political Priority for Global Health Initiatives: A Framework and Case Study of Maternal Mortality', *The Lancet*, vol. 370, no. 9595: 1370–9.

Silberschmidt, M. and V. Rasch (2001) 'Adolescent Girls, Illegal Abortions and "Sugar Daddies" in Dar es Salaam: Vulnerable Victim and Active Social Agents', *Social Science & Medicine*, vol. 52, no. 12: 1815–26.

Singer, P. W. (2002) 'AIDS and International Security', *Survival*, vol. 44, no. 1: 145–58.

Skinner, J., C. Underwood, H. Schwandt and A. Magambo (2013) 'Transitions to Adulthood: Examining the Influence of Initiation Rites on HIV Risk of Adolescent Girls in Mangochoi and Thyolo Districts of Malawi', *AIDS Care*, vol. 25, no. 3: 291–301.

Smith, J. H. and A. Whiteside (2010) 'The History of AIDS Exceptionalism', *Journal of the International AIDS Society*, vol. 3: 13–47.

Solar, O. and A. Irwin (2007) *A Conceptual Framework for Action on the Social Determinants of Health* (Geneva: World Health Organization).

Sparke, M. (2012) 'Entwined Lives and Enclaved Medicine: Globalization and the Targets-turned-territories of Global Health', paper presented at the International Studies Association Conference, San Diego, 1–4 April.

Spencer, L. A., A. Faulkner and J. Keegan (1988) *Talking about Sex* (London: Social and Community Planning Research).

Spike Peterson, V. (1992) 'Introduction', in V. S. Peterson (ed.) *Gendered States: Feminist (Re)Visions of International Relations Theory* (Boulder, CO: Lynne Rienner), 1–30.

Spike Peterson, V. and A. S. Runyan (1998) *Global Gender Issues* (Oxford: Westview Press).

Spring, A. (1995) *Agricultural Development and Gender Issues in Malawi* (London: University Press of America).

Spring, A. and A. Hansen (1985) 'The Underside of Development: Agricultural Development and Women in Zambia', *Agriculture and Human Values*, vol. 2, no. 1: 60–7.

Squires, J. (1990) *Gender in Political Theory* (Cambridge: Polity).

Squires, J. and J. Weldes (2007) 'Beyond Being Marginal: Gender and International Relations in Britain', *British Journal of Politics and International Relations*, vol. 9, no. 2: 185–203.

Stake, R. (1995) *The Art of Case Study Research* (Thousand Oaks, CA: Sage).

Steans, J. (1998) *Gender and International Relations: An Introduction* (Cambridge: Polity).

Stewart, D. W., P. N. Shamdasani and D. W. Rook (2007) *Focus Groups: Theory and Practice*, 2nd edn (Thousand Oaks, CA: Sage).

Stillwaggon, E. (2006a) 'The Ecology of Poverty: Nutrition, Parasites and Vulnerability to HIV/AIDS', in S. Gillespie and S. R. Gillespie (eds) *AIDS, Poverty and Hunger: Challenges and Responses* (Washington, DC: International Food Policy Research Institute), 167–260.

Stillwaggon, E. (2006b) *AIDS and the Ecology of Poverty* (Oxford University Press).

Stromquist, N. P. (1995) 'The Theoretical and Practical Bases for Empowerment', in C. Medel-Añonuevo (ed.) *Women's Education and Empowerment: Pathways towards Autonomy* (Hamburg: UNESCO Institute), 13–22.

Susser, I. (1998) 'Inequality, Violence, and Gender Relations in a Global City: New York, 1986–1996', *Identities: Global Studies in Culture and Power*, vol. 5, no. 2: 219–47.

Swidler, A. and S. C. Watkins (2007) 'Ties of Dependence: AIDS and Transactional Sex in Rural Malawi', *Studies in Family Planning*, vol. 38, no. 3: 147–62.

Swidler, A. and S. C. Watkins (2009) ' "Teach a Man to Fish": The Doctrine of Sustainability and its Effects on Three Strata of Malawian Society', *World Development*, vol. 37, no. 7: 1182–96.

Sylvester, C. (2006) 'Bringing Art/Museums to Feminist International Relations', in B. A. Ackerley, M. Stern and J. True (eds) *Doing Feminist International Relations: A Guide* (Cambridge University Press), 201–20.

Tango International (Technical Assistance to Non-Governmental Organisations) (2004) 'Theme Paper IV: Gender Exploitation in Malawi' (Lilongwe: CARE).

Thomas, C. (1989) 'On the Health of International Relations and the International Relations of Health', *Review of International Studies*, vol. 15, no. 3: 273–80.

Thomas, J. (2005) 'Women's Lack of Control in Relationships May Lead to Inconsistent Condom Use', *International Family Planning Perspectives*, vol. 31: 1.

Thompson, T. J. (2005) 'Presbyterians and Politics in Malawi: A Century of Interaction', *The Round Table*, vol. 94, no. 382: 575–87.

Tickner, J. A. (1992) *Gender in International Relations: Feminist Perspectives on Achieving Global Security* (New York: Columbia University Press).

Tickner, J. A. (1997) " 'You Just Don't Understand": Troubled Engagements Between Feminists and IR Theorists', *International Studies Quarterly*, vol. 41, no. 4: 611–32.

Tickner, J. A. (2005) 'Gendering a Discipline: Some Feminist Methodological Contributions to International Relations', *Signs: Journal of Women in Culture and Society*, vol. 30, no. 4: 2173–88.

Tinker, A., K. Finn and J. Epp (2000) 'Improving Women's Health: Issues and Interventions', Health, Nutrition and Population (HNP) Discussion Paper (Washington, DC: World Bank).

Trevithick, P. (2005) *Social Work Skills: A Practice Handbook* (Maidenhead: Open University Press).

Türmen, T. (2003) 'Gender and HIV/AIDS', *International Journal of Gynecology and Obsterics*, vol. 82: 411–18.

UN (2000) Millennium Development Goals, http://www.un.org/millenniumgoals/aids.shtml, accessed 10 June 2009.

UN (2001) 'Secretary-General Proposes Global Fund for Fight against HIV/AIDS and Other Infectious Diseases at African Leaders Summit', 26 April, http://www.un.org/press/en/2001/SGSM7779R1.doc.htm, accessed October 2014.

UN (2004a) UN Joint Gender Policy Statement – Malawi: section 1, http://www.sdnp.org.mw/gender/un_pol_sec1.html, accessed 10 June 2009.

UN (2004b) 'Secretary-General, Marking Women's Day, Hails Heroic Leaders of Fight against HIV/AIDS, Urging their Further Empowerment: Society's Inequalities Put Women at Unjust, Unconscionable, Untenable Risk, He Says', Press Release, http://www.un.org/News/Press/docs/2004/sgsm9186.doc.htm, accessed 1 October 2005.

UN (2006) Political Declaration on HIV/AIDS (New York: UN).

UN General Assembly Special Session on HIV/AIDS (UNGASS) (2001) Declaration of Commitment on HIV/AIDS (Geneva: UN).

UNAIDS (2006) *Report on a Global Epidemic* (Geneva: UNAIDS).

UNAIDS (2008) *UNAIDS' Terminology Guidelines* (Geneva: UNAIDS).

UNAIDS (2009) *AIDS Epidemic Update* (Geneva: UNAIDS).

UNAIDS (2010) *Report on a Global Epidemic* (Geneva: UNAIDS).

UNAIDS (2011) *Report on a Global Epidemic* (Geneva: UNAIDS).

UNAIDS (2012) 'World AIDS Day Message: 1 December 2012', http://www.unaids.org/en/media/unaids/contentassets/documents/speech/2012/wad2012/20121201_EXD_WAD_Message_en.pdf, accessed 30 Dec. 2012.

UNAIDS (2013) *Report on a Global Epidemic* (Geneva: UNAIDS).

UNAIDS, UNFPA and UNIFEM (2004) *Women and HIV/AIDS: Confronting the Crisis* (Geneva: UN).

UNDP (1994) *Human Development Report: New Dimensions of Human Security* (New York: UNDP).

UNDP (2003) *Malawi Millennium Development Goals Report* (Lilongwe: UNDP Malawi).

UNDP (2005) *Malawi Human Development Report: Reversing HIV/AIDS in Malawi* (Lilongwe: UNDP).

UNFPA (1995) *Report of the International Conference on Population and Development* (New York: UN).

UNICEF (1987) *Adjustment with a 'Human Face'* (Geneva: UNICEF).

UNICEF and NSO Malawi (2006) Malawi Multiple Indicator Cluster Survey (MICS), http://medcol.mw/commhealth/publications/MICS%20Report.pdf, accessed 22 October 2014.

US National Intelligence Council (2000) *Global Infectious Disease and its Implications for the United States* (Washington, DC: NIC).

USAID Malawi (2008) *Gender Assessment*, June (Lilongwe: USAID Malawi).

Van den Borne, F. (2005) *Trying to Survive in Times of Poverty and AIDS: Women and Multiple Partner Sex in Malawi* (Amsterdam: Het Spinhuis).

van Eerdewijk, A. (2014) 'The Micropolitics of Evaporation: Gender Mainstreaming Instruments in Practice', *Journal of International Development*, vol. 26: 345–55.

Vaughn, S., J. S. Schumm and J. Sinagub (1996) *Focus Group Interviews in Education and Psychology* (Thousand Oaks, CA: Sage).

Verheijen, J. (2011) 'Complexities of the "Transactional Sex" Model: Non-providing Men, Self-providing Women and HIV Risk in Rural Malawi', *Annals of Anthropological Practice*, vol. 35: 116–31.

Vromen, A. (2010) 'Debating Methods: Rediscovering Qualitative Methods', in D. Marsh and G. Stoker (eds) *Theory and Methods in Political Science* (Basingstoke: Palgrave Macmillan), 249–66.

Watkins, S. C. (2004) 'Navigating AIDS in Rural Malawi', *Population and Development Review*, vol. 30, no. 4: 673–705.

Watkins, S., H. P. Kohler, J. Behrman and A. Chimbiri (2004) 'The Malawi Diffusion and Ideational Change Project (MDICP)' (Philadelphia: Population Studies Centre, University of Pennsylvania).

Webb, D. (1997) *HIV and AIDS in Africa* (London: Pluto Press).

Wells, G. (1999) *Dialogic Inquiry: Towards a Socio-cultural Practice and Theory of Education* (Cambridge University Press).

Wengraf, T. (2001) *Qualitative Research Interviewing: Biographic Narrative and Semi-Structured Methods* (London: Sage).

WFP (World Food Programme) (2007) 'Increasing Food Security', Jan. (Lilongwe: WFP).

White, S. (2007) *Malawi Country Gender Profile* (Lilongwe: JICA).

White, S. V. R., T. Kachika, A. L. Chiweza and D. Kamanga (2003) *Dispossessing the Widow: Gender-based Violence in Malawi* (Zomba: Kachere Series).

Whiteside, A. (2006) 'HIV/AIDS and Development: Failures of Vision and Imagination', *International Affairs*, vol. 82, no. 2: 327–43.

Whiteside, M. and S. Carr (1997) *Services and Policies Needed to Support Sustainable Smallholder Agriculture in Malawi* (mimeo). Report to the Overseas Development Agency, UK.

Whiteside, A. and N. Poku (2004a) 'Conclusion', in N. K. Poku and A. Whiteside (eds) *The Political Economy of AIDS in Africa* (Aldershot: Ashgate), 215–20.

WHO (World Health Organization) (2008) 'Closing the Gap in a Generation: Health Equity through Action on the Social Determinants of Health', whqlibdoc.who.int/publications/2008/9789241563703_eng.pdf, accessed 12 Jan. 2014.

WHO (World Health Organization) (2010) *Equity, Social Determinants and Public Health Programmes* (Geneva: WHO).

WHO (World Health Organization) (2011) 'Closing the Gap: Policy into Practice on Social Determinants of Health: Discussion Paper', http://nccdh.ca/resources/entry/closing-the-gap-policy-into-practice-on-social-determinants-of-health, accessed 12 Jan. 2014.

WHO and UNAIDS (2007) *New Data on Male Circumcision and HIV Prevention: Policy and Programme Implications*, http://data.unaids.org/pub/Report/2007/mc_recommendations_en.pdf (accessed 12 Jan. 2014).

Wilkinson, S. (1999) 'How Useful are Focus Groups in Feminist Research?', in R. S. Barbour and J. Kitzinger (eds) *Developing Focus Group Research* (London: Sage), 64–78.

Williams, G. H. (2003) 'The Determinants of Health: Structure, Context and Agency', *Sociology of Health & Illness*, 25: 131–54.

WLSA (Women and the Law in Southern Africa) (2000) *In Search of Justice: Women and the Administration of Justice in Malawi* (Blantyre: Dzuku).

Wodon, Q. and K. Beegle (2006) 'Labour Shortages Despite Underemployment? Seasonality in Time Use in Malawi', in C. M. Blackden and Q. Wodon (eds) *Gender Time Use and Poverty in Sub-Saharan Africa*. World Bank Working Paper 37 (Washington, DC: World Bank), 97–118.

Wolf, A. (2004) 'AIDS and the Discourse on Morality in Malawi', *Religion in Malawi*, vol. 11: 11 9.

World Bank (2010) *World Development Indicators Database*, http://data.worldbank.org/country/malawi, accessed 22 June 2010.

Yates, R., U. Chandan and P. Lim Ah Ken (2010) 'Child-sensitive Social Protection: A New Approach to Programming for Children Affected by HIV and AIDS', *Vulnerable Children and Youth Studies*, vol. 5, no. 3: 208–16.

Young, I. M. (2005) *On Female Body Experience: 'Throwing Like a Girl' and Other Essays* (Oxford University Press).

Yow, V. R. (1994) *Recording Oral History: A Practical Guide for Social Science* (Thousand Oaks, CA: Sage).

Yuval-Davis, N. (2006) 'Intersectionality and Feminist Politics', *European Journal of Women's Studies*, vol. 13, no. 3: 193–209.

Zabin L. S. and K. Kiragu (1998) 'The Health Consequences of Adolescent Sexual and Fertility Behavior in Sub-Saharan Africa', *Studies in Family Planning*, vol. 29, no. 2: 210–32.

ZDA (Zomba District Assembly) (2009) *Zomba District Socio-Economic Profile 2009–2011* (Zomba: Zomba District Assembly).

Zierler, S. (1994) 'Women, Sex and HIV', *Epidemiology*, vol. 5, no. 6: 565–7.

Zulu, E. M. (2001) 'Ethnic Variations in Rationale and Observance of Postpartum Sexual Abstinence in Malawi', *Demography*, vol. 38, no. 4: 467–79.

Zulu, E. M. and G. Chepngeno (2003) 'Spousal Communication about the Risk of Contracting HIV/AIDS in Rural Malawi', *Demographic Research*, Special Collection, vol. 1: 247–78.

Index